Studies in Empirical Economics

Aman Ullah (Ed.)
Semiparametric and Nonparametric Econometrics
1989. VII, 172 pp. Hard cover DM 120,-
ISBN 3-7908-0418-5

Walter Krämer (Ed.)
Econometrics of Structural Change
1989. X, 128 pp. Hard cover DM 85,-
ISBN 3-7908-0432-0

Wolfgang Franz (Ed.)
Hysteresis Effects in Economic Models
1990. VIII, 121 pp. Hard cover DM 90,-
ISBN 3-7908-0482-7

John Piggott and John Whalley (Eds.)
Applied General Equilibrium
1991. VI, 153 pp. Hard cover DM 98,-
ISBN 3-7908-0530-0

Baldev Raj and Badi H. Baltagi (Eds.)
Panel Data Analysis
1992. VIII, 220 pp. Hard cover DM 128,-
ISBN 3-7908-0593-9

Josef Christl
The Unemployment / Vacancy Curve
1992. XVI, 152 pp. Hard cover DM 98,-
ISBN 3-7908-0625-0

Jürgen Kaehler
Peter Kugler (Eds.)

Econometric Analysis of Financial Markets

With 37 Figures

Physica-Verlag
A Springer-Verlag Company

Editors
Dipl.-Vw. Jürgen Kaehler
Z. E. W.
Centre for European Economic Research
Kaiserring 14-16
D-68161 Mannheim, Germany

Professor Dr. Peter Kugler
Institute of Economics
University of Vienna
Hohenstaufengasse 9
A-1010 Vienna, Austria

ISBN-13: 978-3-642-48668-5 e-ISBN-13: 978-3-642-48666-1
DOI: 10.1007/978-3-642-48666-1

CIP-Titelaufnahme der Deutschen Bibliothek
Econometric analysis of financial markets / Jürgen Kaehler;
Peter Kugler (eds.). - Heidelberg : Physica-Verl., 1994
(Studies in empirical economics)
ISBN-13: 978-3-642-48668-5

NE: Kaehler, Jürgen [Hrsg.]

Softcover reprint of the hardcover 1st edition 1994

88/7130-543210 - Printed on acid-free paper

Preface

This volume evolved from a conference on "Financial Markets Econometrics" held at the ZEW (Zentrum für Europäische Wirtschaftsforschung) in Mannheim, Germany in February, 1992. However, not all papers included in this volume were presented at the conference. In some cases the papers are follow-up papers to the ones presented.

The purpose of the conference was to bring together researchers from several European countries to discuss their applications of recent econometric methods to the analysis of financial markets. From a methodological point of view the main emphasis of the conference papers was on *cointegration analysis* and ARCH modelling. In cointegration analysis the links between long-run components of time series are studied and the methods can be applied to the determination of equilibrium relationships between the variables, whereas ARCH models (ARCH is the acronym of autoregressive conditional heteroskedasticity) are concerned with the measurement and analysis of changing variances in time series. These two models have been the most significant innovations for the empirical analysis of financial time series in recent years.

Six papers of this volume apply cointegration analysis (the papers by MacDonald/Marsh, Hansen, Ronning, Garbers, Kirchgässner/Wolters, and Kunst/Polasek) and seven papers deal with ARCH models (Krämer/Runde, Drost, Kunst/Polasek, Kugler, Eggington/Hall, Koedijk/Stork/deVries, and Demos/Sentana/Shah). Other econometric methods and models applied in the papers include *factor analysis* (Eggington/Hall and Demos/Sentana/-Shah), *vector autoregressions* (Kirchgässner/Wolters and Kunst/Polasek), *Markov-switching models* (Garbers and Kaehler/Marnet), *spectral analysis* (Kirchgässner/Wolters), *stable Paretian distributions* (Krämer/Runde and Drost) and ARFIMA models (Drost).

The papers cover a wide range of issues and theories in financial and international economics. Three papers are concerned with the *term structure of interest rates* (Kunst/Polasek, Kugler, and Eggington/Hall) and the papers by Kirchgässner/Wolters and Garbers deal with *international interest-rate linkages* and *interest rate parity*. There are three papers on exchange-rate issues: McDonald/Marsh on *purchasing power parity*, Hansen on the *monetary approach to exchange-rate determination*, and Koedijk/Stork/deVries on *target-zone dynamics*. The stock-market applications include issues of *testing for efficiency* (Krämer/Runde), and of using the CAPM (Ronning) and the APT (Demos/Sentana/Shah). Analysis of derivative instruments is contained in the paper of Kaehler/Marnet who study *option price effects* under stochastic volatility. Finally, the more technical paper by Drost examines the question for several time-series models of whether models which are applied to high-frequency (e.g.) daily data can also consistently be extended to low-frequency (e.g. monthly) data. It is, therefore, of fundamental importance for many applications in empirical finance.

Participants of the ZEW conference were not only academics but also quantitative researchers from financial institutions. Financial economics is probably that area in economics where the flow of methods and models from the academic world to the business world is strongest and quickest. The widespread adoption of the CAPM, the APT, and the Black-Scholes option-pricing approach is evidence of this. There is always a great interest of bankers, investment managers and financial analysts in new developments in theoretical and empirical finance. Therefore, this volume should not only appeal to academics and students working in the fields of finance and international economics but also to professionals from financial institutions who are involved in quantitative research or quantitative orientated investment management.

All papers of this volume went through an anonymous referee process prior to publication. We would like to thank all referees for the time and effort they spent on reviewing the papers. We are also grateful to Julie Kaehler, who read all papers, for her editorial assistance as a native speaker. The word processing in TEX was done at the ZEW and was competently performed by Volker Jankowski, Ingo Fink, Karin Oppolzer and Angelika Neufert. Finally, we wish to thank Wolfgang Franz for his support of this project and Werner A. Müller and Gabriele Keidel of Physica-Verlag for their pleasant cooperation.

J. Kaehler, ZEW and Universität Mannheim
P. Kugler, Universität Bern

Contents

Some Pitfalls in Using Empirical Autocorrelations to Test for Zero Correlation among Common Stock Returns[1]

By Walter Krämer and Ralf Runde[2]

Abstract: We consider the null distribution of empirical autocorrelation coefficients of stationary time series under nonstandard circumstances. We show that this null distribution is not robust to $ARCH$-effects and to non-existing variances, both of which are typical for common stock returns. These results are then applied to several stocks traded on the Frankfurt stock exchange, with the result that the "significance" of empirical autocorrelations is in general reduced.

1 Introduction

We consider empirical autocorrelation coefficients of stationary univariate time-series $\{X_t\}_{t=1,\dots,n}$. In our empirical applications, X_t is the continuously compounded daily return of a common stock, i.e.

$$X_t := ln\left(\frac{S_t}{S_{t-1}}\right), \tag{1}$$

where S_t denotes the daily closing price, and stocks are taken from the Frankfurt stock exchange.

A fundamental assumption respectively requirement in various branches of modern capital market theory is that successive asset returns are independent or at least uncorrelated, as motivated and discussed in e.g. Taylor (1986, p. 9) or Akgiray (1989, pp. 61 ff). A wide-spread rough and ready method to check for this is to compute the empirical first order autocorrelation coefficient

$$r = \frac{\sum_{t=2}^{n}(X_t - \overline{X})(X_{t-1} - \overline{X})}{\sum_{t=1}^{n}(X_t - \overline{X})^2} \tag{2}$$

[1]We are grateful to "Deutsche Finanzdatenbank" (DFDB), in particular to Torsten Lüdeke, for the data used in this report, to an unknown referee for helpful insights and comments, to Victor Ng for providing us with his EZARCH software for the estimation of ARCH-models, and to "Deutsche Forschungsgemeinschaft" (DFG) for additional support.

[2]Walter Krämer and Ralf Runde, Department of Statistics, University of Dortmund, Vogelpothsweg 87, 44227 Dortmund, Germany.

and to reject the null hypothesis of zero autocorrelation when $|r|$ becomes too large.

The problem with this rule is to correctly determine what is meant by "too large". For instance, for VW stocks we found a first order empirical autocorrelation coefficient, based on $n = 3014$ daily returns, of $r = 0.057$. Is this or is this not sufficient to reject the null hypothesis of zero population correlation?

The standard argument assumes independence and finite higher moments of returns, so that we have

$$\sqrt{n}\, r \xrightarrow{d} N(0,1), \tag{3}$$

and we reject H_0 (say at a 1% significance level) whenever $|\sqrt{n}r| > 2.57$. In the VW example, this yields $54.9r = 3.10$, so VW returns are judged serially correlated at 1% significance.

The present paper challenges this view, using two quite unrelated arguments. The first is the obvious one that zero autocorrelation is less restrictive than serial independence, so rejection of the latter does not imply rejection of the former. This is particularly important in the context of stock returns, where large values tend to cluster, in contradiction of the independence assumption, but where returns can still be uncorrelated. We elaborate this point in the context of an $ARCH$-structure in the returns, where the limiting relationship (3) no longer holds. Our second objection is based on infinite variance returns, which likewise lead to a violation of the limiting relationship in equation (3), and which lead to a decidedly non-normal limit law for r. Again, this point is particularly important for stock returns, which in the wake of Mandelbrot (1963) and Fama (1965) are often assumed to follow stable distributions with infinite variance.

More formally, our problem can be phrased like this: How robust is the limit law in (3) to deviations from the standard assumptions of $i.i.d.$ returns with finite higher moments, under which it is usually derived? Can it also be used to test a less restrictive null hypothesis, or do we then need a different decision rule?

For simplicity, we confine our explicit treatment of this question to the first order empirical autocorrelation coefficient r. Extensions to higher order empirical autocorrelation coefficients are obvious. Less obvious are extensions to various summary statistics like the Box-Pierce Q, which we reserve for future work.

Our discussion of the consequences of $ARCH$-type serial dependence draws heavily on Heyde (1981) and Milhoj (1985). The mathematics behind the infinite-variance case are taken from Davis and Resnick (1986), and a preliminary discussion of the present problem is also available in Krämer and Runde (1990, 1991).

2 Empirical Autocorrelation in the Context of ARCH Effects

To better understand the behaviour of the autocorrelation coefficient r in nonstandard situations, it helps to first consider its limiting distribution in the standard case of $i.i.d.(\mu, \sigma^2)$ returns with finite higher moments. To that purpose, define $\tilde{X}_t := X_t - \mu$ and $Z_t = \tilde{X}_t \tilde{X}_{t-1}$ and note that

$$\frac{1}{\sqrt{n}} \sum_{t=2}^{n} (X_t - \overline{X})(X_{t-1} - \overline{X}) = \frac{1}{\sqrt{n}} \sum_{t=2}^{n} \tilde{X}_t \tilde{X}_{t-1} + o_p(1), \tag{4}$$

so the limits in distribution of $\frac{1}{\sqrt{n}} \Sigma\ (X_t - \overline{X})(X_{t-1} - \overline{X})$ and $\frac{1}{\sqrt{n}} \Sigma\ Z_t$ are identical. However, since $\{Z_t\}$ is a martingale difference sequence with

$$Var(Z_t) = E(\tilde{X}_t^2 \tilde{X}_{t-1}^2) = E(\tilde{X}_t^2) E(\tilde{X}_{t-1}^2) = \sigma^2 \sigma^2 = \sigma^4, \tag{5}$$

we deduce from well-known Martingale Central Limit theorems (see e.g. Brown, 1971) that

$$\frac{1}{\sqrt{n}} \sum_{t=2}^{n} Z_t \xrightarrow{d} N(0, \sigma^4). \tag{6}$$

On the other hand, we have from the law of large numbers that

$$\frac{1}{n} \sum_{t=1}^{n} (X_t - \overline{X})^2 \xrightarrow{p} \sigma^2, \tag{7}$$

which in conjunction with (4) and (6) produces the well known result

$$\sqrt{n}\, r = \frac{\frac{1}{\sqrt{n}} \sum_{t=2}^{n} (X_t - \overline{X})(X_{t-1} - \overline{X})}{\frac{1}{n} \sum_{t=1}^{n} (X_t - \overline{X})^2} \xrightarrow{d} \frac{1}{\sigma^2} N(0, \sigma^4) = N(0, 1). \tag{8}$$

Now assume that $\tilde{X}_t$ follows at stationary $ARCH(p)$-process, i.e. that $\tilde{X}_t$ can be written as

$$\tilde{X}_t = \varepsilon_t \sqrt{\sigma^2 + \varphi_1 (\tilde{X}_{t-1}^2 - \sigma^2) + \ldots + \varphi_p (\tilde{X}_{t-p}^2 - \sigma^2)}, \tag{9}$$

where the ε_t are $i.i.d.(0,1), \varphi_i \geq 0\ (i = 1, \ldots, p)$ and $\Sigma \varphi_i < 1$. From

$$\begin{aligned} & E(Z_t | \tilde{X}_{t-1}, \varepsilon_{t-1}, \tilde{X}_{t-2}, \varepsilon_{t-2}, \ldots) \\ = \ & \sqrt{\sigma^2 + \varphi_1 (\tilde{X}_{t-1}^2 - \sigma^2) + \ldots + \varphi_p (\tilde{X}_{t-p} - \sigma^2)} \\ & \cdot \tilde{X}_{t-1} E(\varepsilon_t | \tilde{X}_{t-1}, \varepsilon_{t-1} \ldots) \\ = \ & 0, \end{aligned} \tag{10}$$

we see that $\{Z_t\}$ is still a martingale difference sequence, so an analogue of the limiting relationship in (6) still holds (given the fourth moment of $\tilde{X}_t$ exists; for the additional conditions on the φ_i and the distribution of ε_t to ensure this see Milhoj, 1985). However, we now have

$$\begin{aligned} Var(Z_t) &= E(\tilde{X}_t^2 \tilde{X}_{t-1}^2) \\ &= E(\tilde{X}_t^2)E(\tilde{X}_{t-1}^2) + Cov(\tilde{X}_t^2 \tilde{X}_{t-1}^2) \\ &= \sigma^4 + Cov(\tilde{X}_t^2, \tilde{X}_{t-1}^2) =: \omega, \end{aligned} \tag{11}$$

which differs from the standard case by the term $Cov(\tilde{X}_t^2, \tilde{X}_{t-1}^2)$. This is zero when returns are independent, but is different from zero in the presence of $ARCH$ effects.

Since (7) continues to hold with $ARCH$, the limiting distribution of $\sqrt{n}r$ is now $N(0, \frac{\omega}{\sigma^4})$ – still normal, but with different variance.

Next we demonstrate that $Cov(\tilde{X}_t^2, \tilde{X}_{t-1}^2)$ cannot be negative. This is obvious for $ARCH(1)$-processes, but requires some second thoughts for $ARCH(p)$ with $p > 1$. To that extent, define $\rho_i := cor(\tilde{X}_t^2, \tilde{X}_{t-i}^2)$ $(i = 1, \ldots, p)$ and note that these correlation coefficients satisfy the following equation system (see Milhoj, 1985, p. 281):

$$\begin{array}{lclclclcl} \rho_1 & = & \varphi_1 & + & \varphi_2\rho_1 & + & \cdots & + & \varphi_p\rho_{p-1} \\ \rho_2 & = & \varphi_1\rho_1 & + & \varphi_2 & + & \cdots & + & \varphi_{p-1}\rho_{p-2} \\ \vdots & & \vdots & & \vdots & & \ddots & & \vdots \\ \rho_p & = & \varphi_1\rho_{p-1} & + & \varphi_2\rho_{p-2} & + & \cdots & + & \varphi_p. \end{array}$$

After some rearranging, this can in matrix notation be written as

$$\varphi = (I - \psi)\rho, \tag{12}$$

where $\varphi = (\varphi_1, \ldots, \varphi_p)'$, $\rho = (\rho_1, \ldots, \rho_p)'$ and $\psi_{ij} = \varphi_{i+j} + \varphi_{i-j}$, and where $\varphi_k = 0$ for $k \leq 0$ and $k > p$. Since we can easily check that for each row of ψ, the sum of all elements is always less than $\varphi_1 + \ldots + \varphi_p$, which in turn is by assumption less than one, we deduce that the largest eigenvalue of the nonnegative matrix ψ is less than one. From well known theorems in matrix algebra (see e.g. Takayama, 1985, p. 392, Theorem 4.D.2), we now have that $(I - \psi)^{-1}$ and thus $\rho = (I - \psi)^{-1}\varphi$ is nonnegative. In particular, this implies that the correlation between $\tilde{X}_t^2$ and $\tilde{X}_{t-1}^2$ i.e. the first element of ρ, and thus the covariance between $\tilde{X}_t^2$ and $\tilde{X}_{t-1}^2$ is nonnegative.

The upshot is that the variance of the limiting distribution of $\sqrt{n}r$ can only increase with $ARCH$, or equivalently, that the significance of a given observed value of r is invariably and always *reduced* when we allow for $ARCH$.

In our empirical analysis below, we estimate the unknown ω by its empirical counterpart $\hat{\omega}$, and replace the standard test statistic $\sqrt{n}\, r$ by $\sqrt{n\hat{\sigma}^4/\hat{\omega}}\, r$. Since $\hat{\omega} \xrightarrow{p} \omega$, we have

$$\sqrt{n\hat{\sigma}^4/\hat{\omega}}\, r \xrightarrow{d} N(0,1) \tag{13}$$

and an asymptotically valid test despite of $ARCH$.

In the VW example, we obtained from $n = 3014$ daily returns an $\hat{\omega}/\hat{\sigma}^4 = 10.65$ and a newly standardized $\sqrt{n\hat{\sigma}^4/\hat{\omega}}r$ of 0.95. This implies that $r = 0.057$ is no longer significantly different from zero if we take account of $ARCH$ effects.

3 Empirical Autocorrelation in the Context of Stable Return Distributions

Next we consider the distribution of r when returns are independent, but without a finite variance. In particular, we assume a symmetric stable distribution for the returns, with characteristic exponent $\alpha < 2$. Such distributions have great appeal as models of stock returns, since they capture two additional empirical features of stock returns at the same time: tails are fat, and sums of stable variables retain a stable distribution with the same characteristic exponent α. This accords well with the observation from stock markets that daily, weekly and monthly returns have almost identical distributions, apart from scaling factors, and justifies an investigation of the consequences of stable returns for various statistics that are derived from them.

Consequently, in this section we assume that returns X_t are i.i.d., with characteristic function

$$E(e^{iX_t}) = exp(i\,t\,\mu - c|t|^\alpha), \tag{14}$$

where $\alpha < 2$, and μ and $c > 0$ are location and scale parameters, respectively. This has various implications. First, there is no analogue of (7), as the population variance does not exist, and the empirical variance, i.e. the denominator of the conventional test statistic $\sqrt{n}\, r$, tends to infinity. Second, there is also no analogue of (6), as the $Z_t = \tilde{X}_t\tilde{X}_{t-1}$ have likewise no finite variance and therefore cannot have sums which tend to a normal limiting distribution. Rather, it follows from well known results in mathematical statistics (e.g. Davis and Resnick, 1986, p. 550, Theorem 4.4) that

$$\frac{\sum_{t=2}^{n}(X_t - \overline{X})(X_{t-1} - \overline{X})}{[nln(n)]^{\frac{1}{\alpha}}} \xrightarrow{d} S(\alpha), \tag{15}$$

where $S(\alpha)$ is a symmetric stable random variable with the same characteristic exponent and scale parameter as X_t and location parameter $\mu = 0$. This shows that both the norming constant and the limiting distribution are now different from the standard case.

As to the denominator of r, we now have

$$\frac{\sum_{t=1}^{n}(X_t - \overline{X})^2}{n^{\frac{2}{\alpha}}} \xrightarrow{d} S(\frac{\alpha}{2}), \tag{16}$$

where $S(\frac{\alpha}{2})$ is strictly positive and independent of $S(\alpha)$. Together, (15) and (16) therefore imply that

$$\left[\frac{n}{ln(n)}\right]^{\frac{1}{\alpha}} r \xrightarrow{d} \frac{S(\alpha)}{S(\frac{\alpha}{2})}, \tag{17}$$

where the limiting distribution is a ratio of two independent stable variables which is uniquely determined by the characteristic exponent α.

The evaluation of the corresponding distribution function is a computer job. Similar to stable variates themselves, there are in general no known closed functional forms. For illustration, Figure 1 plots some selected densities of $\frac{S(\alpha)}{S(\frac{\alpha}{2})}$ for various α (for computational details, see Krämer and Runde, 1990).

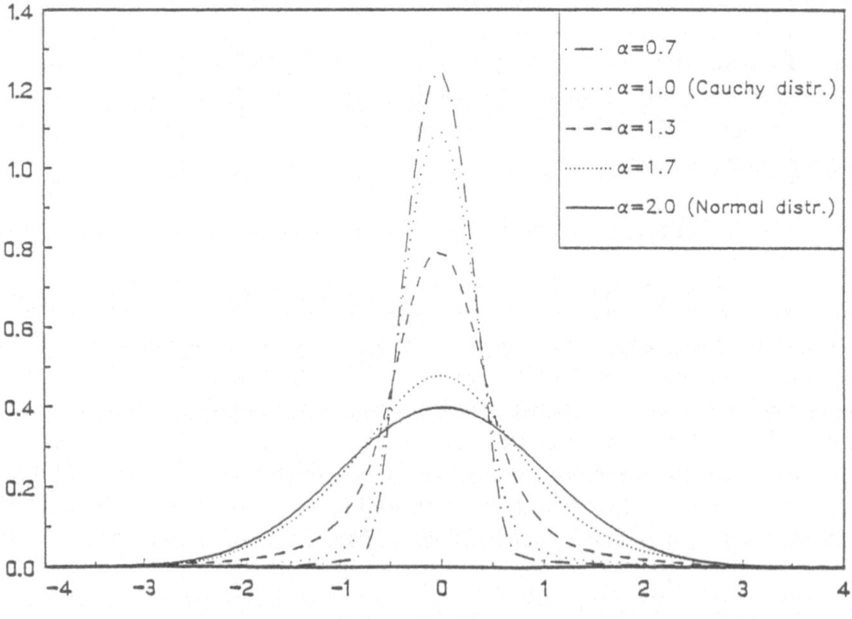

Figure 1 Estimated densities for various α

The relationship (17) has some disturbing implications. First, the limit law of r, after suitable normalisation, is not normal. Second, the limit law depends on the unknown parameter α. And third, and most disturbingly, the norming constant is likewise different from the standard case and depends on an unknown parameter as well.

In addition, we have for any $\alpha < 2$ that

$$\lim_{n\to\infty} \frac{\left[\frac{n}{ln(n)}\right]^{\frac{1}{\alpha}}}{\sqrt{n}} = \infty, \tag{18}$$

i.e. the new norming factors are eventually much larger than the old. In particular, this implies that

$$\sqrt{n}\, r \xrightarrow{p} 0 \tag{19}$$

if returns are stable with infinite variance, which seems to indicate that the significance of a given value of r is now *increased.*

As a closer inspection of the ratio $\left[\frac{n}{ln(n)}\right]^{\frac{1}{\alpha}} / \sqrt{n}$ reveals, this need not be so, however. In fact, for almost all cases of practical interest, the significance of a given r decreases, similar to what we have found in the presence of $ARCH$ effects, since the convergence to infinity of new over old norming constants is neither monotone in n nor uniform in α. For instance for $n \leq 10000$ and $\alpha > 1.4$ (i.e. for the cases most relevant for empirical research), the new norming constant is *smaller* than the old, implying that the significance of a given value of r is ceteris paribus *reduced.*

4 Empirical Application

This section reports empirical autocorrelations for the German stocks that make up the DAX (except Henkel, Veba and Viag, for which no uninterrupted series of returns could be obtained). Time ranges from Jan. 1, 1980 until Jan. 31, 1992, comprising $n = 3014$ trading days on the Frankfurt stock exchange.

Table 1 presents empirical autocorrelations of $z_t := (x_t - \hat{x})^2$, of order $1, \ldots, 5$, computed along the lines of (2). We see that these are much larger than what is consistent with serial independence for almost all stocks, providing ample evidence of ARCH-effects. This was confirmed by direct estimation of specific ARCH and GARCH models, with results similar to Schlag (1991, tables 3 and 4) or Funke (1992), so the serial dependence of higher moments of German common stock returns can certainly not be ignored.

Table 2 summarizes the results for the returns themselves, with the estimation of the critical exponent α of the stable distribution done along the lines of Arad (1980). We see that for almost all stocks, correlation is positive, and significantly so if judged by the standard argument (** denotes

Table 1 Empirical autocorrelations of selected squares of stock returns

	order of autocorrelation coefficient				
	i = 1	i = 2	i = 3	i = 4	i = 5
BASF	0.1327	0.0946	0.1024	0.0718	0.0764
BMW	0.2169	0.2106	0.1495	0.1121	0.1049
Continental	0.3022	0.2689	0.1884	0.0910	0.0933
Daimler	0.2484	0.2149	0.1743	0.1128	0.1129
Deutsche Babcock	0.2954	0.0565	0.0199	0.0054	0.0051
Degussa	0.3221	0.0569	0.0505	0.0213	0.0193
Bayer	0.3258	0.2381	0.2046	0.1452	0.1038
Hoechst	0.1085	0.0851	0.1328	0.0795	0.0647
MAN	0.2833	0.0786	0.0685	0.0301	0.0357
Karstadt	0.2468	0.0478	0.0709	0.0369	0.0200
Linde	0.1365	0.0483	0.1158	0.0881	0.0705
Mannesmann	0.1746	0.0665	0.1105	0.0638	0.0309
Metallgesellschaft	0.2678	0.0498	0.0483	0.0349	0.0136
Preussag	0.1329	0.1317	0.1692	0.0633	0.0626
RWE	0.1576	0.0693	0.0485	0.0539	0.0307
Schering	0.2627	0.3243	0.1687	0.1699	0.1601
Siemens	0.1579	0.1475	0.1494	0.1142	0.1410
Thyssen	0.1559	0.0784	0.0719	0.0667	0.0665
VW	0.1962	0.0705	0.0685	0.0679	0.0585
Kaufhof	0.2591	0.0653	0.0819	0.0410	0.0309
Bayr. Hypo.	0.1395	0.1680	0.1116	0.0703	0.0878
Bayr. Vereinsbank	0.2595	0.1122	0.1041	0.0801	0.0611
Commerzbank	0.1095	0.0739	0.0989	0.0310	0.0252
Deutsche Bank	0.2594	0.1796	0.1334	0.0683	0.0856
Dresdner Bank	0.1682	0.1407	0.1254	0.0461	0.0603
Lufthansa	0.1854	0.1657	0.1102	0.1124	0.0552
Allianz	0.2071	0.1804	0.1802	0.1489	0.1097
DAX	0.1800	0.1984	0.1716	0.1189	0.1227

significance at 1%, * denotes significance at 5%). Once we allow for $ARCH$, however, this significance evaporates, with the sole exception of Dresdner Bank.

Significance is also reduced if we allow for stable distributions. Our estimates for α are all in the range that one expects from previous investigations, and lead to statistics which now testify less strongly against the null hypothesis. The table therefore shows that our theoretical results are no mere mathematical curiosity, but do affect the outcome of empirical research.

5 Directions for Further Research

In this paper, we have focused on possible deviations from the $i.i.d.(0, \sigma^2)$ assumption one at a time. An obvious generalization is to consider $ARCH$-effects and stable distributions of returns together, as in de Vries (1991). The

Table 2 Empirical first order autocorrelations for selected German common stock returns

	r	$\sqrt{n}\,r$	$\sqrt{n\hat{\sigma}^4/\hat{\omega}}\,r$	$\hat{\alpha}$	$\left[\frac{n}{ln(n)}\right]^{1/\hat{\alpha}} r$
BASF	0.022	1.21	0.45	1.83	0.56
BMW	0.073	3.98**	1.29	1.73	2.23**
Continental	0.037	2.01*	0.79	1.81	0.97
Daimler	0.060	3.32**	0.97	1.75	1.79*
Deutsche Babcock	-0.022	-1.21	-0.22	1.84	-0.55
Degussa	0.042	2.31*	0.51	1.87	1.00
Bayer	0.010	0.55	0.19	1.79	0.27
Hoechst	0.066	3.63**	1.21	1.82	1.72*
MAN	0.031	1.68	0.39	1.82	0.79
Karstadt	0.021	1.15	0.28	1.84	0.52
Linde	-0.019	-1.07	-0.29	1.80	-0.53
Mannesmann	0.048	2.66**	0.76	1.83	1.24
Metallgesellschaft	0.004	0.24	0.06	1.86	0.11
Preussag	0.075	4.11**	1.42	1.78	2.09**
RWE	0.026	1.43	0.37	1.81	0.69
Schering	0.077	4.25**	1.39	1.88	1.82*
Siemens	0.069	3.84**	1.33	1.82	1.81*
Thyssen	0.038	2.11*	0.97	1.90	0.87
VW	0.057	3.10**	0.95	1.78	1.58
Kaufhof	0.047	2.59**	0.78	1.83	1.20
Bayr. Hypo.	0.028	1.53	0.46	1.89	0.64
Bayr. Vereinsbank	-0.034	-1.87	-0.58	1.87	-0.81
Commerzbank	0.039	2.14*	0.78	1.89	0.89
Deutsche Bank	0.075	4.09**	1.19	1.81	1.94*
Dresdner Bank	0.103	5.67**	2.25*	1.86	2.00*
Lufthansa	0.009	0.48	0.16	1.84	0.22
Allianz	0.022	1.21	0.29	1.58	0.94
DAX	0.023	1.24	0.32	1.88	0.53

** denotes significance at 1%, * denotes significance at 5%

implications of such return processes for empirical autocorrelations appear quite complicated and might lead to still another limit law.

Less ambitions generalizations, with probably quite similar results, are *GARCH* or *EGARCH* or other conditionally heteroskedastic return processes, as described in e.g. Engle and Bollerslev (1986) or Bollerslev et. al. (1992), and we hope to report on these at some later stage.

References

Akgiray V (1989) Conditional Heteroskedasticity in Time Series of Stock Returns: Evidence and Forecasts, Journal of Business 62, 54 - 80

Arad R W (1980) Parameter Estimation for Symmetric Stable Distributions, Interna-

tional Economic Review 21, 209 - 220
Bollerslev T, Chou R Y and Kroner K P (1992) ARCH Modelling in Finance: A Review of the Theory and Empirical Evidence, Journal of Econometrics 52, 5 - 59
Brown B N (1971) Martingale Central Limit Theorems, Annals of Mathematical Statistics 42, 59 - 66
Davis R and Resnick S (1986) Limit Theory for Moving Averages of Random Variables with Regularly Varying Tail Probabilities, The Annals of Statistics 14, 533 - 558
de Vries C G (1991) On the Relation between GARCH and Stable Processes, Journal of Econometrics 48, 313 - 324
Engle R F and Bollerslev T (1986) Modelling the Persistence of Conditional Variances, Econometric Reviews 5, 1 - 50
Fama E (1965) The Behaviour of Stock Market Prices, Journal of Business 36, 394 - 419
Funke G (1992) The Message in Daily German Stock Returns: Empirical Evidence Using GARCH, Paper given at ESEM 1992, Brussels
Heyde C C (1981) Invariance Principles in Statistics, International Statistical Review 49, 143 - 152
Krämer W and Runde R (1990) Die Autokorrelation von Aktienkursen, Forschungsbericht Nr. 90/10, Department of Statistics, University of Dortmund
Krämer W and Runde R (1991) Testing for Autocorrelation among Common Stock Returns, Statistical Papers 32, 311 - 320
Mandelbrot B (1963) The Variation of Certain Speculative Prices, Journal of Business 36, 394 - 419
Milhoj A (1985) The Moment Structure of ARCH Processes, Scandinavian Journal of Statistics 12, 281 - 292
Schlag C (1991) Return Variances of Selected German Stocks: An Application of ARCH and GARCH Processes, Statistical Papers 32, 353 - 361
Takayama A (1985) Mathematical Economics (2nd ed.), Cambridge (Cambridge University Press)
Taylor S (1986) Modelling Financial Times Series, New York (Wiley)

Temporal Aggregation of Time-Series[1]

By Feike C. Drost[2]

Abstract: The effect of temporal aggregation on several time-series is considered. For several classes of time-series models it is well-known that the classes are closed under temporal aggregation, i.e., aggregation of a high frequency process yields a corresponding low frequency process in the same class. Examples are wide stationary ARMA and weak GARCH. We use two simple lemmas to obtain these results in a more direct way. The lemmas allow for generalizations in several directions. Discussed are fractionally differenced time-series, heavy tailed stable type processes, and GARCH-M.

1 Introduction

In empirical work one often uses some family of models to describe a certain phenomenon, e.g., one chooses the class of ARMA models. Generally this choice is not motivated by the frequency of the data. The same family is used for daily, weekly, and monthly data and the same estimation techniques are used. To avoid departures from the model due to temporal aggregation it seems desirable to use families that are closed under aggregation, i.e., if the model is true at some high frequency level, say daily, then the model is also true at low frequency levels, say weekly and monthly. Such closed classes are robust in the sense that the available data frequency does not invalidate the methods of the researcher. Our interest is mainly devoted to wide stationary processes. Some results are obtained for stable type time-series via pseudo spectral distributions. It is the purpose of this paper to give a unified approach for several models using spectral techniques. The ARMA model, where the spectral density is rational, plays a crucial role in our derivations.

Two aggregation types are considered. In case of *stock* variables, aggregation over m periods yields a low frequency process only recording the $m-$th, the $2m-$th, etc. observations of the original process. The remaining values of the high frequency process are skipped. In case of *flow* variables, the aggregated process records the sum of the first m, the second m, etc. observations of the original time-series. Flow variables apply, e.g., if one considers differenced time-series of stock variables.

---

[1]The author would like to thank Theo E. Nijman and Arie L. Rijkeboer for valuable discussions and helpful suggestions.

[2]Feike C. Drost, Department of Econometrics, Tilburg University, P.O. Box 90153, 5000 LE Tilburg, The Netherlands.

The remainder of this paper is organized as follows. In Section 2 two preparatory lemmas show the connection of the spectral distribution of a high frequency time-series with the corresponding low frequency spectral distribution. The case of flow variables is a corollary of the stock variable case, using a theorem of Brockwell and Davis (1987). Several examples illustrate the lemmas in Section 3. We include the well-known ARMA model and obtain new results for the class of fractionally differenced time-series and the class of stable ARMA processes. We show that the class of fractionally differenced processes is not closed under temporal aggregation, but that the order of fractional differencing is still uniquely determined. The multivariate versions of the lemmas in Section 2 have a wide range of applications. The scope is not limited to multivariate generalizations of the previous examples. We give an overview of the results obtainable in a conditional heteroskedastic framework. Discussed are GARCH and GARCH-M.

2 Two Preparatory Lemmas

In this section the low frequency spectrum is derived from the corresponding high frequency spectrum both in the case of stock and flow variables. We first introduce some notation. Let $\{x_t\}$ be some high frequency n-variate time-series and denote the spectrum of $\{x_t\}$ by $f(\lambda)$. Extend the domain $(-\pi, \pi]$ of the spectrum to the real line by defining

$$f(\lambda + 2k\pi) = f(\lambda), \ \lambda \in (-\pi, \pi], \ k = \pm 1, \pm 2, \ldots .$$

Aggregation of $\{x_t\}$ over m periods yields a corresponding low frequency time-series. For stock and flow variables this aggregated process is denoted by $\{y_t\}$ and $\{\overline{y}_t\}$ respectively, i.e.,

$$\begin{aligned} y_t &= x_{mt} \text{ and} \\ \overline{y}_t &= x_{mt} + x_{mt-1} + \ldots + x_{mt-m+1}. \end{aligned}$$

The following two lemmas derive the spectra of aggregated low frequency processes in case of stock and flow variables [compare also Hansen and Sargent (1983)]. Interpret $\gamma(k)$ and $\gamma^{(m)}(k)$ as autocovariance $(n \times n)$-matrix functions and integrals as a system of n^2 integrals.

Lemma 2.1 (Stock variables) Suppose $\{x_t\}$ is a stochastic process of stock variables with spectrum $f(\lambda)$. Then the aggregated process $\{y_t\}$ has spectrum

$$f^{(m)}(\lambda) = \frac{1}{m} \sum_{j=0}^{m-1} f(\{\lambda + 2\pi j\}/m). \tag{1}$$

Proof: Let $\gamma(k)$ and $\gamma^{(m)}(k)$ denote the autocovariance function of $\{x_t\}$ and $\{y_t\}$ respectively. It suffices to show that the autocovariance function of $\{y_t\}$ satisfies $\gamma^{(m)}(k) = \int_{(-\pi,\pi]} \exp\{k\lambda i\} f^{(m)}(\lambda) d\lambda$ for all $k = 1, 2, \ldots$.

$$
\begin{aligned}
\gamma^{(m)}(k) = \gamma(mk) &= \int_{(-\pi,\pi]} \exp\{km\lambda i\} f(\lambda) d\lambda \\
&= \sum_{j=0}^{m-1} \int_{(-\pi+2\pi j/m, -\pi+2\pi(j+1)/m]} \exp\{km(\lambda - 2\pi j/m)i\} f(\lambda) d\lambda \\
&= \sum_{j=0}^{m-1} \int_{(-m\pi, -m\pi+2\pi]} \exp\{k\lambda i\} \frac{1}{m} f(\{\lambda + 2\pi j\}/m) d\lambda \\
&= \int_{(-\pi,\pi]} \exp\{k\lambda i\} f^{(m)}(\lambda) d\lambda
\end{aligned}
$$

[the integral boundaries can be taken over any interval of length 2π on the right hand side (RHS)]. The proof is complete. □

Remark 2.1 Note that the number of zeros of $f^{(m)}(\lambda)$ declines rapidly as m increases. Moreover, if $m \to \infty$, $f^{(m)}(\lambda) \to \int_{(-\pi,\pi]} f(\nu) d\nu$ = constant if $f(\lambda)$ is an integrable continuous function. The pointwise convergence in the previous sentence implies convergence of $f^{(m)}(\lambda)$ in L^1. This suggests that aggregating more and more leads to processes close to white noise processes.

Lemma 2.2 (Flow variables) Suppose $\{x_t\}$ is a stochastic process of flow variables with spectrum $f(\lambda)$. Then the aggregated process $\{\overline{y}_t\}$ has spectrum

$$
\overline{f}^{(m)}(\lambda) = \frac{1}{m} \sum_{j=0}^{m-1} f(\{\lambda + 2\pi j\}/m) \frac{\sin^2(\lambda/2 + \pi j)}{\sin^2(\{\lambda/2 + \pi j\}/m)}. \tag{2}
$$

Proof: Obtain the time-series $\{x_t^*\}$ by applying the time-invariant linear filter $\{\psi_j = I_{n\times n}\delta_{\{0,1,\ldots,m-1\}}(j)\}$ to $\{x_t\}$. According to Theorem 4.10.1 of Brockwell and Davis (1987) the spectrum $\{x_t^*\}$ is given by

$$
f^*(\lambda) = f(\lambda) \mid \psi(\lambda) \mid^2,
$$

with $\mid \psi(\lambda) \mid^2 = \sin^2(m\lambda/2)/\sin^2(\lambda/2)$. Stock type aggregation over m periods of $\{x_t^*\}$ yields the desired aggregated process $\{\overline{y}_t\}$. Hence application of Lemma 2.1 completes the proof. □

3 Aggregation of Several Time-Series Models

Various univariate examples illustrate the theory presented in Section 2. A trivial case is the class of processes with continuous positive spectral densities. Next we discuss the well-known aggregation result for ARMA time-series. These two examples are used several times in the other examples. Subsections 3.2 and 3.3 discuss long memory processes and time-series with infinite variance. These classes are motivated by the empirical fact that shocks often have a long persistence (which cannot be captured by ARMA models) or that series exhibit several sharp spikes. We refer, e.g., to Fama (1965), Granger and Joyeux (1980), Geweke and Porter-Hudak (1983), De Vries (1991), Diebold and Rudebusch (1991,1992) and Sowell (1992). We show that the class of ARFIMA (fractionally integrated ARMA) models is not closed under temporal aggregation. Despite this fact we show that fractionally differencing is still a useful tool to obtain a more parsimonious parameterization of a given time-series even if this series, strictly spoken, does not belong to the ARFIMA family. For the long memory class of models with stable errors we need a slight adaptation of the theory of Section 2. Next we illuminate the scope of the multivariate versions of Lemma 2.1 and 2.2. We do not pretend to be complete. E.g., multivariate generalizations of the previous examples are skipped. Instead, we present as an interesting area of application some examples of conditional heteroskedastic models. Conditional heteroskedastic models have attracted a lot of attention since the introduction of the ARCH model by Engle (1982) and the GARCH extension by Bollerslev (1986). The range of applications is large, see the survey paper of Bollerslev et al. (1992). Two GARCH type examples are discussed and some indications are given how to generalize these examples to multivariate conditional heteroskedastic models.

3.1 ARMA Processes

Consider the class of wide stationary ARMA time-series

$$\rho(L)x_t = \theta(L)\varepsilon_t, \tag{1}$$

where $\rho(L) = 1 - \rho_1 L - \ldots - \rho_p L^p$ and $\theta(L) = 1 + \theta_1 L + \ldots + \theta_q L^q$ (p, q fixed integers) are time-invariant linear filters having no common roots and no roots on the unit circle and where $\{\varepsilon_t\}$ is white noise with variance σ^2. This family is identical to the class of processes with rational spectral densities [Brockwell and Davis (1987), Theorem 4.4.2]. The family of ARMA models is closed under temporal aggregation. We present the proof for flow variables (the proof for stock variables is similar). Roughly speaking we show that sums of rational spectral densities are also rational. With some abuse of notation denote $1 - \rho_1 \exp\{-i\lambda\} - \ldots - \rho_p \exp\{-ip\lambda\}$ by $\rho(\lambda)$ and let $\theta(\lambda)$ have a similar interpretation. Using Lemma 2.2 observe that, with $\mid \psi(\lambda) \mid^2 = \sin^2(m\lambda/2)/\sin^2(\lambda/2)$,

$$\overline{f}^{(m)}(\lambda) = \frac{1}{m}\frac{\sigma^2}{2\pi}\frac{\sum_{j=0}^{m-1} \mid \psi\left(\frac{\lambda+2\pi j}{m}\right) \mid^2 \mid \theta\left(\frac{\lambda+2\pi j}{m}\right) \mid^2 \prod_{k\neq j} \mid \rho\left(\frac{\lambda+2\pi k}{m}\right) \mid^2}{\prod_{k=0}^{m-1} \mid \rho\left(\frac{\lambda+2\pi k}{m}\right) \mid^2} \tag{2}$$

To show that $\overline{f}^{(m)}(\lambda)$ is rational we use the following easy lemma. Let $[x]$ denote the largest integer smaller than or equal to x.

Lemma 3.1 Suppose $g(\lambda) = \sum_{j=-n}^{n} a_j \exp\{-ij\lambda/m\}$ and assume that

$$g(\lambda) = g(\lambda + 2\pi k), \ k = 0, \ldots, m-1.$$

Then $g(\lambda) = \sum_{j=-[n/m]}^{[n/m]} a_{jm} \exp\{-ij\lambda\}$. □

Both the numerator and the denominator on the RHS of (2) satisfy the conditions of this lemma and hence $\overline{f}^{(m)}(\lambda)$ is rational.

A closer inspection of the spectral density yields also upper bounds on the ARMA orders of an aggregated ARMA(p,q) time-series. For stock variables the aggregated low frequency process is ARMA$(p, p + [(q-p)/m])$ and in case of flow variables it is ARMA$(p, p + [(q-p+m-1)/m])$. The corresponding parameters of the low frequency process are easily obtained: apply the algorithm of Theorem 3 or Lemma 1 of Engwerda et al. (1991) to both the numerator and the denominator in the RHS of (2).

3.2 Fractionally Differenced Processes

Consider the class of wide stationary fractionally differenced time-series

$$(1-L)^d x_t = \varepsilon_t, \tag{3}$$

where $d \in (-\frac{1}{2}, \frac{1}{2})$ and $\{\varepsilon_t\}$ is white noise with variance σ^2. The autocovariance function $\gamma(k)$ of $\{x_t\}$ is slowly decaying at rate k^{2d-1} [Brockwell and Davis (1987), Theorem 12.4.1]. The family (3) is introduced to make a more parsimonious parameterization possible for long memory processes. We show that this class is not closed under temporal aggregation. Even if we assume that the RHS of (3) belongs to the ARMA processes discussed in the previous example, the class is not closed. Recall that the spectral density of (3) is given by

$$f_d(\lambda) = \frac{\sigma^2}{2\pi} \mid 1 - \exp\{-i\lambda\} \mid^{-2d}.$$

In case of stock variables aggregation over $m = 2$ periods yields a process $\{y_t\}$ with spectral density

$$
\begin{aligned}
f_d^{(2)}(\lambda) &= \frac{1}{2}\frac{\sigma^2}{2\pi}\left(|\,1-\exp\{-i\lambda/2\}\,|^{-2d} + |\,1-\exp\{-i(\lambda/2+\pi)\}\,|^{-2d}\right) \\
&= \frac{1}{2}\frac{\sigma^2}{2\pi}\,|\,1-\exp\{-i\lambda\}\,|^{-2d} \times \\
&\quad \left(|\,1-\exp\{-i\lambda/2\}\,|^{2d} + |\,1-\exp\{-i(\lambda/2+\pi)\}\,|^{2d}\right).
\end{aligned}
$$

It is obvious that the autocovariance function of the low frequency process $\{y_t\}$ decays at the same rate k^{2d-1} as the original high frequency time-series. If one observes this rate in applications, one tries to remove the long memory character by pre-multiplying the series with $(1-L)^d$. This does not help for $\{y_t\}$, since $\{\tilde{y}_t = (1-L)^d y_t\}$ has spectral density

$$
\begin{aligned}
\tilde{f}_d^{(2)}(\lambda) &= \frac{1}{2}\frac{\sigma^2}{2\pi}(|\,1-\exp\{-i\lambda/2\}\,|^{2d} + |\,1-\exp\{-i(\lambda/2+\pi)\}\,|^{2d}) \\
&= f_{-d}^{(2)}(\lambda)
\end{aligned}
$$

and this is just the spectral density of an aggregated fractionally differenced time-series of order $-d$ and hence the autocovariance function decays at rate k^{-2d-1}. Thus $\{\tilde{y}_t\}$ is still a long memory process. Moreover, it seems that our goal is overshooted by a fractional differencing coefficient d. This coefficient, however, was motivated by the autocovariance function of $\{y_t\}$. One easily verifies that other fractional differencing coefficients cannot do the job either. According to Theorem 12.4.2 of Brockwell and Davis (1987) we have the same situation if we replace the RHS of (3) by an ARMA process.

This has some repercussions for applications. Observe that the spectral density of an ARFIMA model at $\lambda = 0$ is equal to zero if $d < 0$ and equal to infinity if $d > 0$. Methods for estimating d are concentrated on the estimated spectral density near zero [cf., e.g., Fox and Taqqu (1986)]. Aggregation of a high frequency process with $d < 0$ removes the singularity at zero and hence it is doubtful if the practitioner will find the true underlying d based on aggregated data. Probably he will fit an ARMA process to the series although the autocovariance function does not decay exponentially but rather at the rate k^{2d-1} (between k^{-2} and k^{-1}). If $d > 0$ there is still a singularity in the spectral density of the aggregated process and pre-multiplying the aggregated series with $(1-L)^d$ removes the singularity. Similar to the situation with negative d the practitioner will fit an ARMA process to this remaining series although the covariance function decays at the rate k^{-2d-1} (between k^{-2} and k^{-1}). Whether d is negative or positive, a process with an autocovariance function decaying at a rate between k^{-2} and k^{-1} is approximated by an ARMA time-series. Hence, even in the case of aggregated data, fractionally differencing increases the speed of convergence of the autocorrelation function from a rate between k^{-1} and 1 to a rate between k^{-2} and k^{-1} (if $d > 0$). This suggests that the goal of fractionally differencing (a more parsimonious parameterization) is still reached although the model is not precisely correct in a mathematical sense.

We conclude this example by formally closing the family of fractionally differenced processes. The discussion above suggests the class of processes with positive continuous spectral densities for the RHS of (3). The proof is straightforward. Note that the coefficient d is uniquely defined in this family.

3.3 Stable ARMA Processes

Consider the class of time-series

$$\rho(L)x_t = \sigma\theta(L)\varepsilon_t, \tag{4}$$

where $\rho(L)$ and $\theta(L)$ are time-invariant linear filters satisfying the conditions of Subsection 3.1 and where $\{\varepsilon_t\}$ is an i.i.d. sequence of stable distributions of order α ($\alpha \in (0,2]$ fixed). The scale of the time-series is determined by $\sigma > 0$. Observe that these processes are not square integrable if $\alpha < 2$. Let the coefficients $\{\psi_j\}$ be determined by

$$\psi(\lambda) = \sum_{j=-\infty}^{\infty} \psi_j \exp\{-ij\lambda\} = \theta(\lambda)/\rho(\lambda)$$

and define the pseudo autocorrelation function by

$$\gamma(k) = \sigma^2 \sum_{j=-\infty}^{\infty} \psi_j\psi_{j+k} \;/\; \sum_{j=-\infty}^{\infty} \psi_j^2.$$

These notations are motivated by the following result of Davis and Resnick (1986)

$$\sum_{t=1}^{n-k} x_t x_{t+k} \;/\; \sum_{t=1}^{n} x_t^2 \xrightarrow{P} \gamma(k).$$

Finally define the pseudo spectral density

$$f(\lambda) = \sigma^2 \mid \theta(\lambda) \mid^2 \;/\; \mid \rho(\lambda) \mid^2 .$$

One easily verifies that each pseudo autocorrelation function or each pseudo spectral density uniquely determines a member of the family (4) and vice versa. If the pseudo spectral density is merely used as a short-hand notation for the pseudo autocorrelations, the one-one relation between $f(\lambda)$ and $\gamma(\lambda)$ implies that the proofs of deriving low frequency (pseudo) spectral densities are still valid. The same answers as in the ARMA example are obtained.

Unfortunately, this does not suffice to conclude that the family (4) is closed in a strict stationary sense: aggregated processes do not necessarily satisfy the i.i.d. assumptions following equation (4). Due to temporal aggregation the i.i.d. assumption on the stable variables $\{\varepsilon_t\}$ is lost (except for $\alpha = 2$) and hence the family (4) is not closed in a strict stationary sense. This is not very surprising if we reconsider, e.g., the ARMA family. It is well-known that, if we add an i.i.d. assumption on the innovations errors in the wide stationary ARMA model of Subsection 3.1, the family is not closed anymore in a strict stationary sense (unless the innovations are normal). So the ARMA model is closed only in a wide stationary sense as is shown in Subsection 3.1. The same problem occurs for ARMA models with symmetric stable errors. Aggregation of stable ARMA time-series of the form (4) leads to aggregated processes of the same form but the i.i.d. condition upon $\{\varepsilon_t\}$ in the aggregated series transfers to

$$E\varepsilon_t\varepsilon_{t-i}\delta_{A\times B}(\varepsilon_t, \varepsilon_{t-i}) = 0$$

for all t, i and all bounded, symmetric intervals A, B. Hence the innovation errors of the aggregated process are only 'uncorrelated' but not necessarily independent.

3.4 GARCH Processes

The classical GARCH definition is given by

$$\begin{aligned} x_t &= \sqrt{h_t}\,\varepsilon_t, &(5)\\ B(L)h_t &= \psi + A(L)x_t^2, &(6)\end{aligned}$$

where $B(L) = 1-\beta_1L-\ldots-\beta_pL^p$ and $A(L) = \alpha_1L+\ldots+\alpha_qL^q$ and where $\{\varepsilon_t\}$ is an i.i.d. sequence with zero mean and unit variance. Put $r = \max(p, q)$. Bollerslev (1988) observes that $\{x_t^2\}$ satisfies the following ARMA(r,p) equation

$$\rho(L)x_t^2 \equiv \{B(L) - A(L)\}x_t^2 = \psi + B(L)\eta_t \equiv \psi + \theta(L)\eta_t,$$

where $\{\eta_t = x_t^2 - h_t\}$ is a sequence of uncorrelated random variables. We assume that the polynomials $\rho(L)$ and $\theta(L)$ satisfy the same conditions as in Subsection 3.1. Drost and Nijman (1993) show that the classical GARCH family is not closed under temporal aggregation, neither in case of stock variables nor in case of flow variables. Define the bivariate time-series $\{X_t = (x_t, x_t^2)'\}$ and observe that the components of this multivariate process exhibit the following features:

1. $\{x_t\}$ is white noise,

2. $\{x_t^2\}$ has a rational spectral density

and, if the finite dimensional distributions of $\{\varepsilon_t\}$ are symmetric,

3. the cross-spectrum of $\{x_t\}$ and $\{x_t^2\}$ is zero.

Drost and Nijman (1993) define a time-series to be weak GARCH if it satisfies the properties 1–3, i.e., they restrict attention to the spectrum of the bivariate process $\{X_t\}$. The original characteristics of GARCH - stationary but conditional heteroskedastic processes- are still valid in this class. The class of weak GARCH models is closed under temporal aggregation. Define the aggregated processes $\{Y_t = X_{tm} = (x_{tm}, x_{tm}^2)'\}$ and $\{\tilde{Y}_t = X_{tm} + \ldots + X_{tm-m+1} = (x_{tm} + \ldots + x_{tm-m+1}, x_{tm}^2 + \ldots + x_{tm-m+1}^2)'\}$. These are the aggregated processes corresponding to $\{X_t\}$ if we consider the latter series as stock and flow variables respectively. Application of the multivariate versions of Lemmas 2.1 and 2.2 and recalling Subsection 3.1 show that the aggregated processes satisfy the conditions 1–3, too. Hence the class of weak GARCH models is closed under temporal aggregation in case of stock variables. The same conclusion for flow variables cannot be obtained from the process $\{\tilde{Y}_t\}$. This process is an intermediate case. In fact we want that the process $\{\overline{Y}_t = (\overline{y}_t, \overline{y}_t^2)' = (x_{tm} + \ldots + x_{tm-m+1}, [x_{tm} + \ldots + x_{tm-m+1}]^2)' = \tilde{Y}_t + (0, \sum\sum_{i \neq j \in \{0,\ldots,m-1\}} x_{tm-i}x_{tm-j})'\}$ satisfies the conditions 1–3. Compared to $\{\tilde{Y}_t\}$ this process contains several cross-products. In principle these cross-products may invalidate the requirements 2 or 3. Therefore we impose the following condition

$$\forall 0 \leq i \leq j \leq k, 0 \neq i \text{ or } j \neq k : \; Ex_t x_{t-i} x_{t-j} x_{t-k} = 0. \tag{7}$$

This regularity condition seems to be harmless. If we assume, e.g., that the expected observation at time t does not depend upon past observations (and equals zero) and that the expected observation at time t is not influenced by future conditional variances, i.e.,

$$\begin{aligned} Ex_t \mid x_{t-1}, x_{t-2}, \ldots &= 0, \text{ and} \\ Ex_t x_{t+k}^2 \mid x_{t-1}, x_{t-2}, \ldots &= 0, \; k = \pm 1, \pm 2, \ldots, \end{aligned}$$

condition (7) is fulfilled. Moreover, the argument leading to condition 3 also implies (7).

Similar to the ARMA class, the spectral density also provides upper bounds on the GARCH orders of aggregated high frequency GARCH(p,q) processes. For stock variables the aggregated low frequency process is GARCH$(r+[(p-r)/m],r)$ and for flow variables it is GARCH(r,r). Low frequency parameter values are also obtained along the lines of Subsection 3.1.

Extensions to ARMA models with GARCH errors are straightforward, compare Drost and Nijman (1993). Another extension is the class of quadratic GARCH models of Sentana (1991). He includes also cross products of type $x_{t-i}x_{t-j}$ in the definition of the conditional volatility h_t. Under condition (7), one easily verifies that our analysis carries over to this class. Hence, in a weak sense, the quadratic GARCH models are also closed under temporal aggregation. Moreover, it is easy to extend the analysis of this example to multivariate GARCH type models, see Nijman and Sentana (1993).

3.5 GARCH-M Processes

Adopt the notation of the previous example and consider the GARCH-M family

$$x_t = \delta h_t + \nu_t, \tag{8}$$

where $\{\nu_t\}$ is weak GARCH $(h_t = \nu_t^2 - \eta_t)$. Observe

$$\{B(L) - A(L)\}x_t = \delta\psi + \delta A(L)\eta_t + \{B(L) - A(L)\}\nu_t.$$

Since $\{\eta_t\}$ and $\{\nu_t\}$ are orthogonal, the spectral density of the RHS is the spectral density of a moving average. Hence GARCH-M time-series have rational spectral densities and are therefore indistinguishable from classical ARMA models. In principle one would add conditions similar to those in the GARCH section, i.e., assume some GARCH-M specific characteristic for the squared process. Investigations into this direction are still missing. More research is necessary to obtain a suitable formulation of the GARCH-M class of models such that this family is closed under temporal aggregation. Of course this remark applies to many other models as well.

References

Bollerslev T (1986) Generalized Autoregressive Conditional Heteroskedasticity, Journal of Econometrics 31, 307–327

Bollerslev T (1988) On the Correlation Structure for the Generalized Autoregressive Conditional Heteroskedastic Process, Journal of Time Series Analysis 9, 121–131

Bollerslev T, Chou R Y and Kroner K F (1992) ARCH Modeling in Finance: a Review of the Theory and Empirical Evidence, Journal of Econometrics 52, 5–60

Brockwell P J and Davis R A (1987) Time Series: Theory and Methods, Springer

Davis R A and Resnick S I (1986) Limit Theory for the Sample Covariance and Correlation Functions of Moving Averages, Annals of Statistics 14, 533–558

De Vries C G (1991) On the Relation between GARCH and Stable Processes, Journal of Econometrics 48, 313–324

Diebold F X and Rudebusch G P (1991) Is Consumption too Smooth? Long Memory and the Deaton Paradox, The Review of Economics and Statistics 73, 1–9

Diebold F X and Rudebusch G P (1992) On the Power of the Dicky-Fuller Test Against Fractional Alternatives, Economics Letters 35, 155–160

Drost F C and Nijman T E (1993) Temporal Aggregation of GARCH Processes, Econometrica, to appear

Engle R F (1982) Autoregressive Conditional Heteroskedasticity with Estimates of the Variance of U.K. Inflation, Econometrica 50, 987–1008

Engwerda J C, Ran A C M and Rijkeboer A L (1991) Necessary and Sufficient Conditions for the Existence of a Positive Definite Solution of the Matrix Equation $X + A'X^{-1}A = I$, Working Paper FEW 482, Tilburg University

Fama E (1965) Behavior of Stock Market Prices, Journal of Business 38, 34–105

Fox R and Taqqu M S (1986) Large Sample Properties of Parameter Estimates for Strongly Dependent Stationary Gaussian Time Series, Annals of Statistics 14, 517–532

Geweke J and Porter-Hudak S (1983) The Estimation and Application of Long-Memory Time Series Models, Journal of Time Series Analysis 4, 221–238

Granger C W and Joyeux R (1980) An Introduction to Long-Memory Time Series Models and Fractionally Differencing, Journal of Time Series Analysis 1, 15–29

Hansen L P and Sargent T J (1983) The Dimensionality of the Aliasing Problem in Models with Rational Spectral Densities, Econometrica 51, 377–388

Nijman T E and Sentana E (1993) Marginalization and Contemporaneous Aggregation in Multivariate GARCH Processes, CentER Discussion Papers 9312, Tilburg University

Sentana E (1991) Quadratic ARCH Models: a Potential Re-Interpretation of ARCH Models, Preprint, LSE

Sowell F (1992) Maximum likelihood Estimation of Stationary Univariate Fractionally Integrated Time Series Models, Journal of Econometrics 53, 165–188

On Long- and Short-Run Purchasing Power Parity[1]

By Ronald MacDonald and Ian W. Marsh[2]

Abstract: We use the Johansen maximum likelihood estimation procedure to test for long-run purchasing power parity (PPP) for a variety of exchange rates over the recent float. We find considerable evidence of weak-form PPP in contrast to most of the extant literature. Such long-run relationships are then used to form dynamic error correction models for each currency. In many cases our dynamic PPP models are able to outperform a random walk alternative in out-of-sample tests of forecast accuracy.

1 Introduction

The recent empirical exchange rate literature has produced (at least) two stylised facts[3]: exchange rate models do not seem to provide a long-run relationship between exchange rates and the relevant 'fundamentals', and it is impossible to outperform a random walk in an out-of-sample forecasting contest. In this paper we address these two 'facts' using the simplest 'structural' model of exchange rate determination, namely purchasing power parity (PPP). We demonstrate, *inter alia*, that such a model does, for some currencies, offer a 'tie-down' for the long-run exchange rate and that this long-run relationship can be used to formulate a short-run dynamic equation which outperforms a random walk. Given that these findings contrast with practically all of the extant empirical literature, we believe that they should be of considerable interest to the profession.

The outline of the remainder of this paper is as follows. In the next section we present a brief summary of the concept of PPP and some of the recent empirical evidence. In Section 3 the econometric methodology used for conducting our tests is presented. The data set used and our econometric results are reported in Section 4. The paper closes with a concluding section.

---

[1]An earlier version of this paper was presented at the ZEW Conference on "Financial-Markets Econometrics". We are most grateful to conference participants, Juergen Kaehler and an anonymous referee for helpful comments. We also acknowledge financial support from the ESRC (grant R000232945).

[2]Ronald MacDonald and Ian W. Marsh, Department of Economics, The University of Strathclyde, Curran Building, 100 Cathedral Street, Glasgow, Scotland.

[3]See MacDonald and Taylor (1992).

2 Purchasing Power Parity: A Review of the Recent Evidence

If the home and foreign country produce a tradeable homogeneous good, i, and there are no impediments to international trade, such as tariffs or transactions costs, then the 'law' of one price must hold:

$$P_t^i = P_t^{i*} S_t \tag{1}$$

where P^i denotes the price of good i in the domestic country, S denotes the spot exchange rate (home currency price of a unit of foreign exchange) and an asterisk denotes a foreign magnitude. Arbitrage is assumed to ensure that the equality (1) is continually maintained (see Hallwood and MacDonald (1993) for a further discussion). If both countries produce n goods (where i runs from 1 to n), we may sum across the n goods to obtain absolute PPP:

$$S_t = P_t / P_t^* \tag{2}$$

or

$$s_t = p_t - p_t^* \tag{2'}$$

where the prices now have the interpretation of price levels and lower case letters denote natural logarithms. Absolute PPP implies that an increase (decrease) in the home (foreign) price level should result in an equiproportionate rise (fall) in the exchange rate. Absolute PPP may be motivated in an equivalent way. Thus if we define the log of the real exchange rate, q_t , as $s_t - p_t + p_t^*$, then for absolute PPP to continually hold, q_t should equal zero:

$$q_t \equiv s_t - p_t + p_t^* = 0 \tag{3}$$

However, few proponents of PPP (see, for example, Officer (1976) for a useful discussion of the views of the traditional proponents of PPP) would argue for a strict adherence to PPP. Rather, PPP is usually seen as determining the exchange rate in the long-run[4], whilst a variety of other factors, such as trading restrictions, productivity and preference changes, may influence the exchange rate in conditions of disequilibrium. With this view, shocks to the exchange rate which cause non-zero values of q_t will be corrected in the long-run; the real exchange is a mean-reverting process.

[4]In an hyper-inflation scenario, PPP is also expected to hold in the short-run as well - see Frenkel, 1980.

Much of the empirical evidence on PPP has utilised aggregate price indices to test absolute PPP[5]. One extremely popular way of testing PPP has involved the use of regression analysis. For example, Krugman (1978) and Frenkel (1981) present regression estimates of absolute PPP, based on a selection of aggregate price indices, for part of the recent experience with floating exchange rates. Frenkel and Krugman test absolute PPP using a regression equation of the following form[6]:

$$s_t = \alpha + \beta p_t + \beta^* p_t^* + u_t \tag{4}$$

where u_t is a disturbance term. If PPP holds, it is expected that $\beta = -\beta^* = 1$ and that $\alpha = 0$ (if price indices are used instead of price levels, the intercept term need not be zero). Frenkel (1981) uses wholesale and cost of living indices from the recent floating exchange rate experience for the dollar-pound, dollar-French franc and dollar-Deutschmark exchange rates. It is demonstrated, *inter alia*, that absolute PPP is not supported by the data, since the *a priori* restrictions on β and β^* are not satisfied. Similar results are reported by Krugman (1978) using 1970's data[7].

A further battery of tests of PPP relies on examining the time series properties of the real exchange rate. Such tests may be viewed as tests of the efficient markets view of PPP (EMPPP), against a more traditional view of PPP. The EMPPP, which is derived using parity conditions from the capital account of the balance of payments, suggests that the real exchange rate should follow a random walk process. The EMPPP was originally proposed by Roll (1979) and may be motivated around the following first-order autoregressive process for the real exchange rate:

$$q_t = \alpha_0 + \alpha_1 q_{t-1} + u_t \tag{5}$$

where u_t is a white noise process. In terms of (5), long-run PPP requires $\alpha_0 = \alpha_1 = u_t = 0$; that is, q_t must be a zero-mean stationary process. (again, if price indices are used instead of price levels, q_t may equal the constant, α_0). A less strict interpretation of PPP would, as we have indicated, additionally allow for short-run deviations from PPP which are eventually extinguished in the long-run. In terms of equation (5) such behaviour may be accommodated by a value of α_1 which is less than unity in absolute value. Thus with α_1 less than 1, short-run deviations from PPP are allowed but such deviations are corrected at a rate equal to $(1 - \alpha_1)$: the real exchange rate is mean reverting.

---

[5]Isard (1977) and Kravis and Lipsey (1978) examine the law of one price relationship using disaggregated prices for the 1970's and find that the relationship is not upheld.

[6]These authors also use a first differenced version of (4) to test *relative* PPP; similar results to those for absolute PPP are reported.

[7]Interestingly, both Frenkel (1980) and Krugman (1978) find support for PPP using data from the 1920's experience with floating exchange rates.

Alternatively, a proponent of EMPPP would argue that $\alpha_1 = 1$, indicating that the real exchange rate follows a random walk with possible non-zero drift of α_0.

A number of researchers have tested whether the real exchange rate, for a number of currencies, follows a random walk by running regression equations of the form:

$$\Delta q_t = \gamma + \beta_1 \Delta q_{t-1} + \beta_2 \Delta q_{t-2} + \ldots + \beta_k \Delta q_{t-k} + u_t \tag{6}$$

where Δ is the first difference operator and k is the lag length. The random-walk behaviour of the real exchange rate is usually assessed by testing the hypothesis that the β coefficients are zero. The majority of this evidence is unable to reject the random-walk hypothesis[8]. However, Abuaf and Jorion (1990) have argued that such tests, since they involve only the differences of the variables, are likely to have low power against the alternative of a near-random-walk model. By estimating (5) directly for a number of bilateral US dollar exchange rates, and by additionally accounting for the potential cross correlation of the error terms across the equations using a generalised least squares estimator, Abuaf and Jorion show that the value of α_1 lies in a range of 0.98 to 0.99 for monthly data. Although these point estimates are extremely close to one, they are not *exactly* one, indicating that there is some evidence of mean reversion[9].[10] Using annual data (which in the context of a test of a long-run relationship like PPP may be a more appropriate observational frequency) over the period 1901-1972, Abuaf and Jorion report an average slope coefficient of around 0.78. This allows statistical rejection of the null of a random-walk[11] and defines a half life of 3.3 years, similar to that implied by the monthly data base.

The problematic nature of testing the stationarity of the real exchange rate using equations like (6) has been further emphasised by Huizinga (1987). Huizinga's (1987) insight follows on from the work of Cochrane (1988) and is that an equation like (6) is typically specified with only a relatively short lag length. However, the long-run behaviour of the real exchange rate may be affected by much longer lags than are usually modelled, and it is possible that the inclusion of such longer lags could force the real exchange rate back to its equilibrium level. In particular, if the changes in the real exchange rate are negatively serially correlated, the real exchange rate will be mean-reverting. One simple way of capturing the effects of such long lags is to

---

[8]See *inter alia* Roll (1979), Frenkel (1981), Darby (1980), Mishkin (1984) and MacDonald (1985) for papers which present evidence supportive of the random walk view.

[9]With these numbers, it would take between 3 and 5 years for a 50 per cent overvaluation of a currency to be cut in half.

[10]The statistical significance of this result is, however, somewhat weak.

[11]Interestingly, Adler and Lehmann (1983) used the same annual data set and could not reject the random walk model.

take the ratio of the variance of a long difference of the real exchange rate to the variance of its first difference (scaled by the reciprocal of the long lag length). If the real exchange rate is truly a random walk then this ratio will equal unity. If, however, real exchange rates exhibit mean-reverting behaviour the variance-ratio will fall below unity. Applying this methodology to ten dollar bilateral rates, for the recent floating period, Huizinga finds evidence of mean reversion. This is indicated by the fact that after ten years the average variance ratio across the ten currencies is 0.65. Although this ratio seems to indicate substantial mean reversion, the deviation from one is not significant. To quote: "While the magnitude of these deviations form random walk behaviour is obviously large in an economic sense, it is not significant in a statistical sense. Someone with strong *a priori* information that real exchange rates are random walks need not be persuaded otherwise by the data. Nonetheless, those who look to the data to obtain a reasonable 'best guess' are unlikely to select a random walk specification to describe the long run behaviour of real exchange rates." (Huizinga (1987)).

An alternative way of testing whether real exchange rates obey a random walk process has involved exploiting the cointegration methodology proposed by Engle and Granger (1987). For example, if three variables, such as an exchange rate and the corresponding relative prices, are cointegrated then it means that in the long-run they settle down together in a unique way. More specifically, this means that in terms of equation (4) the estimated residuals (i.e. the $\hat{u}$'s) should form a stationary series. If they do not, there will be no tendency for the exchange rate and relative prices to settle down; they will move apart without bound. The cointegration methodology is in some ways similar to tests discussed above of whether the real exchange rate is stationary. However, using (4) instead of (5) is slightly different since it does not restrict β to equal one and β^* to equal minus one. As Taylor (1988) and Patel (1990) have pointed out, the corresponding results may differ because of measurement error (i.e. the observed price indices are not the 'true' indices, rather they are the observable indices related to the true series by measurement error) and transportation costs.

For the recent experience with flexible exchange rates the cointegration methodology has been applied to aggregate price data by Taylor (1988) and Enders (1988). Both these authors test for cointegration between bilateral dollar exchange rates and a relative price measure (thus the restriction $\beta = -\beta^*$ is imposed) using the Engle-Granger two-step methodology and monthly data. Both Enders and Taylor find that the null hypothesis of non-cointegration cannot be rejected: there is no long-run tendency for exchange rates and relative prices to settle down on an equilibrium track[12].

[12]Taylor and McMahon (1989) apply this methodology to the early 1920's experience with floating exchange rates and find some limited evidence in favour of the hypothesis.

In contrast to these studies, Patel (1990) uses the two-step methodology to test for long-run PPP without imposing $\beta = -\beta^*$; however, little evidence of cointegration is reported and the use of the two-step methodology precludes testing for proportionality of the β's with respect to the exchange rate. Fraser, Taylor and Webster (1991) use the two-step cointegration methodology to test the law-of-one price for the sterling/US dollar exchange rate and a disaggregated industry price base over the period 1975-80; little evidence of cointegration is established. As is evident from the above discussion, most of the recent time series tests of PPP involve some form of hypothesis test in a univariate setting (i.e. testing whether the real exchange rate has a unit root or testing for cointegration between a nominal exchange rate and relative prices). Relatively little work has been conducted recently on *modelling* the exchange rate in terms of relative prices. One exception is the paper by Edison (1985), in which the dynamic error correction methodology of Hendry *et al.* (1984) is utilised. However, the methodology is not used to test how well a dynamic PPP model works relative to, say, the random walk model; rather it is simply used to test a number of propositions regarding symmetry of the exchange rate with respect to relative prices.

In this paper we present some further tests of the PPP hypothesis using cointegration techniques. Our approach has, however, a number of novel features compared to previous tests. First, and as we have seen, other researchers generally impose the restriction $\beta = -\beta^*$; however, transportation or measurement errors may drive a wedge between these two coefficients and they should therefore be estimated unconstrained. We estimate the β's in an unconstrained cointegration framework and indeed test for the validity of the restriction. Such tests are facilitated, despite the fact that we are dealing with non-stationary variables, by our use of the multivariate cointegration methodology proposed by Johansen (1988, 1991).

The Johansen technique is superior to the simpler regression-based tests, noted above, because it fully captures the underlying time series properties of the data, provides estimates of *all* the cointegrating vectors that exist within a vector of variables (i.e. using ordinary least squares to estimate a cointegration relationship for an N dimensional vector does not clarify whether one is dealing with a unique cointegrating vector or simply a linear combination of all the distinct cointegrating vectors which exist within the system) and offers a test statistic for the number of cointegrating vectors (again, this contrasts with the regression-based methodology). This test may therefore be viewed as more discerning in its ability to reject a false null hypothesis.

A further feature of our work is that, in contrast to much of the recent literature on PPP, we push the cointegration tests further by engaging in some exchange rate modelling. In particular, we utilise estimated cointegrating relationships to model the dynamic behaviour of exchange rates using the general-to -specific methodology of Hendry *et al.* (1984). One critical feature of this part of the work is whether the estimated dynamic equations can outperform a simple random walk model in an out-of-sample forecasting contest. We now turn to a brief description of the econometric technique used in our cointegration tests.

3 Econometric Method

Let $X_t = (s_t, p_t, p_t^*)'$, where the elements in X are assumed to be integrated of order 1 (I(1)), and assume that this vector has an autoregressive representation with Gaussian errors u_t[13]:

$$X_t = \Pi_1 X_{t-1} + \Pi_2 X_{t-2} + \ldots + \Pi_k X_{t-k} + u_{t'} \qquad t = 1, 2, \ldots, T. \tag{7}$$

where, for expository reasons, we have excluded a constant. The long-run static[14] equilibrium corresponding to (7) is

$$\Pi X = 0, \tag{8}$$

where the long-run coefficient matrix Π is defined:

$$I - \Pi_1 - \Pi_2 - \ldots - \Pi_k = \Pi. \tag{9}$$

Π is an nxn matrix whose rank determines the number of distinct cointegrating vectors which exist between the variables in X and $I$is the identity matrix. Define two nxr matrices, α and β, such that

$$\Pi = \alpha\beta' \tag{10}$$

The rows of β' form the r distinct cointegrating vectors such that, if β' is the ith row of β':

$$\beta_i' X_t \sim I(0) \tag{11}$$

that is, despite all the variables entering X_t are I(1) there is some linear transformation of the variables, defined by β_i', which is stationary (I(0)).

The elements of α have the interpretation of error correction terms: they indicate the average speed of adjustment towards equilibrium. In the current context, for example, they indicate how rapidly a current deviation from PPP is offset in the future. Johansen (1988) demonstrates that the likelihood

---

[13]Phillips (1987) suggests that the Johansen technique may also be applicable in the presence of heteroskedastic error processes. In our empirical analysis, an intercept term and seasonal dummies were included in the VARs, as in Johansen and Juselius (1990).

[14]Dynamic steady state equilibrium simply involves the addition of a term in the constant vector of steady-state growth rates to (7), which we omit here for expositional purposes; this does not affect the subsequent discussion.

ratio, or trace, test statistic (LR1) for the hypothesis that there are at most r distinct cointegrating vectors is

$$LR1 = T \sum_{i=r+1}^{n} ln(1 - \hat{\lambda}_i) \tag{12}$$

where $\hat{\lambda}_{r+1}, \ldots, \hat{\lambda}_n$ are the $n - r$ smallest squared canonical correlations between the X_{t-k} and ΔX_t series, corrected for the effect of the lagged differences of the X_t process (for details of how to extract the $\hat{\lambda}_i$'s see Johansen 1988,1991). Additionally, the likelihood ratio statistic for testing at most r cointegrating vectors against the alternative of $r + 1$ cointegrating vectors is given by

$$LR2 = Tln(1 - \lambda_{r+1}) \tag{13}$$

Johansen (1988) shows that (12) and (13) have a non-standard distribution under the null hypothesis. He does, however, provide approximate critical values for the statistic, generated by Monte Carlo methods[15].

An additional advantage of using the Johansen methodology is that it allows direct hypothesis tests on the coefficients entering the cointegrating vectors. We may therefore test the proportionality of the exchange rate to relative prices. The novel feature of the present tests is that they are robust to the non-stationarity of the data; previous tests, which used the levels of the variables and standard t-tests or F ratios, are not. Using the notation of Johansen and Juselius (1990), the hypothesis tests which we implement are of the general form:

$$H_3 : \Pi = \alpha\varphi' H' (or \beta = H\varphi) \tag{14}$$

where H is an nxs matrix, with $s \geq r$ and φ is the corresponding sxr weighting matrix.

In this paper we use the above methodology to test what we refer to as strong-form and weak-form PPP. Strong-form PPP refers to the situation where there is at least one cointegrating vector between an exchange rate and the corresponding relative prices and the proportionality restrictions are satisfied. As we have indicated, such restrictions may not be satisfied because of factors such as measurement error and transportation costs. Given the high probability that the price series used in our empirical analysis are not the 'true' price series, we would tend to emphasize the weak-form version of PPP. The latter places no restrictions on the cointegrating vector and simply

---

15 The critical values recorded in Johansen's (1988) paper are for a VAR without an intercept term or seasonal dummies. Since these were included in our empirical analysis, we used the critical values for (12) and (13) reported in Johansen and Juselius (1990).

requires that the exchange rate and relative prices be cointegrated. This latter definition of PPP is, we believe, of considerable importance since if it does not hold, as other researchers have found, it implies that exchange rates and relative prices have no long-run equilibrium relationship.

4 Data and Results on Unit Roots and Cointegration

The data for this study were obtained from Datastream who, in turn, use International Financial Statistics (IFS) as their original source. The exchange rates used consist of five US dollar bilateral rates - the German mark, Japanese yen, French franc, Italian lira and UK pound - and three German mark bilateral rates - the French franc, the Italian lira and UK pound. All US dollar bilateral rates are sourced as IFS line RF; the German mark bilateral rates are constructed using the familiar triangular arbitrage condition[16]. Two alternative price series were used, namely a wholesale price index, IFS line 63, and a consumer price index, IFS line 64.[17] The data period runs from January 1974 to June 1991 (all lags are generated within this sample period) and all the variables are converted into natural logarithms.

As a preliminary exercise to our multivariate cointegration tests we investigated the orders of integration of our series. In order to do this, we estimated standard Augmented Dickey -Fuller (ADF) statistics, which correct for autocorrelation using an autoregressive representation[18] , and Phillips-Perron (PP) statistics, which adjust for autocorrelation using a non-parametric correction. The estimated values of the relevant t-ratios (constructed, alternatively, with a constant and with a constant and time trend) are reported in Table 1. The ADF statistics indicate that all of the exchange rate series contain a unit root. In line with previous studies the ADF statistics suggest that the price indices - with the exception of the Japanese CPI - are only stationary in second differences. In contrast, a number of the PP statistics indicate that some of the price series are stationary in either levels or first differences. We attribute this finding for the price series to the point made by Schwert (1987) that Phillips -Perron statistics may reject the null of a unit root too often in the presence of a first-order moving average process.

---

[16]The UK pound rate is in fact taken as line RH. All currencies are originally expressed as the home currency price of one unit of foreign currency, except for the UK pound. The reciprocal of the published UK pound rate was utilised.

[17]The wholesale price measures are not available for France and Italy.

[18]The reported statistics have up to 12 lags. The lag length was chosen to ensure residual whiteness.

Table 1 Unit Root Tests on (Log of) Variables

	Dickey Fuller		Philipps Perron	
	τ_μ	τ_τ	$Z(\tau_\mu)$	$Z(\tau_\tau)$
Exchange Rates				
FR/US	-1.59	-1.85	-1.27	-0.69
GE/US	-1.92	-1.99	-1.49	-0.91
IT/US	-1.53	-1.56	-1.68	-0.52
JA/US	-1.42	-2.38	-0.90	-1.04
UK/US	-2.10	-2.72	-1.87	-1.16
FR/GE	-1.24	-3.29	-0.95	-1.08
IT/GE	-2.70	-1.03	-2.52	-1.45
UK/GE	-1.72	-2.61	-1.68	-1.74
Consumer Prices				
FR	-1.35	-0.49	-3.44	1.87
GE	-1.29	-1.19	-2.85	0.32
IT	-1.99	0.32	-3.58	1.50
JA	-2.87	-3.10	-6.49	-2.22
UK	-2.57	-2.17	-5.28	-1.85
US	-1.31	-1.35	-2.35	0.31
Wholesale Prices				
GE	-1.33	-1.06	-1.60	0.32
JA	-1.85	-1.44	-1.62	-0.15
UK	-3.20	-2.46	-9.02	-2.61
US	-1.34	-1.72	-2.02	-0.15

Unit Root Tests on First Difference of Variables

	Dickey Fuller		Philipps Perron	
	τ_μ	τ_τ	$Z(\tau_\mu)$	$Z(\tau_\tau)$
Exchange Rates				
FR/US	-2.67	-2.71	-14.01	- 9.83
GE/US	-2.92	-2.92	-13.86	-10.01
IT/US	-3.48	-3.56	-12.80	- 9.28
JA/US	-2.95	-2.87	-12.04	- 9.86
UK/US	-3.27	-3.26	-12.02	-10.10
FR/GE	-3.45	-3.49	-12.51	-10.95
IT/GE	-6.26	-6.79	-12.14	-14.16
UK/GE	-3.55	-3.59	-11.13	-11.16
Consumer Prices				
FR	-1.32	-1.83	- 4.93	- 4.81
GE	-1.66	-1.78	- 8.37	- 6.31
IT	-1.87	-3.10	- 5.73	- 5.44
JA	-3.27	-3.56	-13.54	-11.38
UK	-2.17	-3.03	- 7.28	- 7.01
US	-1.62	-1.92	- 5.41	- 4.78
Wholesale Prices				
GE	-2.68	-2.85	- 9.50	- 5.47
JA	-2.92	-2.85	- 5.77	- 4.76
UK	-2.19	-2.99	- 6.32	- 7.02
US	-1.70	-1.78	- 6.58	- 5.32

Approximate critical value at 5% level for τ_μ and $Z(\tau_\mu)$ is -2.89; the 5% critical value for τ_τ and $Z(\tau_\tau)$ is approximately -3.43. Up to 12 lags were used in computing the ADF statistics and 12 lags were used in computing the Phillips-Perron statistics. The mnemonics in the first column have the following interpretation: FR = France, GE = Germany, IT = Italy, JA = Japan, UK = United Kingdom and US = United States.

Since the autocorrelation functions of our price series indicated that such moving average errors were present, we preferred to correct for this using relatively long lags in the autoregressive representation of the Augmented Dickey Fuller statistics (also there is now a growing consensus that ADF statistics have better small sample properties than Phillips-Perron statistics).

Though *two* series of different orders of integration cannot be cointegrated, this apparent mixture of different order series is valid when we are considering *three* (or more) series (see Cuthbertson, Hall and Taylor, 1992). However, we present both sets of unit root statistics more for motivational purposes than as a definitive statement since, following Hendry and Mizon (1990), it is not entirely clear that inferences from unit root tests are reliable in small samples. We believe that a better basis for examining the number of unit roots in a vector of variables is given by the multivariate cointegration methodology of Johansen, to which we now turn.

Table 2 Multivariate Cointegration Results

	Lambda-max (LR2)			Tracetest (LR1)		
	$r=0$	$r\leq 1$	$r\leq 2$	$r=0$	$r\leq 1$	$r\leq 2$
74:1 89:6						
UK/US CPI	32.03**	11.79	8.14†	51.95**	19.93†	8.14†
UK/US WPI	20.79†	13.22	6.80	40.80**	20.02	6.80
GE/US CPI	31.43**	12.54	7.98†	51.96**	20.52*	7.98†
GE/US WPI	25.51*	6.51	4.05	36.07*	10.56	4.05
JA/US CPI	20.73†	11.19	2.83	34.75†	14.02	2.83
JA/US WPI	15.29	5.95	0.79	22.03	6.73	0.79
UK/GE CPI	19.69	12.62	8.69†	40.01**	21.32*	8.69†
UK/GE WPI	27.64**	18.27*	8.02†	53.94**	26.29**	8.02†
FR/GE CPI	22.53*	13.97†	3.12	36.92*	17.09	3.12
IT/GE CPI	16.55	13.25	7.13	36.93*	20.38*	7.13
79:3 89:6						
FR/GE CPI	32.16**	27.24**	4.25	63.65**	31.49**	4.25
IT/GE CPI	18.99	11.32	4.05	34.38†	15.38	4.05

†, * and ** denote significance at 10, 5 and 1% levels respectively.

All of our multivariate cointegration tests were implemented using a twelfth-order lag in the underlying VAR; the VAR also contained a constant and twelve seasonal dummies. The choice of a twelfth-order system was sufficient to ensure residual whiteness and account for any seasonality not captured by the seasonal dummies[19]. In Table 2 we report the trace and

[19]The exception is the UK pound - US dollar rate, in which a ten lag autoregressive system proved sufficient.

maximum eigenvalue statistics derived from our estimates of (7) for our full sample period. The trace statistic is the stochastic matrix trace test for at most r cointegrating vectors and is an estimate of (12) - LR1. The maximum eigenvalue statistic is a test for at most r cointegrating vectors against the alternative of $r + 1$ cointegrating vectors, and is an estimate of (13) - LR2. Interestingly, for the 'full sample' period practically all of the exchange-rate/ price combinations reveal some evidence of cointegration using one or other of the two tests statistics. This, we believe, is an interesting finding which contrasts with much of the literature referred to in Section 2, but confirms the findings of MacDonald (1992) for a range of bilateral US dollar rates. In the last two rows of the table we present estimates of (12) and (13) for the French franc and Italian lira against the German mark (using CPI's) for a period corresponding to the operation of the ERM; the evidence for the former currency seems stronger for the sub-period, whereas the evidence for the latter currency is somewhat weaker. It would therefore be difficult to draw any inferences about the operation of the ERM on the basis of these results.

Table 3 Maximum Likelihood Estimates of Normalised Cointegration Vectors

	Consumer Prices		Wholesale Prices	
	β_0	β_1	β_0	β_1
74:1 89:6				
UK/US	0.998	-1.503	0.368	-1.390
GE/US	14.717	-7.597	312.770	-177.818
JA/US	5.161	-4.722	2.562	-1.812
UK/GE	1.274	-2.970	1.071	-1.910
FR/GE	-1.573	5.080	N/A	N/A
IT/GE	1.797	-4.519	N/A	N/A
79:3 89:6				
FR/GE	2.048	-2.675	N/A	N/A
IT/GE	0.968	-1.541	N/A	N/A

The results presented in Table 2 suggest that, what we have called, the weak-form version of PPP finds considerable support from the data. What about the strong-form version? In Table 3 maximum likelihood estimates of the normalised cointegration vectors are presented. Notice that all of these vectors contain coefficients which are correctly signed in terms of PPP, apart from the French franc - German mark rate. Interestingly, the latter becomes correctly signed when the EMS sub-sample is considered. Also notice that some of the point estimates are *numerically* close to plus and minus one, particularly for rates containing the UK pound. But are these estimates *statistically* close to plus and minus unity?

In Table 4 we present maximum likelihood tests of this and other hy-

Table 4 Tests of Homogeneity Restrictions

	$1,1,-1$	$1,\beta_0,-\beta_0$	$1,\beta_0,-1$	$1,1,\beta_1$
74:1 89:6				
UK/US CPI	20.99 (0.00)	11.46 (0.00)	19.54 (0.00)	21.44 (0.00)
WPI	6.41 (0.04)	4.78 (0.03)	0.17 (0.68)	0.84 (0.36)
GE/US CPI	19.64 (0.00)	18.66 (0.00)	18.83 (0.00)	18.75 (0.00)
WPI	15.21 (0.00)	15.15 (0.00)	14.10 (0.00)	14.69 (0.00)
JA/US CPI	16.64 (0.00)	0.05 (0.82)	3.87 (0.05)	1.34 (0.25)
WPI	N/A	N/A	N/A	N/A
UK/GE CPI	10.35 (0.03)	3.74 (0.15)	2.53 (0.28)	0.45 (0.79)
WPI	7.65 (0.10)	7.63 (0.02)	6.58 (0.04)	0.26 (0.89)
FR/GE CPI	12.42 (0.00)	5.48 (0.02)	5.75 (0.02)	6.13 (0.01)
IT/GE CPI	8.46 (0.08)	6.71 (0.03)	6.89 (0.03)	7.38 (0.02)
79:3 89:6				
FR/GE CPI	4.15 (0.38)	0.60 (0.74)	1.07 (0.58)	1.57 (0.46)
IT/GE CPI	9.94 (0.01)	2.66 (0.10)	1.18 (0.28)	0.03 (0.86)

Marginal significance levels are given in brackets. Note that the degrees of freedom depend on the number of significant cointegrating vectors found. No restrictions tests are performed for the yen-dollar WPI model since no significant cointegrating relationships are found.

potheses. Notice that though the null hypothesis that the vector of coefficients is (1, -1, 1) is rejected in most cases, it is accepted for certain price indices over one or other of the time periods for the European cross rates. Estimated likelihood ratio tests for less restrictive null hypotheses are also reported in Table 4. Here there is more evidence of non-rejection of the null, and a good example of this is the case of the ERM combinations, where none of the alternative null hypotheses can be rejected.

5 Dynamic Error Correction Models and Out-of-Sample Forecasting

We have established above that weak-form PPP gains considerable support from the data, but that the evidence for strong-from is mixed. Given the various problems with measured price series, the lack of conclusive evidence in favour of the stronger form of PPP is, perhaps, not surprising. However, the existence of weak-form PPP for many currency/price combinations means that an error correction representation must exist for these combinations. The next part of our testing methodology involves using the general-to-specific methodology, popularised by Hendry *et al* (1984), to obtain a parsimonious dynamic equation for each exchange rate and then use this equation to construct out-of-sample predictions for the exchange rate which we then compare to the performance of the random walk model. As we mentioned in the Introduction, one of the stylised facts of the recent exchange rate literature, attributable to Meese and Rogoff (1983), is the finding that structural exchange rate models fail to outperform a random walk in an out-of-sample forecasting contest. Can the simplest of structural models, namely PPP, do any better?

In Table 5 we present our final parsimonious dynamic error correction models (ECM) for each of the currency/price combinations[20]. In each case the dynamics are rather complicated, and certainly much more complicated than previous estimates of PPP equations in differences. The equations pass a battery of diagnostic tests, suggesting that they have good in-sample properties. The coefficients of determination are all, apart from one instance, above twenty per cent, a reasonable level given that the variables entering the equations are stationary[21] and also given Mussa's (1979) dictum regarding goodness of fit for exchange rate equations.

Table 5 The Dynamic Model Specifications

74:10 89:6
UK/US CPI

$$
\begin{array}{llllll}
\Delta s_t = & 0.089\Delta s_{t-1} & + & 0.161\Delta s_{t-2} & + & 0.005(\Delta s_{t-4} + \Delta s_{t-5}) \\
 & (0.074) & & (0.076) & & (0.051) \\
- & 0.581\Delta p^c_{t-4} & - & 0.764(\Delta p^c_t - \Delta p^c_{t-3}) & - & 1.004(\Delta p^c_{t-7} - \Delta p^c_{t-8}) \\
 & (0.436) & & (0.346) & & (0.407) \\
- & 1.634\Delta p^{c*}_{t-1} & - & 3.101\Delta p^{c*}_{t-7} & + & 2.075\Delta p^{c*}_{t-8} \\
 & (0.910) & & (1.089) & & (1.073) \\
- & 2.044(\Delta p^{c*}_{t-4} - \Delta p^{c*}_{t-5}) & - & 0.056 ecm_{t-1} & + & 0.097 \\
 & (0.996) & & (0.019) & & (0.041)
\end{array}
$$

$R^2 = 0.218; \sigma = 0.03; \eta_1[24,154] = 1.59; \eta_2[4,150] = 0.75; \eta_3[4,146] = 0.48;$

$\xi[2] = 0.945; \eta_4[29,127] = 1.355; \chi[24]/24 = 1.86$

[20]We were not successful in modelling all of the currency/price combinations, and the reasons for this are noted in Table 6.

[21]That is, the coefficients of determination are not merely reflecting a 'spurious' regression.

Table 5 cont.

UK/US WPI

$$
\begin{array}{rlllll}
\Delta s_t = & 0.100(\Delta s_{t-2} + \Delta s_{t-4} + \Delta s_{t-5}) & + & 0.835(\Delta p^{w}_{t-4} - \Delta p^{w}_{t-5}) & + & 1.124\Delta p^{w*}_{t-1} \\
 & (0.043) & & (0.633) & & (0.543) \\
- & 0.777\Delta p^{w*}_{t-4} & - & 0.593\Delta p^{w*}_{t-6} & - & 0.012 ecm_{t-1} \\
 & (0.466) & & (0.459) & & (0.010) \\
+ & 0.044 & & & & \\
 & (0.042) & & & &
\end{array}
$$

$R^2 = 0.125; \sigma = 0.03; \eta_1[24,159] = 1.52; \eta_2[4,155] = 0.33; \eta_3[4,151] = 1.17;$

$\xi[2] = 6.954; \eta_4[23,135] = 1.129; \chi[24]/24 = 1.52$

GE/US CPI

$$
\begin{array}{rlllll}
\Delta s_t = & 0.131\Delta s_{t-2} & + & 0.088(\Delta s_{t-5} + \Delta s_{t-7}) & - & 1.300\Delta p^{c}_{t-7} \\
 & (0.076) & & (0.052) & & (1.179) \\
- & 2.565(\Delta p^{c}_{t-6} - \Delta p^{c}_{t-8}) & + & 2.620(\Delta p^{c}_{t-1} + \Delta p^{c}_{t-3}) & + & 1.579(\Delta p^{c*}_{t} - \Delta p^{c*}_{t-2}) \\
 & (0.921) & & (0.832) & & (0.813) \\
- & 1.264(\Delta p^{c*}_{t-3} - \Delta p^{c*}_{t-5}) & - & 0.024 ecm_{t-1} & - & 0.760 \\
 & (0.800) & & (0.020) & & (0.661)
\end{array}
$$

$R^2 = 0.239; \sigma = 0.03; \eta_1[24,157] = 1.54; \eta_2[4,153] = 0.20; \eta_3[4,149] = 0.92;$

$\xi[2] = 1.456; \eta_4[27,129] = 0.668; \chi[24]/24 = 1.76$

UK/GE CPI

$$
\begin{array}{rlllll}
\Delta s_t = & 0.189\Delta s_{t-1} & + & 0.226\Delta s_{t-7} & - & 0.090\Delta s_{t-8} \\
 & (0.076) & & (0.074) & & (0.077) \\
+ & 0.447\Delta p^{c}_{t} & - & 0.910\Delta p^{c}_{t-6} & - & 2.375\Delta p^{c*}_{t} \\
 & (0.386) & & (0.387) & & (1.183) \\
+ & 1.177\Delta p^{c*}_{t-6} & - & 1.783(\Delta p^{c*}_{t-4} + \Delta p^{c*}_{t-8}) & - & 0.089 ecm_{t-1} \\
 & (1.174) & & (0.737) & & (0.029) \\
+ & 0.592 & & & & \\
 & (0.192) & & & &
\end{array}
$$

$R^2 = 0.244; \sigma = 0.03; \eta_1[24,156] = 0.61; \eta_2[4,152] = 0.10; \eta_3[4,148] = 0.50;$

$\xi[2] = 5.293; \eta_4[27,129] = 0.912; \chi[24]/24 = 0.70$

Table 5 cont.

UK/GE WPI

$$\begin{aligned}\Delta s_t = & \ 0.181\Delta s_{t-1} + 0.247\Delta s_{t-7} - 0.104\Delta s_{t-8} \\ & \ (0.078) \quad (0.076) \quad (0.077) \\ & + 1.308\Delta p_t^w + 0.736\Delta p_{t-3}^w - 0.799(\Delta p_{t-6}^w + \Delta p_{t-8}^w) \\ & \ (0.582) \quad (0.578) \quad (0.310) \\ & - 2.586\Delta p_t^{w*} - 0.697\Delta p_{t-5}^{w*} - 0.131 ecm_{t-1} \\ & \ (0.681) \quad (0.638) \quad (0.036) \\ & + 0.344 \\ & \ (0.092)\end{aligned}$$

$R^2 = 0.266; \sigma = 0.03; \eta_1[24,156] = 0.71; \eta_2[4,152] = 0.27; \eta_3[4,148] = 0.70;$

$\xi[2] = 1.028; \eta_4[28,128] = 1.5125; \chi[24]/24 = 0.71$

IT/GE CPI

$$\begin{aligned}\Delta s_t = & \ 0.112\Delta s_{t-1} - 0.299\Delta s_{t-4} + 0.133(\Delta s_{t-2} + \Delta s_{t-6}) \\ & \ (0.076) \quad (0.072) \quad (0.061) \\ & + 0.916\Delta p_t^c + 0.728\Delta p_{t-4}^c - 0.875\Delta p_{t-6}^c \\ & \ (0.361) \quad (0.316) \quad (0.369) \\ & + 0.459\Delta p_{t-7}^c - 1.035\Delta p_{t-1}^{c*} - 1.831\Delta p_{t-3}^{c*} \\ & \ (0.338) \quad (0.618) \quad (0.664) \\ & + 2.042\Delta p_{t-4}^{c*} - 1.575\Delta p_{t-5}^{c*} - 0.070 ecm_{t-1} \\ & \ (0.691) \quad (0.661) \quad (0.024) \\ & + 0.627 \\ & \ (0.220)\end{aligned}$$

$R^2 = 0.342; \sigma = 0.02; \eta_1[24,153] = 0.36; \eta_2[4,149] = 0.59; \eta_3[4,145] = 13.27;$

$\xi[2] = 373.4; \eta_4[30,126] = 2.492; \chi[24]/24 = 0.42$

79:3 89:6
FR/GE CPI

$$\begin{aligned}\Delta s_t = & \ 0.081\Delta s_{t-7} - 0.202(\Delta s_{t-1} + \Delta s_{t-2}) + 0.968\Delta p_{t-8}^c \\ & \ (0.079) \quad (0.068) \quad (0.256) \\ & + 0.487(\Delta p_t^c - \Delta p_{t-5}^c) + 0.614(\Delta p_{t-6}^c - \Delta p_{t-7}^c) - 0.575(\Delta p_{t-1}^{c*} - \Delta p_{t-3}^{c*}) \\ & \ (0.224) \quad (0.271) \quad (0.218) \\ & - 0.523(\Delta p_{t-5}^{c*} + \Delta p_{t-7}^{c*}) - 0.017 ecm_{t-1} + 0.064 \\ & \ (0.200) \quad (0.009) \quad (0.035)\end{aligned}$$

$R^2 = 0.312; \sigma = 0.01; \eta_1[24,104] = 0.88; \eta_2[4,100] = 0.11; \eta_3[4,96] = 1.60;$

$\xi[2] = 7.034; \eta_4[27,76] = 1.750; \chi[24]/24 = 1.02$

Table 5 cont.

IT/GE CPI

$$\begin{array}{rllll} \Delta s_t = & -0.224\Delta s_{t-3} & - \; 0.105(\Delta s_{t-4} - \Delta s_{t-5}) & + & 0.256\Delta p^c_{t-7} \\ & (0.086) & \quad (0.043) & & (0.120) \\ + & 0.414(\Delta p^c_{t-5} - \Delta p^c_{t-6}) & - \; 0.414(\Delta p^{c*}_{t-1} - \Delta p^{c*}_{t-2}) & - & 0.586(\Delta p^{c*}_{t-3} - \Delta p^{c*}_{t-4}) \\ & (0.163) & \quad (0.258) & & (0.259) \\ + & 0.452(\Delta p^{c*}_{t-6} - \Delta p^{c*}_{t-7}) & - \; 0.034 ecm_{t-1} & + & 0.307 \\ & (0.263) & \quad (0.020) & & (0.186) \end{array}$$

$R^2 = 0.352; \sigma = 0.01; \eta_1[24,104] = 1.76; \eta_2[4,100] = 0.90; \eta_3[4,96] = 0.44;$

$\xi[2] = 8.029; \eta_4[27,76] = 1.129; \chi[24]/24 = 2.11$

Where R^2 is the coefficient of determination, σ is the standard error of the regression, figures in parentheses below coefficient estimates are standard errors. η_1 is the Chow test of parameter constancy, η_2 is a Lagrange multiplier test statistic for 4th order serial correlation, η_3 is a 4th order ARCH test statistic, ξ is a test statistic for residual normality and η_4 is a heteroscedasticity test statistic based on the quadratic form of the regressors. χ is a test statistic of structural change between sample and forecast periods. A RESET test for misspecification could not be carried out because of the large number of right hand side variables.

The equations presented in Table 5 are estimated by OLS using PC-GIVE, version 7.0. It should be noted that since many of our equations contain contemporaneous domestic or foreign price terms as independent variables the normalisation with respect to the exchange rate is valid only if these price terms are weakly exogenous. Following Hendry and Ericsson (1991) we test for this by reestimating using instrumental variables[22]. With just one exception, the CPI model of the pound-mark rate, the estimated coefficients and standard error of the equation are little changed and the instruments pass Sargan's test of validity. The poor performance of the consumer price based model of the Sterling-Deutschmark rate may explain its subsequent inferior out-of-sample forecasting record.

So far, we have accepted the so-called LSE approach uncritically. Those who choose to question this methodology often point out that the determination of the parsimonious equations is subject to criticism as a form of data mining. However, we feel that our results are robust for three reasons[23]. First, most of the models pass the two forecast period tests (η_1 and χ) indicating good out-of-sample properties. The Chow test, η_1 , examines parameter constancy out-of-sample whilst the χ value is a test of structural change between

[22] Additional instruments used were a time trend term, time squared and time cubed.

[23] We thank the referee for drawing our attention to these considerations.

sample and forecast periods. As further confirmation, the one-month-ahead forecasts of three of these models, together with error bands corresponding to ±2 standard errors, are shown in Figures 1, 2 and 3. Only rarely do the actual changes in the rates lie outside the error bands. Second, recursive estimation of the models shows reasonable stability in the coefficients of our models. As an example, estimates of four coefficients from the consumer price based model of the sterling-dollar rate are plotted in Figure 4. Finally, reestimation of the models over different sample periods also yields similar models. Reestimating the CPI model of the sterling-dollar rate, including calculating the new cointegrating vector, over the full data period of January 1974 to June 1991 produces an equation with eleven explanatory variables besides constants, seasonals and the ECM term. Of these eleven, ten were also present in the 'old' model of the pound-dollar rate derived with twenty-four fewer observations.

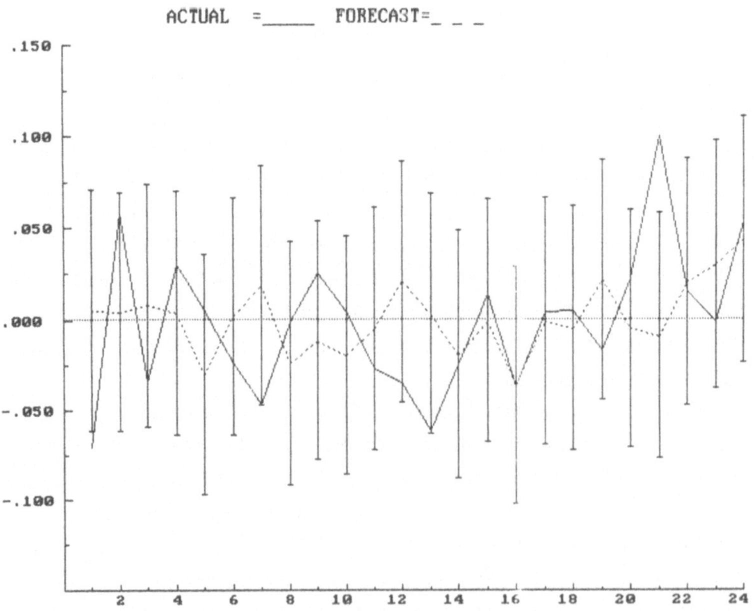

Figure 1 UK/US CPI One Step Ahead Forecasts
Sample Period is 1989(7) - 1991(6)

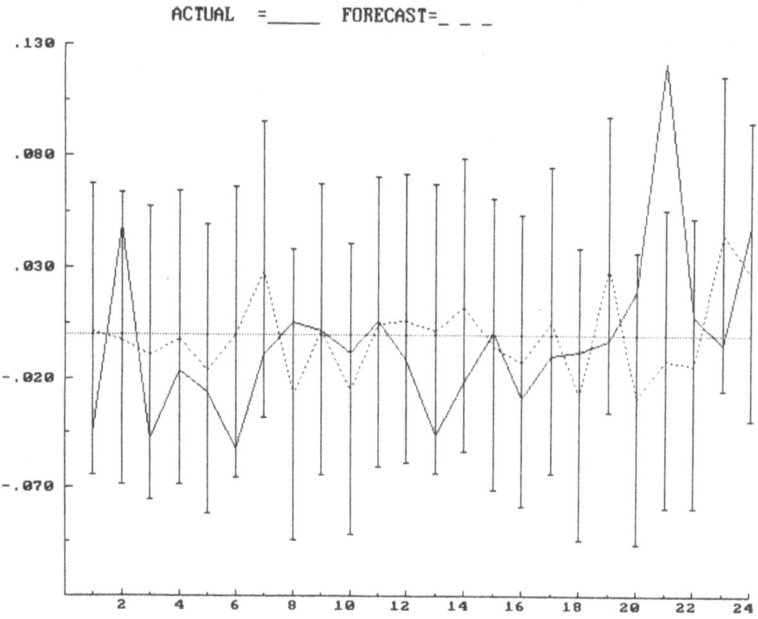

Figure 2 GE/US CPI One Step Ahead Forecasts
Sample Period is 1989(7) - 1991(6)

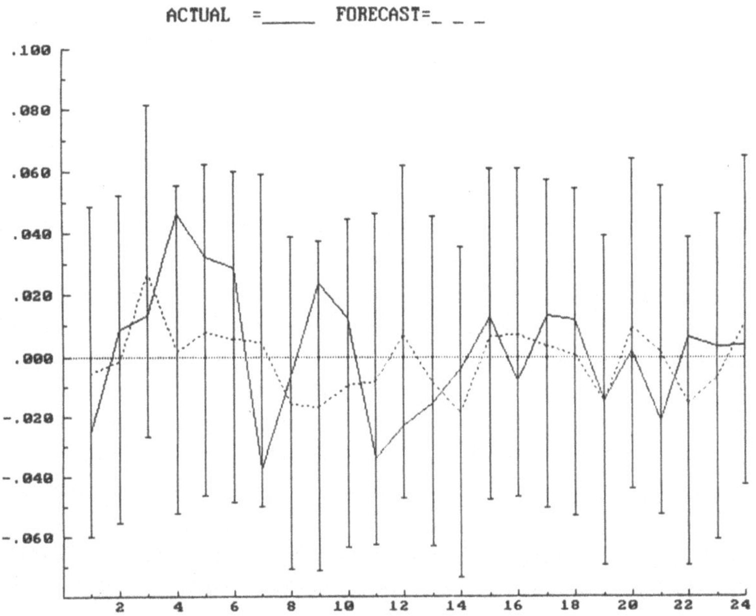

Figure 3 UK/GE WPI One Step Ahead Forecasts
Sample Period is 1989(7) - 1991(6)

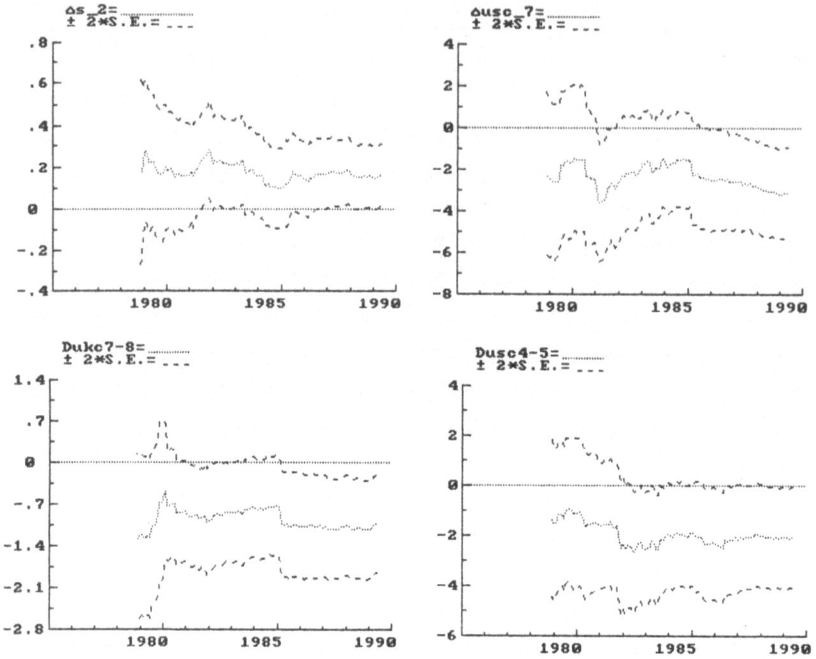

Figure 4 Recursive Estimates of UK/US CPI Coefficients

A further test of out-of-sample forecasting performance of the equations reported in Table 5 is to compare the forecast errors for 5 different out-of-sample forecast horizons (namely one, three, six, twelve and twenty four months) with that of a simple random walk. Following Meese and Rogoff (1983) we use actual realised values of price level changes as explanatory variables in computing our forecasts. This allows us to test the validity of the PPP model rather than our ability to predict price levels.

We calculate the forecasts in the following way. The models are first estimated up to June 1989. These estimated equations are then used to forecast the exchange rate one month ahead. For multi-month forecasts, this estimated exchange rate is then fed back into the model and further forecasts made. The forecasts are therefore partially dynamic[24]. The model is then reestimated using data up to July 1989 and the process repeated for all twenty-three remaining observations. Again following Meese and Rogoff (1983) we evaluate the forecasts using root mean squared errors (RMSE), mean absolute errors (MAE) and mean errors (ME). As they note, RMSE's may be an inappropriate test criteria if exchange rates follow non-normal Paretian distributions

[24]A fully dynamic model would also use forecast values of exogenous variables. We chose not to follow this route for the reason given in the text.

Table 6 Out-of-Sample Forecast Statistics

			1	3	6	12	24
1974:01 1989:06							
UK/US	RW	RMSE	0.0388	0.0696	0.1006	0.1400	0.0450
		MAE	0.0301	0.0556	0.0869	0.1255	0.0450
		ME	-0.0019	-0.0072	-0.0338	-0.1145	-0.0450
	CPI	RMSE	0.0491	0.0708	0.0783*	0.0966*	0.0293*
		MAE	0.0371	0.0563	0.0661*	0.0845*	0.0293*
		ME	-0.0026	-0.0043*	-0.0218*	-0.0771*	0.0293*
	WPI	RMSE	0.0427	0.0857	0.1301	0.1471	0.0425*
		MAE	0.0340	0.0692	0.1084	0.1246*	0.0425*
		ME	0.0011*	0.0047*	-0.0139*	-0.0992*	0.0425*
GE/US	RW	RMSE	0.0367	0.0712	0.1057	0.1383	0.0747
		MAE	0.0251	0.0562	0.0970	0.1216	0.0747
		ME	-0.0031	-0.0126	-0.0386	-0.0994	-0.0747
	CPI	RMSE	0.0415	0.0687*	0.0999*	0.1218*	0.0065*
		MAE	0.0274	0.0515*	0.0870*	0.1100*	0.0065*
		ME	-0.0015*	-0.0045*	-0.0203*	-0.0748*	-0.0065*
	WPI		no short-term model - ECM term positive				
JA/US	CPI		no short-term model - ECM term positive				
	WPI		no significant cointegration vector				
UK/GE	RW	RMSE	0.0209	0.0420	0.0532	0.0434	0.0297
		MAE	0.0172	0.0296	0.0430	0.0396	0.0297
		ME	0.0012	0.0054	0.0048	-0.0151	0.0297
	CPI	RMSE	0.0292	0.0531	0.0668	0.0599	0.1336
		MAE	0.0240	0.0422	0.0596	0.0550	0.1336
		ME	0.0078	0.0265	0.0454	0.0550	0.1336
	WPI	RMSE	0.0274	0.0435	0.0424*	0.0132*	0.0171*
		MAE	0.0226	0.0319	0.0334*	0.0101*	0.0171*
		ME	0.0021	0.0092	0.0130	0.0006*	0.0171*
FR/GE	CPI		no valid cointegrating vector				
IT/GE	RW	RMSE	0.0077	0.0147	0.0198	0.0165	0.0277
		MAE	0.0061	0.0124	0.0173	0.0145	0.0277
		ME	0.0012	0.0040	0.0070	0.0145	0.0277
	CPI	RMSE	0.0137	0.0175	0.0186*	0.0107*	0.0165*
		MAE	0.0116	0.0136	0.0155*	0.0086*	0.0165*
		ME	-0.0009*	-0.0017*	-0.0050*	-0.0075*	-0.0165*
1979:03 1989:06							
FR/GE	RW	RMSE	0.0060	0.0088	0.0107	0.0091	0.0023
		MAE	0.0047	0.0066	0.0091	0.0085	0.0023
		ME	-0.0001	0.0001	-0.0002	-0.0020	-0.0023
	CPI	RMSE	0.0091	0.0105	0.0134	0.0122	0.0071
		MAE	0.0071	0.0085	0.0122	0.0103	0.0071
		ME	-0.0003	0.0000*	-0.0007	-0.0045	-0.0071
IT/GE	RW	RMSE	0.0077	0.0147	0.0198	0.0165	0.0277
		MAE	0.0061	0.0124	0.0173	0.0145	0.0277
		ME	0.0012	0.0040	0.0070	0.0145	0.0277
	CPI	RMSE	0.0091	0.0145*	0.0165*	0.0167	0.0267*
		MAE	0.0078	0.0118*	0.0139*	0.0137*	0.0267*
		ME	-0.0017	-0.0037*	-0.0068*	-0.0130*	-0.0267*

Note: * denotes a smaller (absolute) value than random walk reading.

with infinite variance, as has been suggested by Westerfield (1977). MAE's are less influenced by large errors and, hence, are more robust to fat-tailed distributions. Furthermore, comparison of MAE and ME statistics may indicate whether the models systematically under- or over-predict. These error statistics for the various PPP equations are presented in Table 6.

The first thing to note from this table is that in terms of RMSE and MAE none of the dynamic ECM equations outperforms a random walk at the shortest of horizons, namely one month. However, as we move away from this period some of the PPP models start to do better than the simple random walk. At the three month horizon, for example, the PPP model for the Deutschmark-dollar rate (using consumer prices) outperforms a random walk on all three criteria, as it also does at the six, twelve and twenty-four month horizons. It is interesting to note that for the UK sterling -German mark rate the dynamic equation using the wholesale price measure outperforms a random walk from the six month horizon, whereas the equivalent expression using the CPI fails to outperform the random walk at any forecast horizon. This finding would seem to shed some light on one of the key issues in the PPP literature, namely the appropriate price measure to use in the construction of a PPP test. The other models which display some evidence of outperforming a random walk are the sterling-US dollar rate (for consumer prices and, to a lesser extent, wholesale prices) and the Italian Lira-German mark model both over the full- and ERM-estimation periods. Notice that although the ERM model predicts better over short horizons (1, 3 and 6 months), the full sample model performs better in long horizon comparisons. No model for the French franc-Mark rate is capable of beating a random walk. For those models which do perform well there is no evidence of systematic bias since the mean errors are typically much lower than the mean absolute error statistics.

6 Summary and Conclusions

In this paper we have reexamined the Purchasing Power Parity concept using both long- and short-run frameworks. The long-run framework consisted of testing for cointegration using the multivariate methodology of Johansen. We argued that this methodology has distinct advantages over the simpler regression-based tests conducted by other researchers. Using this technique we demonstrated that weak-form PPP found considerable support from the data, but that the strong-form version of the hypothesis did not. The long-run cointegration estimates unearthed using the multivariate methodology were then used in a dynamic error correction modelling exercise. One interesting outcome of this exercise was the finding that dynamic PPP equations could outperform a simple random walk model in an out-of-sample forecasting context. This finding contrasts with many of the findings from the empirical exchange rate literature. Finally, the various tests conducted in this paper did not indicate any particular evidence of an EMS effect, although our testing methodology in this respect should not be regarded as comprehensive.

References

Abuaf N, Jorion P (1990) Purchasing power parity in the long run, The Journal of Finance 45: 157 - 174

Adler M, Lehmann B (1983) Deviations from purchasing power parity in the long run, The Journal of Finance 38: 1471 - 83

Cochrane J H (1988) How big is the random walk in GNP? Journal of Political Economy 96: 893 - 920

Cuthbertson K, Hall S G, Taylor M P (1992) Applied Econometric Techniques, Hemel Hempstead: Philip Allen

Darby M (1980) Does purchasing power parity work? NBER Working Paper No. 607

Edison H J (1985) Purchasing power parity: a quantitative reassessment of the 1920's experience, Journal of International Money and Finance 4: 361 - 372.

Enders W (1988) ARIMA and cointegration tests of PPP under fixed and flexible exchange rates, Review of Economics and Statistics: 505-508

Engle R, Granger C W J (1987) Cointegration and error correction: representation, estimation and testing, Econometrica 55: 251-76

Fraser P, Taylor M P, Webster A (1991) An empirical analysis of long-run purchasing power parity as a theory of international commodity arbitrage, Applied Economics 23: 1749-1760

Frenkel J A (1980) Exchange rates, prices and money, lessons from the 1920's, American Economic Association, Papers and Proceedings 70: 235-242

Frenkel J A (1981) Flexible exchange rates, prices and the role of 'news': lessons from the 1970's, Journal of Political Economy 89: 665-705

Fuller W A (1976) Introduction to Statistical Time Series, New York: Wiley

Hallwood P, MacDonald R (1993) International Money and Finance, Second Edition, Oxford: Blackwell

Hendry D F, Ericsson N R (1991) An econometric analysis of U.K. money demand in Monetary trends in the United States and United Kingdom by Milton Friedman and Anna J. Schwartz, American Economic Review 81: 8-38

Hendry D F, Mizon G (1990) Evaluating dynamic econometric models by encompassing the VAR, in P.C.B. Phillips and V.B. Hall (eds.), Models, methods, and applications of econometrics. Essays in honor of Rex Bergstrom

Hendry D F, Pagan A R, Sargan J D (1984) Dynamic specification in Z. Grilliches and M. Intrilligator (eds.), Handbook of Econometrics Amsterdam (North Holland): 1023-1100

Huizinga J (1987) An empirical investigation of the long-run behaviour of real exchange rates, in K. Brunner and A.H. Meltzer (eds.) Carnegie Rochester Conference Series on Public Policy, Amsterdam (North Holland): 149-214

Isard P (1977) How far can we push the law of one price? American Economic Review 67: 942-948

Johansen S (1988) Statistical analysis of cointegration vectors, Journal of Economic Dynamics and Control 12: 231-54

Johansen S (1991) Estimation and hypothesis testing of cointegration vectors in gaussian vector autoregressive models, Econometrica 59: 1551-1580

Johansen S, Juselius K (1990) Maximum likelihood estimation and inference on cointegration - with applications to the demand for money, Oxford Bulletin of Economics and Statistics 52: 169-210

Kravis I, Lipsey R (1978) Price behaviour in the light of balance of payments theory, Journal of International Economics 8: 193-246
Krugman P (1978) Purchasing power parity and exchange rates: another look at the evidence, Journal of International Economics 8: 397-407
MacDonald R (1985) Do deviations of the real effective exchange rate follow a random walk? Economic Notes 14: 63-9
MacDonald R (1988) Floating Exchange Rates: Theories and Evidence, London: Unwin Hyman
MacDonald R (1992) Long-run purchasing power parity: is it for real? Review of Economics and Statistics, forthcoming
MacDonald R, Taylor M P (1990) International parity conditions, in A.S. Courakis and M.P. Taylor (eds.) Policy Issues for Interdependent Economies, Oxford (Oxford University Press)
MacDonald R, Taylor M P (1992) Exchange rate economics, International Monetary Fund Staff Papers 39: 1-57
Meese R, Rogoff K (1983) Empirical exchange rate models of the seventies: Do they fit out of sample? Journal of International Economics 14: 3-24
Mishkin F (1984) Are real interest rates equal across countries? An empirical investigation of international parity conditions, Journal of Finance 39: 1345-58
Mussa M (1979) Empirical regularities in the behavior of exchange rates and theories of the foreign exchange market, in K. Brunner and A.H. Meltzer (eds.) Policies for Employment, Prices and Exchange Rates, Amsterdam (North Holland)
Officer C H (1976) The purchasing power parity theory of exchange rates: a review article, IMF Staff Papers 23: 1-60
Patel J (1990) Purchasing power parity as a long-run relation, Journal of Applied Econometrics 5: 367-79
Phillips P C B (1987) Time series regression with a unit root, Econometrica 55: 277-301
Roll R (1979) Violations of purchasing power parity and their implications for efficient international commodity markets, in M.Sarnat and G.Szego (eds.), International Finance and Trade 1, Cambridge, Mass (Ballinger)
Schwert G W (1987) Effects of model specification on tests for unit roots in macroeconomic data, Journal of Monetary Economics 20: 73-103
Taylor M P (1988) An empirical examination of long-run purchasing power parity using cointegration techniques, Applied Economics 20: 1369-82
Taylor M P, McMahon P C (1988) Long-run purchasing power parity in the 1920's, European Economic Review 32: 179-197
Westerfield J M (1977) An examination of foreign exchange risk under fixed and floating regimes, Journal of International Economics 7: 181-200

Cointegration and the Monetary Model of the Exchange Rate[1]

By Gerd Hansen[2]

Abstract: Within this paper methods to estimate partial cointegration systems, as well as complete systems like the Johansen procedure, are applied to the monetary model of the exchange rate. The partial system gives some evidence in favour of the purchasing power parity hypothesis, which is especially supported by Lagrange multiplier tests for weak exogeneity. It is shown that cointegration vectors may be sensitive with respect to parametric restrictions.

1 Introduction

Most econometric studies of the DM/\$–rate published since the mid seventies estimate a single reduced form equation for the exchange rate. These studies quite often show that the best explanation is the random walk hypothesis (see for example Meese, Rogoff (1983)). The same conclusion results from most of the studies which try to estimate a cointegration relation for the DM/\$–rate.

The Phillips procedure starts from a partial set of cointegration relations (partial system) and assumes weak exogeneity of a subset of the variables (Phillips (1991)). This weak exogeneity can be tested.

One of the more popular procedures to estimate these cointegration relations is the Johansen procedure applied to a VAR(p) model (Johansen (1988)). This procedure starts instead of the exogeneity assumption with tests of the cointegration rank and tries to identify the cointegration relations later on. There are some serious problems in identifying the cointegration relations and therefore to interpret the results in terms of meaningful economic relations. The paper by Johansen (1992b) deals with this problem and demonstrates that there is no simple method to estimate such a system. Furthermore the Johansen procedure does not allow to restrict a single cointegration parameter with respect to theoretical assumptions to be tested. As a consequence the procedure does not provide significance levels of cointegration parameters. This paper shows that the results of a cointegration analysis are quite sensitive with respect to the statistical procedure and especially with respect

[1]I would like to thank two anonymous referees whose comments led to several improvements of this paper.

[2]Gerd Hansen, Institute for Statistics and Econometrics, University of Kiel, Olshausenstr. 40–60, D-24118 Kiel, Germany.

to the order of succession, in which different assumptions are tested. Therefore, different conclusions can be drawn from the analysis of a partial system in contrast to that of a complete VAR model. The results are also sensitive with respect to the lag order.

The paper is organized in the following way. Section 2 gives a short discussion of the theoretical model and its consequences for the specification of the empirical model. In Section 3 we discuss the difference between Johansen's VAR(p) model and the analysis within a SUR framework of a partial model. Alternative parametrizations and tests for exogeneity are defined. Section 4 gives the empirical results. Section 5 summarizes the results.

2 The Monetary Model of the Exchange Rate

Our starting point is the following monetary model (1)–(4) for a small country (all variables in logarithms except r and r^*):

$$\begin{aligned} y^d &= -\gamma(r-\dot{p}) + \delta(e+p^*-p) + \theta\bar{y} && (1)\\ m &= p + \kappa y - \eta r && (2)\\ \dot{p} &= \Phi(y^d - \bar{y}) && (3)\\ \mathrm{E}_t\dot{e} &= r - r^* && (4) \end{aligned}$$

with y^d and $\bar{y}$ as goods demand and supply respectively, r and r^* domestic versus foreign interest rate, p and p^* domestic versus foreign price level, $\dot{e}$ and e the rate of change versus the level of the exchange rate, $\dot{p}$ the rate of inflation and m the domestic money supply.

Equations (1) and (2) describe an IS–LM model, equation (3) is the Walras condition for stability of the goods market (Phillips curve) whereas equation (4) is the uncovered interest rate parity, which defines the capital market equilibrium, if domestic and foreign assets are perfect substitutes.

Substituting r and $\dot{p}$ in equation (1) by means of the equations (2) and (3) gives the reduced IS–LM system (5) and (6), if output supply $\bar{y}$ is assumed to be fixed in the short run:

$$\begin{aligned} r &= -\frac{1}{\eta}(m-p-\kappa y) && (5)\\ y^d &= -\frac{1}{\xi}\left(\gamma m - (\gamma+\delta\eta)p + \delta\eta e + \delta\eta p^* + \eta(\theta - y\Phi)\bar{y}\right) && (6)\\ &\quad \text{with} \quad \xi = \gamma(\Phi\eta-\kappa) - \eta < 0. \end{aligned}$$

For simplicity we assume $\bar{y} = 0$.

Substituting these equations into (3) and (4) gives a dynamic subsystem for the (expected) exchange rate (e) and the price level p as in (7):

$$\begin{pmatrix} \dot{p} \\ \mathrm{E}_t\dot{e} \end{pmatrix} = \frac{1}{\xi}\begin{pmatrix} \Phi(\gamma+\delta\eta) & -\Phi\delta\eta \\ \gamma\Phi - 1 + \delta\kappa & -\delta\kappa \end{pmatrix}\begin{pmatrix} p \\ e \end{pmatrix} + \frac{1}{\xi}\begin{pmatrix} -\gamma\Phi & -\delta\eta\Phi & 0 \\ 1-\gamma\Phi & -\delta\kappa & -\xi \end{pmatrix}\begin{pmatrix} m \\ p^* \\ r^* \end{pmatrix} \tag{7}$$

Under rational expectations with respect to $\dot{e}$ ($\dot{e} = \mathrm{E}_t\dot{e} + \epsilon$) and white noise errors u_1 and $u_2 = u_2^* - \epsilon$ this dynamic system can be be written as in (8) or (9):

$$\begin{pmatrix} \dot{p} \\ \dot{e} \end{pmatrix} = \begin{pmatrix} \gamma_{11} & \gamma_{12} \\ \gamma_{21} & \gamma_{22} \end{pmatrix}\begin{pmatrix} p \\ e \end{pmatrix} + \begin{pmatrix} \theta_{11} & \theta_{12} & 0 \\ \theta_{21} & \theta_{22} & \theta \end{pmatrix}\begin{pmatrix} m \\ p^* \\ r^* \end{pmatrix} + \begin{pmatrix} u_1 \\ u_2 \end{pmatrix} \tag{8}$$

$$\dot{y} = \Gamma y + \theta x + u \tag{9}$$

$$\text{with} \quad y' = (p, e) \quad \text{and} \quad x' = (m, p^*, r^*).$$

Therefore, the system subdivides into the dynamic transition system (9) and the static IS–LM system of equations (5) and (6) given by (10) or (11):

$$\begin{pmatrix} 1 & -\kappa\eta^{-1} \\ 0 & 1 \end{pmatrix}\begin{pmatrix} r \\ y \end{pmatrix} = \begin{pmatrix} \eta^{-1} & 0 \\ (\gamma+\delta\eta)\xi^{-1} & -\delta\eta\xi^{-1} \end{pmatrix}\begin{pmatrix} p \\ e \end{pmatrix} + \begin{pmatrix} -\eta^{-1} & 0 & 0 \\ -\gamma\xi^{-1} & -\delta\eta\xi^{-1} & 0 \end{pmatrix}\begin{pmatrix} m \\ p^* \\ r^* \end{pmatrix} + \begin{pmatrix} v_1 \\ v_2 \end{pmatrix} \tag{10}$$

$$w = Ay + Bx + v \tag{11}$$

$$\text{with} \quad w' = (r, y).$$

The long run equilibrium of $y' = (p, e)$ implied by (8) or (9) results from

$$\dot{p} = \dot{e} = 0 \quad \text{and} \quad \mathrm{E}_t u_1 = \mathrm{E}_t u_2 = 0 \quad \text{or} \quad y = \Gamma^{-1}\theta x.$$

These long run effects are restricted with respect to the effects of p^* only. We get after some simple matrix calculations for the long run effect of p^*

$$p = 0p^* \quad \text{and} \quad e = -p^*,$$

that is the purchasing power parity (*ppp*). After adjustments to a shock in p^* are completed, the old terms of trade are reestablished by means of exchange rate appreciations. Purchasing power parity is therefore the fundamental long run relation for the exchange rate in the model.

In reality, this long run *ppp* will show up very fast, if foreign inflation is tremendous compared to domestic inflation, say 100%. Difficulties to estimate the long run *ppp* are mainly due to the fact that differences in inflation are small compared to the variation of the exchange rate and therefore the results are sensitive with respect to the statistical procedure.

Furthermore the system (9) includes exogenous variables $x' = (m, p^*, r^*)$ in the sense that no equations are available from the system for these variables. Especially p^* and r^* will be weakly exogenous in the statistical sense, if the assumption of a small country is valid. In the case of Germany this assumption may be wrong and has therefore to be tested.

The exogeneity of m may be due to the missing money supply function and therefore result from misspecification. We will show later that the weak exogeneity of m is well supported by the data.

In what follows I will refer to the state space system (8) or (9) only. This system corresponds to a *partial error–correction system*, which forms the basis of the statistical cointegration theory. Starting point of the cointegration theory is the vector–autoregressive system (13) or (12):

$$\begin{aligned} \begin{pmatrix} B^*(L) & C^*(L) \\ D^*(L) & E^*(L) \end{pmatrix} \begin{pmatrix} \Delta y_t \\ \Delta x_t \end{pmatrix} &= -\begin{pmatrix} B(1) & C(1) \\ D(1) & E(1) \end{pmatrix} \begin{pmatrix} y_{t-1} \\ x_{t-1} \end{pmatrix} \\ &\quad + \begin{pmatrix} \epsilon_{1t} \\ \epsilon_{2t} \end{pmatrix} \qquad (12) \\ A^*(L)\Delta z_t &= -A(1) z_{t-1} + \epsilon_t \qquad (13) \\ &\quad \text{with} \quad z_t = (y_t, x_t) \end{aligned}$$

In (13), continuous changes $\dot{z}_t$ are substituted by discrete changes Δz_t. The system (13) or (12) is a *cointegration system*, if

1. all the variables in z_t are integrated, say of order one, and
2. the matrix $A(1)$ has a reduced rank in order to make a subset of the linear combinations in $A(1)z_{t-1}$ stationary.

The reduced rank of $A(1)$ may be due to the weak exogeneity of x_{t-1} with respect to the parameters $(B(1), C(1))$. In this case we have $D(1) = E(1) = 0$ and (14)

$$B^*(L)\Delta y_t = -(B(1)y_{t-1} + C(1)x_{t-1}) - C^*(L)\Delta x_t + \epsilon_{1t} \qquad (14)$$

gives a stable subsystem with cointegration vectors

$$B(1)y_{t-1} + C(1)x_{t-1}.$$

We may think of model (8) or (9) as such a stable partial dynamic system with

$$B(1) = \frac{1}{\xi}\begin{pmatrix} \Phi(\gamma+\delta\eta) & -\Phi\delta\eta \\ \gamma\Phi - 1 + \delta\kappa & -\delta\kappa \end{pmatrix} \text{ and} \tag{15}$$
$$C(1) = \frac{1}{\xi}\begin{pmatrix} -\gamma\Phi & -\delta\eta\Phi & 0 \\ 1-\gamma\Phi & -\delta\kappa & -\xi \end{pmatrix}.$$

There are only the trivial conditions $\delta = 0$ or $\Phi = 0$ (no terms of trade effect on goods demand or no price reaction by excess demand on the goods market) which lead to a further reduction of the stable dynamic subsystem according to a reduced rank of $B(1)$. Therefore, a full rank of $B(1)$ in (16) can be seen as a minimum condition for consistency between the data and the monetary model of the exchange rate as given in (1)–(4). A reduced rank of the system matrix $B(1)$ in economic models indicates in general inconsistent behavioural equations or insufficient goals of economic agents. Furthermore, there is no theoretical basis to make other variables dependent on the cointegration vectors in (16) as in the time series literature. In other words: To be consistent with the theoretical model, we cannot even get a single cointegration vector, for example, the first line of $B(1)$ and $C(1)$, explaining Δp.

On the other hand, it may well be that there is an additional cointegration vector for m describing money supply behaviour. From this point of view the monetary theory provides a testable hypothesis for a cointegration analysis of the variables $y' = (p, e)$ and $x' = (m, p^*, r^*)$. The theory does also exclude certain variables from the cointegration vector. For example, there is no effect from r^* on Δp according to the first line of $C(1)$. If the interest elasticity of money demand is zero ($\eta = 0$), the exchange rate (e) as well as the foreign price level (p^*) do not appear in the first line of $B(1)$ and $C(1)$, respectively according to (15).

3 Alternative Estimation and Test Procedures

3.1 Partial Cointegration Systems and Lagrange Multiplier Test for Weak Exogeneity

As shown in Section 2 the monetary model corresponds to a stable partial system (14) in the endogenous variables $y' = (p, e)$ and the weakly exogenous variables $x' = (m, p^*, r^*)$. Empirical cointegration analysis is easier and better based on economic theory, if we start from this model and test, if the implied prior restrictions in terms of weak exogeneity of x are satisfied. Corresponding test statistics are given by Johansen (1992a), Boswijk (1991) and

Urbain (1991). Both procedures test, whether the two stationary cointegration relations of the partial system

$$B(1)y_{t-1} + C(1)x_{t-1} = \begin{pmatrix} u_{1\,t-1} \\ u_{2\,t-1} \end{pmatrix}$$

help to explain the probably weakly exogenous variables $x' = (m, p^*, r^*)$. This is done by estimating (16) without and with restrictions

$$\mathrm{H}_0: \quad \alpha_{i1} = \alpha_{i2} = 0 \quad \text{for} \quad i = 1,2,3.$$

$$\begin{aligned} \Delta x_{it} &= \alpha_{i1}u_{1\,t-1} + \alpha_{i2}u_{2\,t-1} + \epsilon^*_{it} \quad \text{for} \quad i = 1,2,3 && (16) \\ \text{with} \quad u_{1t} &= y_{1t} + \gamma_{12}y_{2t} + \theta_{11}x_{1t} + \theta_{12}x_{2t} + \theta_{13}x_{3t} \\ u_{2t} &= y_{2t} + \gamma_{21}y_{1t} + \theta_{21}x_{1t} + \theta_{22}x_{2t} + \theta_{23}x_{3t} && (17) \\ \epsilon^*_{it} &= b^*_i(L)\Delta y_t + c^*_i(L)\Delta x_t + \epsilon_{it}. \end{aligned}$$

The Lagrange multiplier statistic (LM) can be constructed from the corresponding covariance matrices $\hat{\Sigma}$ and $\hat{\Sigma}_0$ respectively (Boswijk (1991)) as

$$LM = T\,\mathrm{trace}\left((\hat{\Sigma}_0 - \hat{\Sigma})\hat{\Sigma}_0^{-1}\right) \quad \sim \quad \chi^2(6).$$

The likelihood ratio statistic

$$LR = T(\ln \mid \hat{\Sigma}_0 \mid - \ln \mid \hat{\Sigma} \mid) \quad \sim \quad \chi^2(6)$$

can be shown to be asymptotically identical to LM (Boswijk (1991)).

The stationarity of u_{1t} and u_{2t} is tested by means of the augmented Dickey–Fuller test. If this hypothesis is accepted, we can easily obtain standard errors and t–values for cointegration vectors, if we normalize equation (14) as in (18):

$$\begin{aligned} B^*(L)\Delta y_t &= \alpha(\Gamma y_{t-1} + \theta x_{t-1}) + C^*(L)\Delta x_t + \epsilon_{1t} && (18) \\ &\quad \text{with} \quad \alpha = \mathrm{diag}B(1). \end{aligned}$$

In our two equation model this refers to estimating (19) and (20).

$$\begin{aligned} \Delta y_{1t} &= \alpha_{11}(y_{1\,t-1} + \gamma_{12}y_{2\,t-1} + \theta_{11}x_{1\,t-1} + \theta_{12}x_{2\,t-1} + \theta_{13}x_{3\,t-1}) && (19) \\ &\quad + \epsilon^*_{1t} \\ \Delta y_{2t} &= \alpha_{22}(y_{1\,t-1} + \gamma_{21}y_{1\,t-1} + \theta_{21}x_{1\,t-1} + \theta_{22}x_{2\,t-1} + \theta_{23}x_{3\,t-1}) && (20) \\ &\quad + \epsilon^*_{2t} \\ &\quad \text{with} \quad \epsilon^*_{it} = b^*_i(L)\Delta y_t + c^*_i(L)\Delta x_t + \epsilon_{it} \end{aligned}$$

Wickens, Breusch (1988) have shown that estimates of γ_{ij} and θ_{ij} can be obtained by estimating the Bewley transform (21) and (22)

$$\begin{aligned} y_{1t} &= \frac{-(\alpha_{11}+1)}{\alpha_{11}}\Delta y_{1t} + \gamma_{12} y_{2\,t-1} + \theta_{11} x_{1\,t-1} \\ &\quad + \theta_{12} x_{2\,t-1} + \theta_{13} x_{3\,t-1} + \frac{\epsilon^*_{1t}}{\alpha_{11}} \end{aligned} \tag{21}$$

$$\begin{aligned} y_{2t} &= \gamma_{21} y_{1\,t-1} - \frac{-(\alpha_{22}+1)}{\alpha_{22}}\Delta y_{2t} + \theta_{21} x_{1\,t-1} \\ &\quad + \theta_{22} x_{2\,t-1} + \theta_{23} x_{3\,t-1} + \frac{\epsilon^*_{2t}}{\alpha_{22}} \end{aligned} \tag{22}$$

by means of an instrumental variables estimator with the lagged level variables $y_{1\,t-1}$ or $y_{2\,t-1}$ as instruments for Δy_{1t} or Δy_{2t} respectively. Standard errors of this linear estimation are the same as those of the nonlinear least squares estimation of (18).

3.2 SUR Estimation and Test for Weak Exogeneity in A(1)

In contrast to the analysis of the partial system, which starts from the economic exogeneity assumptions, we may first estimate the full vector-autoregressive model (VAR) of equation (13) and test for weakly exogenous variables in $z = (y, x)$.

This can be done by testing for zero rows in $A(1)$ by means of a classical $\chi^2(g)$-test within a SUR estimation of (13) where g is the number of variables and equations in the VAR. Whereas the SUR estimator of the unrestricted ECM (13) is the least squares estimator of each equation due to identical regressors, the restricted ECM has to be estimated simultaneously by means of the SUR procedure.

The likelihood ratio statistic is given by

$$LR = -2\ln\lambda^* = T(\ln \mid \hat{\Sigma}_0 \mid - \ln \mid \hat{\Sigma} \mid)$$

with $\hat{\Sigma}_0$ and $\hat{\Sigma}$ as covariance matrix of the SUR procedure under the H_0-restrictions and unrestricted, respectively.

The test for weak exogeneity will not in general give the same exogenous variables as the LM test in the partial system. Therefore, it may be hard to understand this data-guided specification in terms of economic theory. In our case the US-price level turns out to depend on German money stock m and price level p, which is counter-intuitive.

3.3 Johansen Procedure

One of the most widely used procedures in cointegration analysis is now the Johansen procedure, which is available as a RATS–subroutine for a maximum of five variables.

This procedure starts from the least squares estimates of $A(1)$ in the error–correction model (ECM) of equation (13). This LS estimator can equivalently be written as in (23):

$$\begin{aligned}
\Delta\hat{Z} &= \hat{A}(1)'\hat{Z}_{-1} + u \qquad (23)\\
\text{with} \quad \hat{A}(1)' &= (\hat{Z}_{-1}'\hat{Z}_{-1})^{-1}\hat{Z}_{-1}\Delta\hat{Z}\\
\Delta\hat{Z} &= (I_T - \Delta Z^{*\prime}(\Delta Z^{*\prime}\Delta Z^{*})^{-1}\Delta Z^{*})\Delta Z\\
\hat{Z}_{-1} &= (I_T - \Delta Z^{*\prime}(\Delta Z^{*\prime}\Delta Z^{*})^{-1}\Delta Z^{*})Z_{-1}\\
\text{and} \quad \Delta Z^{*} &= (\Delta Z_{-1}, \Delta Z_{-2}, \ldots, \Delta Z_{-p})
\end{aligned}$$

where $\Delta\hat{Z}$ and $\hat{Z}_{-1}$ are the residual matrices of regressions of ΔZ and Z_{-1}, respectively on the differenced variables in ΔZ^{*}.

The first step of the Johansen procedure is to test for the rank of $A(1)$ and therefore for the number of cointegration relations in the system. Given the residuals $\Delta\hat{Z}$, $\hat{Z}_{-1}$, a test for the number of cointegration vectors in the system is performed on the basis of the trace statistic (24)

$$\begin{aligned}
\text{trace statistic}(m) &= -T\sum_{i=1}^{m}\ln(1-\lambda_{g-m+i}) \qquad (24)\\
&\quad\text{with} \quad \lambda_{g-m+1} > \lambda_{g-m+2} > \ldots > \lambda_g
\end{aligned}$$

where the eigenvalues λ_i can be obtained from solving equation (25)

$$\mid \lambda\hat{Z}_{-1}'\hat{Z}_{-1} - \hat{Z}_{-1}\Delta\hat{Z}(\Delta\hat{Z}'\Delta\hat{Z})^{-1}\Delta\hat{Z}'\hat{Z}_{-1} \mid = 0 \qquad (25)$$

which is identical to solving (26)

$$\mid \lambda I - P\hat{Z}_{-1}\Delta\hat{Z}(\Delta\hat{Z}'\Delta\hat{Z})^{-1}\Delta\hat{Z}'\hat{Z}_{-1}P' \mid = 0 \qquad (26)$$

where $P = W^{-1}$ is the *inverse* from a Choleski–decomposition of $\hat{Z}_{-1}'\hat{Z}_{-1}$

$$\hat{Z}_{-1}\hat{Z}_{-1} = WW'.$$

It can be shown that $\sqrt{\lambda_i}$ are the *singular values* of $A(1)$ with respect to the matrices $\hat{Z}_{-1}'\hat{Z}_{-1}$ and $(\Delta\hat{Z}'\Delta\hat{Z})^{-1}$.

Furthermore the cointegration vectors $\hat{\beta}$ are obtained as the eigenvectors corresponding to the eigenvalues from (26). With $g = 5$ variables (and equations) in (23) there are at most g cointegration vectors. If the number of cointegration vectors m is less than g according to the test in (24), those cointegration vectors, corresponding to the zero eigenvalues, can be dropped. Quantiles for this test are obtained by Johansen (1988) from simulating the asymptotic distribution of the test statistic in (24), which is a Brownian motion. Given m cointegration vectors $\hat{\beta}$ one can easily estimate the loading coefficients $\hat{\alpha}$ in

$$\hat{A}(1) = \hat{\alpha}\hat{\beta}' \quad \text{with} \quad \alpha \quad \text{and} \quad \beta \quad \text{as } (g \times m)\text{–matrices} \tag{27}$$

from regressing

$$\Delta\hat{Z} = \hat{\alpha}(\hat{\beta}'\hat{Z}_{-1}) + u. \tag{28}$$

It is the decomposition in (27) which makes an identification of the parameters in $\hat{\beta}$ so difficult. $\hat{\beta}$ does only span a cointegration space.

The number of cointegration vectors from the trace test does not in general correspond to the number of exogenous variables as discussed under 3.2. Cointegration allows at most that all the g variables depend on the m cointegration vectors and therefore none of the variables is weakly exogenous. Therefore, cointegration is a weaker restriction than the weak exogeneity. As we saw before, this type of restriction cannot be easily derived from economic theory. Within a static economic model a reduced rank normally refers to inconsistency or at least incompleteness of the model. A reduced rank of the system may therefore be resolved by taking certain variables as exogeneous or by adding further equations to complete the model. Therefore, less exogenous variables than unit roots in the system may indicate a misspecification in the number of variables in the model.

Furthermore, the economist would not only like to know the stationary linear combinations between the level variables of the ECM but also the significance of the parameters of these relations.

Stationarity is a necessary condition for an equilibrium relation but it is by no means a sufficient one. The Johansen procedure does not provide significance tests for single elements of $\hat{\beta}$, except $\hat{\beta}$ is identified.

4 Estimation Results

All time series are seasonally adjusted quarterly data from 1975,1 to 1989,4 taken from the IMF International Financial Statistics. p and p^* are German versus US log consumer prices, m is log M1 and r^* is the US treasury bill rate.

As a first step we analyse the lag length of the VAR-system, see equation (13), by means of the AIC, HQ and SC criterion. Results are given in Table 1.

Table 1 Information Criteria for Lag Length in the Five Variable System

Lag	AIC	HQ	SC
1	-46.832	-46.488*	-45.951*
2	-46.590	-45.898	-44.813
3	-46.943*	-45.898	-44.254
4	-46.719	-45.317	-43.102
5	-46.766	-45.001	-42.204

Whereas the HQ and SC criteria prefer lag length $p = 1$, the AIC criterion selects $p = 3$. We use both lag lengths in order to show the sensitivity of the results.

4.1 Partial Error–Correction Model

First we show estimates of the partial system obtained by a SUR estimation of the Bewley transform using level variables as instrumental variables.

Table 2 SUR Estimates of the Partial ECM[a]

	$Z_1 = r^*$	$Z_2 = p^*$	$Z_3 = m$	$Z_4 = p$	$Z_5 = e$	$\hat{\alpha}_{ii}$	ADF(4)
$Z_4 = p$	-.003	.500	.013	-1.000	.078	-.208	-5.57
	(.02)	(12.1)	(.33)		(4.98)	(3.81)	
$Z_5 = e$	1.910	-4.154	-.512	8.844	-1.000	-.249	-6.79
	(.76)	(2.23)	(.87)	(3.15)		(2.97)	

[a] t–values in brackets

The coefficients $\hat{\alpha}_{ii}$ are the diagonal elements of $B(1)$ and therefore the effects of the cointegration vector on the corresponding differenced variables Δp or Δe according to (18). The t–statistic of these coefficients can be used to test for cointegration by means of classical asymptotic critical values, if the $x = (r^*, p^*, m)$–variables are weakly exogenous. Kremers et al. (1992) show that this test has more power than the ADF test for cointegration proposed by Engle, Granger (1987). By means of this test cointegration is accepted for both equations. Augmented Dickey–Fuller tests $ADF(4)$ for lag length four confirm the stationarity of the two long–run relations obtained from the significance of α_{ii}.

The main determinants of the exchange rate seem to be domestic and foreign prices, with domestic prices being much more important. This result seems plausible with respect to the fact that we use consumer prices (instead of prices for tradables) in our model. The wrong signs of the coefficients of r^* and m do not matter because these coefficients are not significant.

The cointegration relation refers to purchasing power parity as the main long run factor. Interest rate effects appear only in the short-run relation. This fits to sticky price theories of the exchange rate where the long run exchange rate is defined in terms of purchasing power parity. The Lagrange multiplier (LM) and the likelihood ratio test (LR) for weak exogeneity of (Z_1, Z_2, Z_3) accept this assumption by means of

$$LR(6) = LM(6) = 7.189 \quad \text{and significance level} = 0.304.$$

For comparison, we compute the static first step Engle–Granger estimates for the domestic price and the exchange rate, which give similar cointegration vectors:

Table 3 Static Cointegration Regressions according to Engle, Granger (1987)[a]

	$Z_1 = r^*$	$Z_2 = p^*$	$Z_3 = m$	$Z_4 = p$	$Z_5 = e$	ADF
$Z_4 = p$	-.288	.529	.002		.072	-3.12
	(7.0)	(0.03)	(.13)		(0.0)	
	-.292	.531			.071	-3.10
	(10.3)	(0.74)			(0.6)	
$Z_5 = e$	1.639	-4.403	-.624	9.364		-3.85
	(2.6)	(7.1)	(3.7)	(10.0)		
	3.446	-6.285		11.801		-3.24
	(8.17)	(16.2)		(9.16)		

[a] t–values in brackets

4.2 Exogeneity Tests within a SUR Estimation and Instrumental Variable Estimates of the ECM

Table 4 gives the alternative test on weak exogeneity within a SUR or LS estimation of the VAR in error–correction parametrization. The LR test refers to the SUR estimation of the restricted and the unrestricted ECM, whereas the F– and t–test refer to LS estimates of each equation of the ECM. The F–tests test for exclusion of all level variables from that equation whereas the t-test checks the significance of the diagonal elements in $\hat{A}(1)$, see Kremers et al. (1992).

It can be seen from Table 4 that all these procedures lead to similar results, namely that $Z_3 = m$ and $Z_1 = r^*$ are weakly exogenous and $Z_2 = p^*$

Table 4 Tests of Weak Exogeneity (lag length = 3)

Excluded Variable	a LR Test: LR stat.	a LR Test: Sign.level	b1 F–Test: F–stat.	b1 F–Test: Sign.level	b2 t–Test: t–stat.	b2 t–Test: Sign.level
Z_1	7.40	0.192	1.488	0.216	-.744	.466
Z_2	20.44	0.001	4.656	0.002	-2.557	.019
Z_3	5.39	0.369	1.066	0.394	-.946	.356
Z_4	25.63	0.0001	6.193	0.00027	-2.256	.036
Z_5	10.0	0.075	2.06	0.092	-1.495	.152

a SUR estimation of the VAR (13) and likelihood ratio tests for zero rows in $\hat{A}(1)$

b LS estimation of the VAR and

b1 F–Test for zero rows in $\hat{A}(1)$

b2 t–Test for significance of the diagonal elements in $\hat{A}(1)$

Table 5 LR Test of Joint Weak Exogeneity

Excluded variables	Lag length= 3: LR stat.	Lag length= 3: Sign.level	Lag length= 1: LR stat.	Lag length= 1: Sign.level
$Z_1 Z_3$	13.29	0.208	59.83	.000
$Z_1 Z_3 Z_5$	25.64	0.042	74.37	.000
$Z_1 Z_2 Z_3$	32.90	0.0048	72.14	.000
$Z_1 Z_2 Z_3 Z_5$	45.49	0.001	79.63	.000

and $Z_4 = p$ depend strongly on the levels and are therefore the cointegration vectors. With respect to the exchange rate the results are somewhat volatile. Expecially the t–test discovers weak exogeneity and therefore a random walk.

Furthermore Table 5 gives LR tests for joint exogeneity. These results show

1. that there are only two weakly exogenous variables, if the lag length is $p = 3$ namely $Z_1 = r^*$ and $Z_3 = m$
2. that only $Z_3 = m$ is weakly exogenous, if lag length is $p = 1$
3. that weak exogeneity of $Z_1 = r^*$, $Z_3 = m$ and $Z_5 = e$ is rejected with a significance level only slightly below the 5% level, if $p = 3$.

Table 6 gives the corresponding cointegration vectors, if we estimate the Bewley transform of the ECM equations by SUR with all level variables as instruments. This procedure gives the corresponding t–statistics.

Table 6 SUR(IV) Estimates of the Cointegration Parameters[a,b]

Table 6a: 5 Cointegration Vectors

	$Z_1 = r^*$	$Z_2 = p^*$	$Z_3 = m$	$Z_4 = p$	$Z_5 = e$
$Z_1 = r^*$	-.113	-1.766	-.117	3.600	-.383
	(-.744)	(.64)	(.526)	(.70)	(.75)
$Z_2 = p^*$	1.226	-.168	.1961	1.334	-.140
	(3.63)	(2.56)	(2.21)	(6.55)	(3.80)
$Z_3 = m$	-3.59	-2.07	-.060	5.346	-.876
	(1.29)	(.48)	(.95)	(.68)	(1.12)
$Z_4 = p$	.503	.435	.018	-.188	.0228
	(1.65)	(7.35)	(.37)	(2.26)	(.83)
$Z_5 = e$	1.843	.857	-1.545	.611	-.172
	(.63)	(.24)	(1.70)	(.11)	(1.49)

Table 6b: 3 Cointegration Vectors

	Z_1	Z_2	Z_3	Z_4	Z_5
$Z_2 = p^*$	1.241	-1.000	0.229	1.255	-.134
	(3.77)		(2.71)	(6.45)	(3.83)
$Z_4 = p$	.459	.438	.0184	-1.000	.028
	(1.51)	(7.47)	(.39)		(1.03)
$Z_5 = e$	.416	2.237	-1.762	-1.561	-1.000
	(.15)	(.68)	(2.11)	(.30)	

Table 6c: 3 Cointegration Vectors with Zero–Restrictions

	Z_1	Z_2	Z_3	Z_4	Z_5
$Z_2 = p^*$	1.183	-1.000	.208	1.300	-.141
	(3.69)		(2.62)	(7.02)	(4.31)
$Z_4 = p$	.615	.431		-1.000	
	(1.51)	(7.47)			
$Z_5 = e$	3.656	-4.167		7.503	-1.000
	(3.20)	(5.15)		(4.50)	

[a] t–values in brackets

[b] estimated as Bewley transform of the ECM

On the diagonal of Table 6a the diagonal elements of $\hat{A}(1)$ are given. Again these results show that the exchange rate equation, as well as the equations for r^* and m, do not provide significant long-run equilibrium relations. Table 6b shows the SUR estimates of the Bewley transform with the equations for $Z_1 = r^*$ and $Z_3 = m$ dropped from the system. This does not help much to improve the significance of the exchange rate parameters. Table 6c shows how sensitive long–run parameters are with respect to zero restrictions. By dropping the domestic money from the exchange rate equation we get significant and plausible coefficients for the effects of $Z_1 = r^*$, $Z_2 = p^*$ and $Z_4 = p$, as in the partial system under 4.1. Obviously more restrictions are needed in the ECM to get reasonable results. It is the main problem of the full ECM that there is no unique order to put additional restrictions on the cointegration vectors. Therefore, it seems to be more attractive to start with the partial system for $y' = (p, e)$ derived from the monetary model of the exchange rate.

4.3 Johansen Procedure

Next we present the Johansen test for the cointegration rank of $A(1)$ and the critical values of the test statistic:

Table 7 Johansen Test for the Cointegration Rank

Numbers of cointegration vectors	$m = 1$	$m = 2$	$m = 3$	$m = 4$	$m = 5$
Trace statistic (lag=1):	170.536*	68.828*	25.926	5.352	1.386
Trace statistic (lag=3):	90.386*	51.203*	22.309	9.306	.556
Crit. values (95%):	70.598	48.280	31.525	17.953	8.176
Crit. values (90%):	66.486	45.229	28.709	15.663	6.503

Significant test statistics are indicated by (*). According to this result there are two cointegration vectors in the system. Estimates of $\hat{A}(1)$, $\hat{\beta}$ and $\hat{\alpha}$ for different numbers of cointegration vectors m and lag length are given in Table 8. Whereas the test of the cointegration rank gives the number of cointegration vectors, it does not give the variables, which are determined by means of these vectors. This information can be found either from the estimated loading matrix $\hat{\alpha}$ or from the change in the diagonal elements of the restricted $\hat{A}(1)$–Matrix according to a reduction in the number of cointegration vectors. The second interpretation assumes that each variable may only be affected by one cointegration vector whereas in the Johansen approach each cointegration vector can be loaded on each variable.

The rank restriction does also heavily effect the estimates $\hat{A}(1)$. Excluding two cointegration vectors ($m = 3$) mainly makes the diagonal elements of $\hat{A}(1)$ for $Z_3 = m$ and $Z_1 = r^*$ equal zero, whereas for $m = 2$ the diagonal element of $Z_5 = e$ becomes zero in addition. This refers to the weak exogeneity of m, r^* and possibly e. Therefore, we understand the two cointegration vectors as belonging to $Z_4 = p$, $Z_2 = p^*$ and $Z_5 = e$.

The third cointegration vector refers to the exchange rate but the coefficients, for example of r^* and m, have the wrong sign. With lag length equal to one, the coefficients do not fit to any prior belief. The results in Table 10 and 9 show that especially the $\hat{\alpha}$– and $\hat{\beta}$–coefficients are extremely sensitive with respect to lag length, although these coefficients should asymptotically be independent of the coefficients of the differenced variables and therefore of

Table 8 Unrestricted and Restricted $\hat{A}(1)$–Matrix [a]

	m^b	$Z_1 = r^*$	$Z_2 = p^*$	$Z_3 = m$	$Z_4 = p$	$Z_5 = e$
	5	-.113	-.199	-.013	.406	-.043
$Z_1 = r^*$	3	-.032	-.294	-.009	.576	-.051
	2	-.089	-.271	.016	.490	-.034
	5	.206	-.168	.033	.224	-.024
$Z_1 = p^*$	3	.180	-.148	.028	.194	-.022
	2	.176	-.151	.025	.207	-.025
	5	-.216	-.124	-.060	.321	-.053
$Z_1 = m$	3	.054	-.332	-.011	.631	-.067
	2	-.090	-.297	.026	.500	-.040
	5	.095	.082	.003	-.188	.004
$Z_1 = p$	3	.124	.054	.007	-.141	.002
	2	.125	.054	.008	-.144	.033
	5	.317	.142	-.266	.105	-.172
$Z_1 = e$	3	.092	.297	-.314	-.098	-.163
	2	.397	-.589	-.000	1.204	.061

[a] lag length = 3

[b] m = cointegration rank

the lag length. The normalisation in Table 10 is due to the effect of a reduced cointegration rank m on the diagonal elements of $\hat{A}(1)$ as given in Table 8.

The loading coefficients of Table 9 show that all three cointegration vectors in case of lag length 3 and only the second cointegration vector in case of lag length 1 do strongly effect the exchange rate. This demonstrates that the interpretation is less clear cut than that of the $A(1)$–Matrix. But given the fact that the first two cointegration vectors include mainly p and p^*, the loading coefficients again support the purchasing power parity. Table 10 gives these cointegration vectors if the rank of $A(1)$ is 3. Again p^* and p seem to be involved in the first two cointegration vectors with half of the weight on p^*.

Table 10 also shows how sensitive the β–coefficients are with respect to the lag length.

Table 11 gives tests for weak exogeneity according to Johansen. With lag length $p = 1$ we would accept that there are no weakly exogenous variables according to the marginal significance level of the test statistic whereas with lag length $p = 3$ at least the domestic money supply is weakly exogenous although it is highly loaded on the first two cointegration vectors. Again domestic and foreign prices (Z_4, Z_2) depend most strongly on the level variables. This result is in conflict with the monetary model.

Table 9 Loading Matrix $\hat{\alpha}^a$

	Lag length = 3			Lag length = 1		
	$Z_4 = p$	$Z_2 = p^*$	$Z_5 = e$	$Z_4 = p$	$Z_2 = p^*$	$Z_5 = e$
$Z_1 = r^*$	.186	-.190	-.017	-.002	-.226	-.003
$Z_2 = p^*$	-.089	-.190	.003	-.038	-.148	.000
$Z_3 = m$	.267	-.254	-.027	.053	-.249	-.006
$Z_4 = p$	-.169	-.019	-.001	-.024	.103	.000
$Z_5 = e$	-.809	.234	-.223	-.085	.675	.003

[a] 3 cointegration vectors

Table 10 Cointegration Vectors $\hat{\beta}^a$

Table 10a: Lag length = 3					
	$Z_1 = r^*$	$Z_2 = p^*$	$Z_3 = m$	$Z_4 = p$	$Z_5 = e$
$Z_4 = p$	.669	.437	.033	-1.000	.032
$Z_2 = p^*$	.615	-1.000	.114	1.684	-.146
$Z_5 = e$	-1.369	-1.304	-1.403	3.545	-1.000
Table 10b: Lag length = 1					
	$Z_1 = r^*$	$Z_2 = p^*$	$Z_3 = m$	$Z_4 = p$	$Z_5 = e$
$Z_4 = p$	5.876	-.302	.808	-1.000	-.048
$Z_2 = p^*$	.344	-1.000	.034	1.832	-.167
$Z_5 = e$	-51.683	38.019	-11.352	-66.239	-1.000

[a] normalized variable -1.000

5 Summary

Cointegration analysis has not been very successful in establishing meaningful long–run relations for the DM/\$–rate. Our exercise tries to show that this is partly due to the atheoretical research strategy chosen in cointegration analysis. Instead of using economic theory to restrict the number of reasonable specifications from the beginning, time series analysts start from a general VAR model in error–correction representation and try to find a plausible specification by means of statistical tests alone.

These statistical tests have widely unknown power, at least if the true data generation process is unknown. This paper demonstrates that this research strategy can easily lead to nonsense results like a long-run relation explaining the U.S. price level by means of German money stock and price level. In contrast, one can make use of the theoretical restrictions and test these restrictions by means of a Lagrange multiplier test. This strategy seems to be more fruitful and much easier, and is supported by the results of this

Table 11 χ_e^2–Test Statistics for Weak Exogeneity due to Johansen[a]

	Lag length = 1		Lag length = 3	
	χ_e^2	Significance level	χ_e^2	Significance level
Z_1	9.572	.088	9.638	.086
Z_2	86.149	.000	26.685	.00007
Z_3	32.212	.000	6.928	.226
Z_4	81.278	.000	33.418	.000003
Z_5	12.404	.029	13.115	.022

[a] 5 degress of freedom according to restrictions on $A(1)$

paper. These results give evidence that the purchasing power parity is an important factor in the long run.

References

Boswijk H P (1991) The LM–Test for Weak Exogeneity in Error Correction Models. University of Amsterdam. Report AE 13/91

Engle R F, Granger C W J (1987) Cointegration and Error Correction: Representation, Estimation and Testing. Econometrica 51:277–304

Johansen S (1988) Statistical Analysis of Cointegration Vectors. Journal of Economic Dynamics and Control 12:132–254

Johansen S (1992a) Cointegration in Partial Systems and the Efficiency of Single Equation Analysis. Journal of Econometrics 52:389–402

Johansen S (1992b) Identifying Restrictions of Linear Equations. Discussion Paper. University of Copenhagen

Kremers J J M, Ericsson N, Dolado J J (1992) The Power of Cointegration Tests. International Finance Discussion Paper 431. Board of Governors of the Federal Reserve System

Meese R A, Rogoff K (1983) Empirical Exchange Rate Models of the Seventies: Do They Fit out of Sample? Journal of International Economics 14:3–24

Phillips P C B (1991) Optimal Inference in Cointegrated Systems. Econometrica 59:283–306

Urbain J P (1991) On Weak Exogeneity in Error Correction Models. CREDEL Research Paper 9103. University of Liege

Wickens M R, Breusch T S (1988) Dynamic Specification, the Long–Run and the Estimation of Transformed Regression Models. Economic Journal 98:189–205

Does Cointegration Matter in the Empirical Analysis of the CAPM?[1]

By Gerd Ronning[2]

Abstract: Nonstationarity and cointegration do not matter in the empirical analysis of CAPM when returns are analysed. The situation is different when risk premia are considered which contain interest rates as one component: These variables are nonstationary but cointegration is satisfied in a trivial manner. However estimates of the empirical CAPM are greatly influenced by these nonstationary variables. Empirical results are given for the German stock market.

1 Introduction

Capital market research has always made intensive use of econometric and statistical methods in order to test hypotheses from the theory of capital markets. One of the most famous models is the 'capital asset pricing model' (CAPM) which has been developed by Sharpe (1964), Lintner (1965) and Mossin (1966) and which by now is a standard tool in assessing the risk of single stocks or portfolios of stocks and other capital assets. Both cross-section and time-series data are used. In the latter case the question arises naturally whether the problem of nonstationarity and cointegration plays a role in the estimation of this model. In this note we present empirical evidence that nonstationarity does *not* matter if returns are used in estimation. However the situation is different if 'risk premia' are employed since interest rates are then involved.

Section 2 presents two versions of the CAPM on which time series regressions are based: Besides the usual specification in which returns are involved we also present a version from which so-called 'abnormal returns' are determined. Section 3 describes the data. Section 4 presents empirical results from

[1]Earlier versions of this paper have been commented by Wolfgang Bühler, Walter Krämer, Jack Wahl and Jürgen Wolters. Jürgen Kaehler and an anonymous referee added further remarks which helped to improve the content of the paper. Data have been provided by Lehrstuhl für Finanzierung at the University of Mannheim and by Karlsruher Datenbank, University of Karlsruhe. This research is related to 'Schwerpunkt "Empirische Kapitalmarktforschung"' financed by Deutsche Forschungsgemeinschaft.

[2]Gerd Ronning, Wirtschaftswissenschaftliches Seminar, Eberhard-Karls-Universität Tübingen, Abteilung Statistik und Ökonometrie I, Mohlstr. 36, D-72074 Tübingen, Germany.

unit root tests based on data from the German stock market for both returns and risk premia. Section 5 adds some concluding remarks.

2 The CAPM

The capital asset pricing model postulates a linear relationship between the expected return $\mathrm{E}(R_i)$ of a single asset and the expected return $\mathrm{E}(R_P) \equiv \mu_P$ of the (efficient) market portfolio P as follows:

$$\mathrm{E}(R_i) = R_f + \beta_i(\mu_P - R_f) \quad . \tag{1}$$

Here R_f denotes the return of the 'riskless' asset which is also used to define the risk premium

$$r_i = R_i - R_f$$

of a single asset. Correspondingly we have

$$r_P = R_P - R_f$$

for the risk premium of a portfolio. β_i is the 'systematic risk' of asset i since it measures the correlation with the market portfolio:

$$\beta_i = \frac{\mathrm{cov}(R_i, R_P)}{\sigma_P^2} = \mathrm{corr}(R_i, R_P)\,\frac{\sigma_i}{\sigma_P} \quad .$$

Roll (1977) has criticized attempts to test the efficiency of portfolios: Since an efficient portfolio is characterized by (1), a test is superfluous if the portfolio used in empirical analysis has this property. On the other hand, a test of efficiency is impossible if the efficient portfolio is not used. Sharpe (1963) has proposed the 'index model'

$$R_i = \alpha_i + \beta_i I + \epsilon_i \quad . \tag{2}$$

which may be seen as an approximation to the true CAPM. Here I is an index of average market return, α_i and β_i are asset–specific parameters and ϵ_i is an error term.

The CAPM may be written in a similar fashion as

$$\mathrm{E}(R_i) = \alpha_i + \beta_i\,\mu_P \tag{3}$$

but in this case α_i and β_i are related by the restriction[3]

$$\alpha_i = R_f(1 - \beta_i) \quad .$$

[3]See (1). Gibbons (1982) has taken account of this restriction.

Disregarding this constraint Fama (1976 Chapter 4) calls (3) the 'market model' which for a certain asset i , $i = 1, \ldots, N$, in empirical analysis takes the form

$$R_{it} = \alpha_i + \beta_i R_{Pt} + \epsilon_{it} \quad , \quad t = 1, \ldots, n \quad . \tag{4}$$

where t denotes the t-th observation.

Alternatively we can write (1) as a linear relation between risk premia of asset i and the portfolio P, respectively, as follows:

$$\mathrm{E}(R_i - R_f) = \alpha_i^\star + \beta_i(\mu_P - R_f) \quad . \tag{5}$$

Comparison of (1) and (5) shows that the 'abnormal return' $\alpha_i^\star$ should be zero, that is

$$\alpha_i^\star = 0 \quad .$$

However, if a positive (negative) abnormal return is identified for asset i, the investor should put higher (lower) weight to it than in the market portfolio[4]. In empirical analysis the following equation is used[5]:

$$r_{it} = \alpha_i^\star + \beta_i r_{Pt} + \epsilon_{it} \quad . \tag{6}$$

Huang and Litzenberger (1988) have extensively discussed the econometric analysis of the CAPM both for cross-section and time series data[6]. But they have not treated the model (6). Moreover there has been no discussion of problems arising from nonstationary variables in time series regressions related to the CAPM so far. The only exception is a paper by Cerchi und Havenner (1988 p. 335) who point out that 'financial asset models that use returns can reasonably be assured of stationarity'. Our paper provides this empirical evidence.

Empirical capital market research and particularly CAPM analysis has payed surprisingly little attention to the question of temporal aggregation[7]. There has been almost no discussion about an adequate or even optimal interval for which price changes and resulting returns should be analysed.

---

[4]See Jegadeesh (1990) and Stehle (1991), Section IV.1. R_i could also characterize the return of a portfolio consisting of a subset of available assets.

[5]See, for example, Berndt (1991) p. 35.

[6]Their presentation is rather irritating from an econometric point of view since the notion of 'parameter' and 'variable' is frequently interchanged. An example is the 'parameter' $\alpha_i^\star$ in equation (6), which contains the return of the riskless asset as a component.

[7]Fama (1976, Chapter 1) prefers monthly data since they provide the best compromise between a large number of observations and approximation to normality. Drost (1993, this issue) reports some new results for the temporal aggregation of fractionally differenced time-series and GARCH processes.

All kinds of data have been used ranging from transaction data which have a period of 5 minutes and less up to yearly changes of share prices. Most researchers have been content with the data they got. On the other hand it is well-known that temporal aggregation has considerable effects on the stochastic behaviour. We shall present some evidence in the next section.

Another problem rarely discussed is the definition of the return variable. Let Π_t be the price of some asset at t. Then – disregarding side payments from dividends and other sources – we may define the profit (per unit invested) by

$$E_t = \Pi_t - \Pi_{t-1}$$

This variable can be modelled by symmetric distributions. However return is usually given as

$$R_t = \frac{\Pi_t - \Pi_{t-1}}{\Pi_{t-1}} = \frac{E_t}{\Pi_{t-1}}$$

which has lower bound -1. Therefore, only asymmetric distributions can describe its stochastic behaviour. To remedy this defect, often the 'continuous' return

$$S_t = \ln(1 + R_t) = \ln(\Pi_t) - \ln(\Pi_{t-1})$$

is analysed. Additional questions arise with regard to the return R_P from a portfolio. Since the CAPM typically considers a weighted[8] arithmetic mean of returns from N assets, that is

$$R_{Pt} = \sum_{j=1}^{N} w_j R_{tj} \quad ,$$

the use of the variable S_t would be inadequate. Moreover, returns from market indexes such as DAX or Dow Jones are commonly computed as

$$R_{Mt} = \frac{I_t - I_{t-1}}{I_{t-1}}$$

which differs from R_{Pt}.

The CAPM is derived from equilibrium arguments and is considered as a model for the aggregate market. This makes the model an attractive candidate for cointegration analysis provided nonstationarity is indicated by the data. We already noted that this is not very likely for return variables which are assumed to be stationary and (almost) uncorrelated over time. This is, however, not true for returns from 'riskless' assets such as interest rates which act as indicators of R_f. As Kirchgässner and Wolters (1990a,b) and

[8]Many empirical researchers prefer equally weighted portfolios, that is $w_j = 1/N$.

others have shown, interest rates exhibit nonstationary behaviour. Therefore risk premia should also have this property. This raises the question whether cointegration exists. From (6) and the definition of the risk premia given above we see that the two risk premia are trivially cointegrated since they both contain the same nonstationary component R_f. This fact has severe consequences on the parameter estimates: Since, roughly speaking, the same variable acts as dependent and as independent variable we can expect that the OLS estimates of the two coefficients satisfy

$$\begin{pmatrix} \hat{\alpha}_i^* \\ \hat{\beta}_i \end{pmatrix} \simeq \begin{pmatrix} 0 \\ 1 \end{pmatrix}$$

and this result will hold almost exactly when returns become white noise and/or the interest rate exhibits a pronounced trend[9]. Therefore the usual interpretation of estimates from this equation seems to be disputable. See Section 4.3 for some illustrative results. To the author's best knowledge this has not been noted in the financial market literature so far.

3 The Data

We use daily quotations of four common stocks (Daimler-Benz, Siemens-Nixdorf, Siemens, VEBA) and three market indexes (FWB, DAX, FAZ) during the years 1986 to 1990 (about 1250 observations)[10]. We excluded those data points for which some of the seven variables were not observed. This reduced the number of observations by 7. We computed all three types of returns (absolute (E), relative (R) and logarithmic(S) - see Section 2) from successive observations. We also constructed time series of weekly quotations from the Wednesday prices (about 250 observations). Correspondingly we determined two-weekly returns, three-weekly returns and four-weekly returns (about 60 observations). As an indicator of the return R_f from the riskless asset we used money market rates ('Geldmarktsätze'). Only weekly (Friday) quotations were available for terms of one day, one month, three months and six months[11]. All rates are given as percentages per annum. Here we use only

[9]The vector of OLS estimates in the simple linear regression model equals

$$\begin{pmatrix} \hat{\alpha} \\ \hat{\beta} \end{pmatrix} = \begin{pmatrix} 0 \\ 1 \end{pmatrix}$$

if the dependent variable is also used as regressor and a constant term is added. The model (6) considered in the text could also be seen as an errors-in-variables model. Note however that in case of trended variables OLS estimation is consistent contrary to the usual textbook result. See, for example, Krämer (1985) or Schneeweiß(1991).

[10]These data were provided by Karlsruher Datenbank.

[11]These data were provided by Lehrstuhl für Finanzierung, University of Mannheim.

monthly rates as an approximation to R_f.[12] From the available ask and bid quotations we formed an arithmetic mean for each term.

4 Results

In this section we perform unit root tests and cointegration tests for the empirical CAPM. In the first subsection, results are given for model (4) which uses returns whereas the second subsection reports corresponding results for risk premia which are used in model (6). For illustrative purpose we also show some estimation results in the third subsection which illustrate the difference between the two specifications.

4.1 Returns

Tables 1 and 2 show results from unit root tests (Dickey-Fuller test) which test for stationarity of the observed time series[13]. This test for variable x is based on OLS estimation of the following equation:

$$\Delta x_t = \gamma_0 + \delta t + \rho x_{t-1} + \sum_{j=1}^{k} \gamma_j \Delta x_{t-j} + u_t \tag{7}$$

where the lag length k should be chosen such that the error term u_t is white noise. We test the hypothesis that the stochastic process which generates x contains a unit root, i.e. it follows a random walk, by the null

$$\rho = 0 \quad .$$

Large negative values of the estimated coefficient indicate that the null should be rejected, i.e. the process is stationary. Critical values have to be obtained from nonstandard distributions[14]. Three options are available: option T estimates the full model as given in (7), option C excludes the trend term from this model and option N additionally drops the constant term. West (1987) has pointed out that option T has to be used if the time series is stationary around a linear trend. Moreover the test has practically no power if the number of lags (k) is too large (Perron 1988).

Table 1 shows results for *daily* returns. For all seven variables the null hypothesis of a nonstationary process (unit root) is strongly rejected. Results

---

[12]Ideally one would use the term which corresponds to the return interval. Since data for one week term are not available we have to use one-day or one-month term rates. One-day money rates seem to be primarily indicators of liquidity shortage and cannot be interpreted as returns on riskless investment.

[13]All computations were done using Micro-TSP (7.0).

[14]Micro-TSP provides these critical values automatically using results from MacKinnon (1991).

Table 1 Results from unit root tests for daily returns

	absolute	relative	logarithmic
Daimler-B.	-15.5***	-15.8***	-15.7***
Nixdorf	-16.2***	-16.6***	-16.5***
Siemens	-14.5***	-14.6***	-14.6***
VEBA	-16.5***	-16.2***	-16.1***
FWB-Index	-14.8***	-15.0***	-14.9***
FAZ-Index	-15.4***	-15.9***	-15.7***
DAX-Index	-15.2***	-15.6***	-15.4***
No. of observations:		1246	

Remarks:
Option "T" (with trend and constant term), k = 4 lags
*** denotes significance at the 1% level.

are only presented for option "T" and lag parameter $k = 4$. (For larger k the test statistic is smaller in absolute value.) The table shows that the differences of the test results with respect to the three types of return variables are not large. Therefore in Table 2 we restrict ourselves to the return variable R_t (relative returns). Results in this table refer to returns from *longer intervals* (1 week up to 4 weeks). Again we only show results for $k = 4$. For intervals larger than 2 weeks the rejection of the null is no longer as clearcut as for short intervals. However Perron and Shiller (1985) and Perron (1988 p. 317) have noticed that this effect is due to the reduced power of the unit root test if intervals are enlarged within a fixed time interval, i.e. the number of observations diminishes. Therefore for larger intervals the time span should be enlarged. However in empirical research very often this is not possible. On the other hand this provokes the question of the adequate length of the time interval in capital market research.

4.2 Risk Premia

Some authors[15] have used model (6) which relates the two risk premia $R_{it} - R_{ft}$ and $R_{Pt} - R_{ft}$ for asset i and portfolio P. As an indicator of the return R_f of the riskless asset, money market interest rates are used[16].

Our analysis uses interest rates from the German money market as described in Section 3. We consider *weekly* intervals since we do not have daily quotations for these rates. As already noted above, we have to recognize that the money rate should correspond to the return both with respect to the term

[15]See, for example, Jegadeesh (1990) and Stehle (1991).

[16]Jegadeesh (1990) uses one-month T–bills, Stehle (1991) uses monthly averages of the "Monatsgeld am Frankfurter Geldmarkt" and FIBOR rates alternatively.

Table 2 Unit root tests for returns from longer intervals

	1 week	2 weeks	3 weeks	4 weeks
Daimler-B.	-6.42***	-5.21***	-4.25***	-3.80**
Nixdorf	-7.49***	-5.34***	-3.55**	-3.66**
Siemens	-6.71***	-4.53***	-3.52**	-3.25*
VEBA	-7.14***	-5.04***	-3.80**	-3.34*
FWB	-6.87***	-5.13***	-4.04**	-3.89**
FAZ	-7.06***	-5.19***	-4.01**	-3.92**
DAX	-6.84***	-5.97***	-4.11***	-4.10**
No. of obs.:	250	125	80	60

Remarks: k = 4 lags.
*** (**,*) denotes significance at the 1% (5% , 10%) level.

and the interval. So ideally for weekly returns we should use the interest paid for a loan to be paid back after one week. But we have only one-day and one-month rates the former being less useful (see above). Therefore we will use one-month rates. We also have to recognize that rates are quoted "per annum" and should therefore be transformed to weekly returns. For this we use the linear approximation

$$W_t = \frac{Y_t}{52}$$

to compute the weekly rate W_t from the yearly rate Y_t since this is common practice in the banking sector . This implies that our regression model becomes of the form

$$(R_t - \frac{1}{c} R_{ft}) = \alpha + \beta(R_{Pt} - \frac{1}{c} R_{ft}) + u_t \quad . \tag{8}$$

Here c is a constant such that c times the interval considered covers one year. In case of weekly data $c = 52$.

We already mentioned recent empirical results indicating nonstationary behaviour of interest rates[17]. Therefore the risk premium combines the – stationary – component R_{it} or R_{Pt} with the – nonstationary – component R_f so that *risk premia are typically nonstationary.* However the nonstationary component is reduced if the p.a. rate is adjusted to the investment interval. Figure 1 shows this for weekly returns of the common stock Daimler-Benz contrasted with the one-month rate.

[17]See Rose (1988) and Kirchgässner and Wolters (1990a,b). The important theoretical question why interest rates should be nonstationary and returns should be stationary has still to be solved.

We will therefore expect that two nonstationary variables will be considered in model (6) especially if shorter intervals are analysed. However cointegration of the two risk premia is trivially satisfied since the same nonstationary component appears in both risk premia.

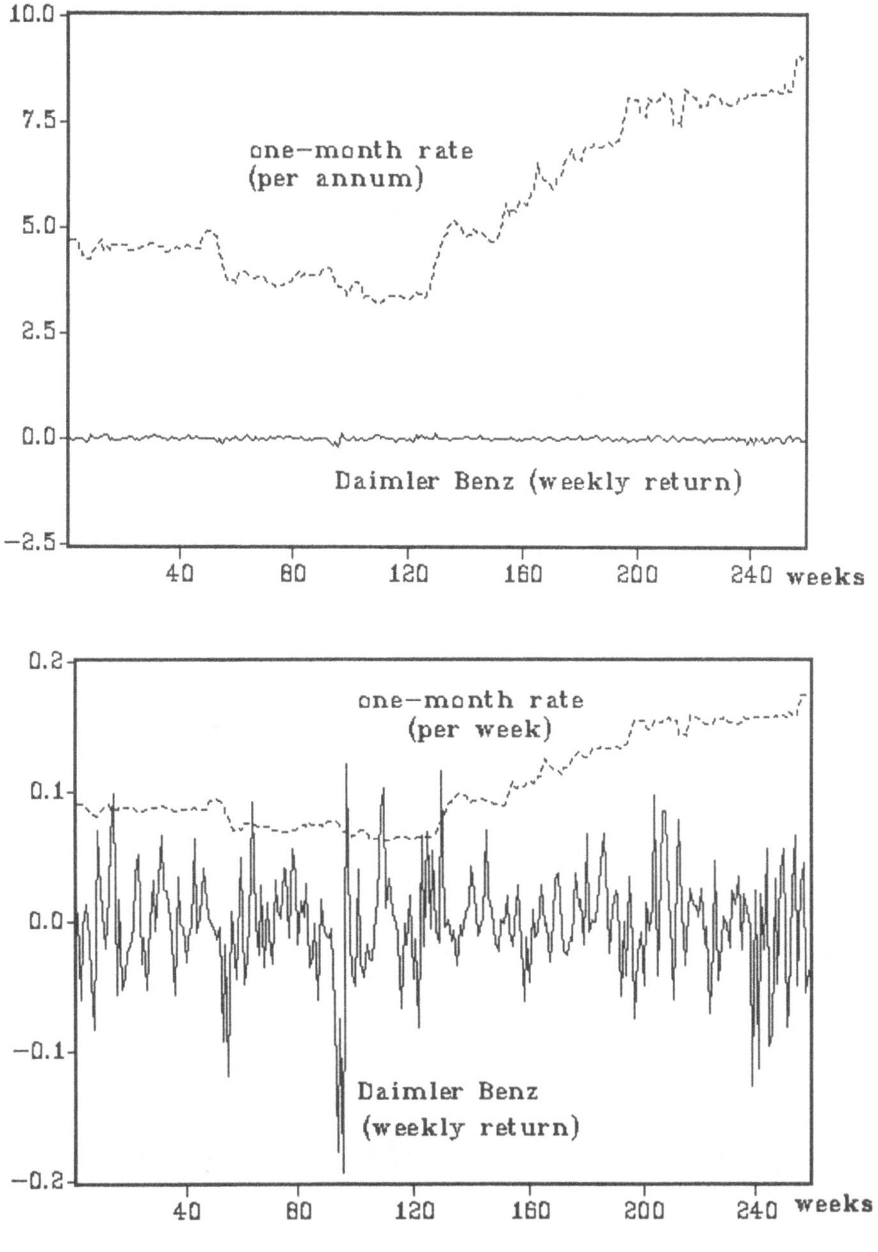

Figure 1 Weekly returns, unadjusted and adjusted money market rate

Our empirical results are given in tables 3 and 4. Table 3 reports results from unit root tests and Table 4 results from Engle-Granger cointegration tests. In the latter case we estimate a linear regression model

$$y_t = \alpha + \beta x_t + \delta t + u_t \tag{9}$$

for the two variables y and x for which cointegration is assumed. In a second step we use the residuals $\hat{u}_t$ from this regression and estimate

$$\Delta \hat{u}_t = \gamma \hat{u}_{t-1} + \sum_{j=1}^{k} \alpha_j \Delta \hat{u}_{t-j} + \epsilon_t \quad . \tag{10}$$

The null hypothesis of "no cointegration" is rejected if the estimated coefficient of γ is significantly smaller than 0. Again critical values have to be obtained from non-standard distributions. Option T includes the trend term in (9), option N excludes it.

Table 3 Unit root tests for weekly risk premia ('one-month' rate)

	T		C	
	$k = 4$	$k = 12$	$k = 4$	$k = 12$
		unadjusted rate		
DB	-1.48	-1.52	0.59	0.43
Nixdorf	-1.49	-1.56	0.61	0.47
Siemens	-1.46	-1.53	0.61	0.42
VEBA	-1.45	-1.54	0.59	0.40
FWB	-1.45	-1.53	0.60	0.42
FAZ	-1.46	-1.53	0.59	0.41
DAX	-1.46	-1.54	0.59	0.42
1 month rate	-1.47	-1.57	0.58	0.43
		adjusted rate		
DB	-5.01***	-2.92	-3.11**	-1.38
Nixdorf	-6.14***	-2.95	-3.48***	-1.14
Siemens	-4.96***	-2.70	-3.21**	-1.28
VEBA	-4.75***	-2.32	-2.60*	-0.88
FWB	-4.31***	-2.10	-2.38	-0.73
FAZ	-4.59***	-2.16	-2.61*	-0.79
DAX	-4.38***	-2.15	-2.45	-0.76

Remarks: k = 4 lags.
*** (**,*) denotes significance at the 1% (5% , 10%) level.

Table 3 indicates nonstationary behaviour of risk premia if the money rate is *not* adjusted[18]. The table contains also the test results for the '1 month rate' which indicate that this variable is responsible for the non-stationary behaviour of the risk premia. The results are more in favour of stationary behaviour when adjusted money rates are used although for larger k nonstationarity still is indicated. Let us then turn to the cointegration test results: Table 4 indicates that the null hypothesis of no cointegration can be rejected in all cases.

Table 4 Engle-Granger tests for risk premia ('one-month' rate)

		FWB		FAZ		DAX	
		$k=4$	$k=12$	$k=4$	$k=12$	$k=4$	$k=12$
		unadjusted rate					
DB	C	-6.65***	-5.63***	-6.82***	-5.66***	-6.51***	-5.56***
	T	-6.73***	-5.87***	-6.90***	-5.91***	-6.59***	-5.80***
Nixdorf	C	-6.50***	-3.44**	-6.53***	-3.56**	-6.59***	-3.56**
	T	-6.87***	-3.98**	-6.85***	-4.07**	-6.72***	-4.06**
Siemens	C	-6.26***	-4.84***	-6.20***	-4.65***	-6.10***	-4.57***
	T	-6.25***	-4.86***	-6.17***	-4.66***	-6.09***	-4.59***
VEBA	C	-7.31***	-4.61***	-7.47***	-4.56***	-7.93***	-4.92***
	T	-7.42***	-4.67***	-7.55***	-4.59***	-8.04***	-8.01***
		adjusted rate					
DB	C	-6.26***	-4.71***	-6.89***	-5.65***	-6.17***	-4.67***
	T	-6.23***	-4.58***	-6.90***	-5.66***	-6.16***	-4.56***
Nixdorf	C	-6.49***	-3.35*	-6.29***	-3.27**	-6.36***	-3.44**
	T	-7.14***	-4.07***	-7.11***	-4.24**	-7.03***	-4.18**
Siemens	C	-6.15***	-4.75***	-6.16***	-4.54***	-6.00***	-4.46***
	T	-6.19***	-4.72***	-6.14***	-4.59***	-6.06***	-4.44***
VEBA	C	-7.11***	-4.20***	-6.53***	-3.30*	-7.73***	-4.51***
	T	-7.49***	-4.50***	-7.17***	-3.87**	-8.08***	-4.86***

Remarks: k = 4 lags. Option T.
*** (**,*) denotes significance at the 1% (5% , 10%) level.

4.3 Estimation Results for both Specifications

In this section we compare the estimation results from the two specifications (4) and (6) which are equivalent in theory. In the first we consider the relation between returns and in the second the relation between risk premia. As we have shown in extenso, both models contain cointegrated variables. However we also already pointed out in Section 2 that estimation results for the second

[18]In a comment to my talk at the conference it was noted that nobody would use this unadjusted specification. Nonetheless I have kept these results in the paper to show the difference with regard to test results.

model will tend to

$$\begin{pmatrix} \hat{\alpha}_i^* \\ \hat{\beta}_i \end{pmatrix} \simeq \begin{pmatrix} 0 \\ 1 \end{pmatrix}$$

because of the 'dominating' money market rate on both sides of the equation. Table 5 shows estimation results for both specifications. As can be seen from the table the estimated coefficient β tends towards 1 if risk premia instead of returns are used, that is if we consider model (6) instead of (4). This illustrates our claim in Section 2 that estimates from both models cannot be interpreted in the same manner.

Table 5 Least-squares estimates for returns and risk premia

	returns		risk premia	
	α	β	α	β
	FWB index			
DB	0.00	1.28***	0.01***	1.13***
Nixdorf	0.00	0.78***	-0.01**	0.89***
Siemens	0.00	1.07***	0.00	1.01***
VEBA	0.00	0.83***	-0.01	0.94***
	FAZ index			
DB	0.00	1.06***	0.00	1.04***
Nixdorf	0.00	0.67***	-0.02***	0.83***
Siemens	0.00	0.91***	-0.01*	0.94***
VEBA	0.00	0.70***	-0.01***	0.86***
	DAX index			
DB	0.00	1.22***	0.01***	1.10***
Nixdorf	0.00	0.74***	-0.02**	0.86***
Siemens	0.00	1.05***	0.00	0.99***
VEBA	0.00	0.85***	-0.01	0.93***

Remark: *** (**,*) denotes significance at the 1% (5% , 10%) level.

5 Concluding Remarks

This short note draws attention to the fact that the two specification of the CAPM as used in the financial literature cannot be viewed as equivalent in empirical analysis: If the study is based on stock returns then the estimates can be seen as reasonable whereas research which uses risk premia has to take care of possible nonstationary behaviour of these variables and also of the bias of estimates towards $\alpha = 0$ and $\beta = 1$. So far empirical financial economics has not taken account of this phenomenon.

References

Berndt E R (1991) The Practice of Econometrics: Classic and Contemporary. Addison-Wesley : Reading (Mass.)

Cerchi M und Havenner A (1988) Cointegration and Stock Prices: The Random Walk on Wall Street Revisited. Journal of Economic Dynamics and Control 12, 333-346

Drost F C (1993) Temporal Aggregation of Time-Series. This volume, 11-21

Fama E F (1976) Foundations of Finance. Portfolio Decisions and Security Prices. Basic Books: New York

Gibbons M (1982) Multivariate Tests of Financial Models: A New Approach. Journal of Financial Economics 10, 3-27

Huang C-f and Litzenberger R H (1988) Foundations for Financial Economics. New York: North-Holland

Jegadeesh N (1990) Evidence of Predictable Behavior of Security Returns. Journal of Finance 45, 881-898

Kirchgässner G and Wolters J (1990a) Uncovered Interest Parity Condition Between the United States and Europe Under Different Exchange Rate Regimes. in: S F Frowen (ed.): Monetary Theory and Monetary Policy. New Tracks for the 1990s. MacMillan: London

Kirchgässner G and Wolters J (1990b) Sind die Realzinsen stationär? Theoretische Überlegungen und empirische Ergebnisse. Kredit und Kapital 23, 468-495

Krämer W (1985) Asymptotische Verteilungen einiger Schätzverfahren bei Trend und Fehlern in den Variablen. Metrika 32, 151-162

Lintner J (1965) The Evaluation of Risk Assets and the Selection of Risky Investments in Stock Portfolios and Capital Budgets. Review of Economic Studies 47, 13-37

MacKinnon J G (1991) Critical Values for Cointegration Tests. In: R F Engle and C W J Granger (eds.) Long-Run Economic Relationships. Oxford University Press

Mossin J (1966) Equilibrium in a Capital Asset Market. Econometrica 34, 768-783

Perron P (1988) Trends and Random Walks in Macroeconomic Time Series: Further Evidence from a New Approach. Journal of Economic Dynamics and Control 12, 297-332.

Perron P and Shiller R J (1985) Testing the Random Walk Hypothesis. Power versus Frequency of Observation. Economics Letters 18, 381-386.

Roll R (1977) A Critique of the Asset Pricing Theorys Tests - Part I: On Past and Potential Testability of the Theory. Journal of Financial Economics 4, 129-176

Rose A K (1988) Is the Real Interest Stable? Journal of Finance 43, 1095-1112

Schneeweiß H (1991) Note on a Linear Model With Errors in the Variables and With Trend. Statistical Papers 32, 261-264

Sharpe W F (1963) A Simplified Model of Portfolio Analysis. Management Science 9, 277-293

Sharpe W F (1964) Capital Asset Prices: A Theory of Market Equilibrium Under Conditions of Risk. Journal of Finance 19, 425-442

Stehle R (1991) Der Size-Effekt am Deutschen Aktienmarkt. Universität Augsburg, mimeo

West K D (1987) A Note on the Power of Least Squares Tests for a Unit Root. Economics Letters 24, 249-252

Constructing an Empirical Model for Swiss Franc Exchange Rates and Interest Rate Differentials[1]

By Hermann Garbers[2]

Abstract: This paper analyses different properties of the Swiss franc/U.S.-\$- and the Swiss franc/DM-exchange rate. The first one behaves according to a switching regime model, while the second rate is part of a linear error correction model.

1 Introduction

It is by now well-known that the Swiss franc/U.S.-\$-rate and the Swiss franc/DM-rate behave rather differently. This paper describes the differences between the two rates and presents some new stylised facts.

2 Data and the VAR-process

Modelling the Swiss franc/U.S.-\$ spot exchange rate (s_t, logarithmic scale, monthly data since 1974.1) and following Fama (1984), we considered in an earlier paper (Garbers(1987)) the equation

$$s_t - s_{t-1} = a + b(f_{t-1} - s_{t-1}) + \varepsilon_t \tag{1}$$

f_{t-1} is the logarithm of the one month forward exchange rate, so that $f_{t-1} - s_{t-1}$ is, from covered interest parity, equal to the one month interest rate differential.

In Garbers (1987, 1992) it was shown that (1) is misspecified. There is some evidence that the short term interest differential should appear in first differences: $[(f_{t-1} - s_{t-1}) - (f_{t-2} - s_{t-2})]$ while a long term interest-differential (in levels) shows some additional influence. Moreover, Swiss monetary policy seems to be even more concerned with the Swiss franc/DM rate (e_t, in logs) and the corresponding interest rate differentials than with the

[1]A first version of the paper was presented at a workshop organised by OLSEN and Associates, Research Institute for Applied Economics, Zürich. Martin Sieg and Danilo Zanetti provided very helpful research assistance. Their comments and those of other members of the econometric staff at the University of Zürich are gratefully acknowledged.

[2]Hermann Garbers, University of Zürich, 8006 Zürich, Blümlisalpstrasse 10, Switzerland

Swiss franc/U.S.-\$- rates. We decided, therefore, to nest (1) within an error correction model which contains s_t, e_t together with the corresponding long- (five years and more) and short-term (one month) interest rate differentials: $il_t^{USA} - il_t^{CH}$, $il_t^{DM} - il_t^{CH}$, $is_t^{USA} - is_t^{CH}$, $is_t^{DM} - is_t^{CH}$.
There is a graph for each of the six time series in figure 1, 2 and 3.

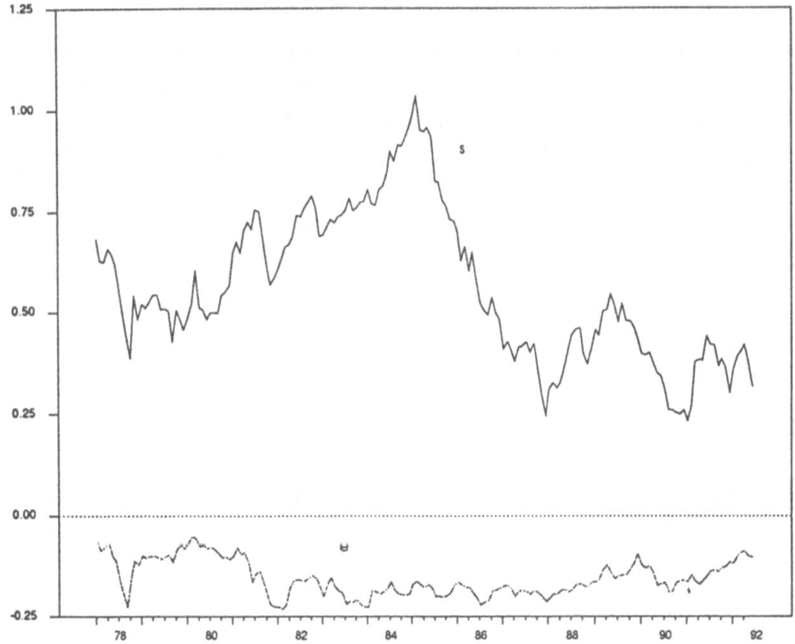

Figure 1 Exchange Rates Sfr/US-\$ (s_t) and Sfr/DM (e_t)

Notice, that there are long swings in the Swiss franc/U.S.-\$ exchange rate, while the SFr/DM-rate appears like a variable under control. From the graphs of the short term interest differentials it can be seen that there was a regime switch during 1983 from a money volume targeting to an interest rate targeting policy. Because of this switch in the policy regimes, we decided to take the period 1983.1-1992.5 for our data set.

We start the analysis of the data by applying Johansen's cointegration procedure, based on a VAR(2)-process. In some unpublished work (Garbers (1991)) we assumed first that the VAR-process is of order 1. The decision to take this order was derived from the computed values of the Schwarz criterion. If we take the Akaike criterion, together with an analysis of the residuals, a VAR(2)-process appears to be the preferred alternative.

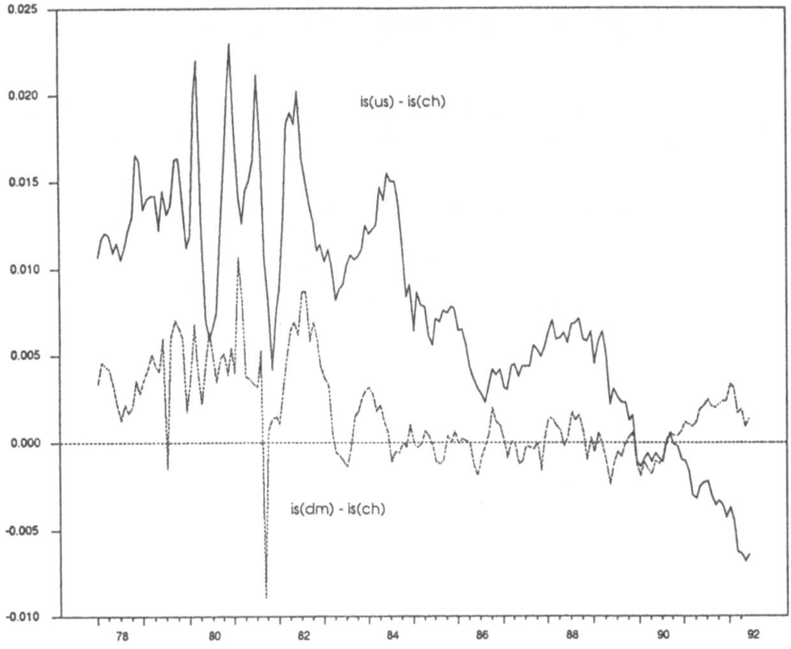

Figure 2 Short-term interest rate (is) differentials

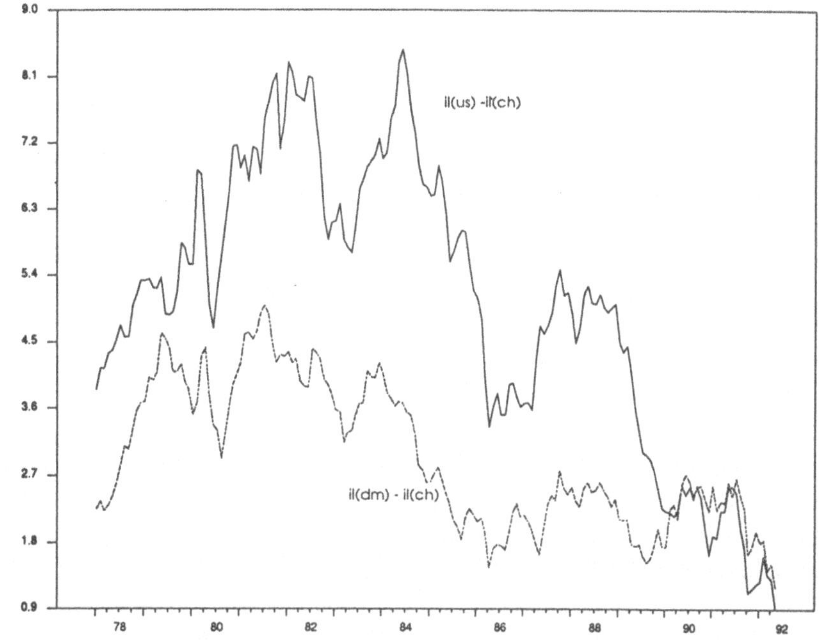

Figure 3 Long-term interest rate (il) differentials

3 The Cointegration Analysis

The Johansen test on the dimension ν of the cointegration space accepts the hypothesis that $\nu = 1$.[3] Moreover, it is accepted that s_t and $il_t^{USA} - il_t^{CH}$ are "passive" variables which are neither *members of the cointegrating relationship nor are they influenced by the cointegrating vector.*

Also e_t does not belong to the cointegrating vector but, most importantly, e_t *is influenced by the cointegrating relationship:*

$$\lambda_1(is_t^{USA} - is_t^{CH}) + \lambda_2(is_t^{DM} - is_t^{CH}) + \lambda_3(il_t^{DM} - il_t^{CH}) := \tilde{\varepsilon}_t \tag{2}$$

To be more precise, assuming a VAR(2)-process:

$$(I - A_1 L - A_2 L^2)\vec{X}_t = \vec{\mu} + \vec{\eta}_t; \qquad \vec{\eta}_t \sim i.i.d \quad N(\vec{0}, \sigma^2 I)$$

where $\vec{X}_t := (s_t, is_t^{USA} - is_t^{CH}, il_t^{USA} - il_t^{CH}, il_t^{DM} - il_t^{CH}, is_t^{DM} - is_t^{CH}, e_t)$ one gets by reparameterising the above equation

$$(1 - L)\vec{X}_t = \Gamma_1(1 - L)\vec{X}_{t-1} + \Pi\vec{X}_{t-2} + \vec{\mu} + \vec{\eta}_t$$

where $\Gamma_1 = -(I - A_1)$, $\Pi = -(I - A_1 - A_2)$.

Now, as according to Phillips-Perron tests (see Garbers (1991)) each of the components of $\vec{X}_t$ is integrated of an order not greater than one, it follows that $rank(\Pi) < 6$. But if $rank(\Pi) = \nu < 6$, there exists a $(6,\nu)$-matrix α and a $(6,\nu)$-matrix β, so that $\Pi = \alpha\beta'$. While β contains the cointegrating vectors in its columns, α measures in its first (second, etc) column the influence of the first (second, etc.) cointegrating vector on $(1 - L)\vec{X}_t$.

Taking then the data set 1983.1-1992.5 we get by the application of the maximum eigenvalue (λ-)test and the trace test the following results: Accepting $\nu = 1$, one gets the following $\alpha-$ and $\beta-$matrices:

$$\vec{\alpha} = (5.47, 23.331, -0.212, -0.324, -45.040, 2.649)$$

$$\vec{\beta} = (-0.001, 0.001, 0.561, 1.000, -0.001, 0.027)$$

We then test in a "top-down" manner by starting with a hypothesis created in Garbers (1991), that s_t and $il_t^{USA} - il_t^{CH}$ are excluded from the α-Matrix while $\vec{\beta}$ is taken unrestricted. The hypothesis is accepted at a significance level of 0.235.

---

[3]The computations were performed by the RATS-procedure written by R. Mosconi and C. Giannini.

Table 1 Tests for cointegration according to Johansen

	λ-statistic	95% critical values
$\nu \leq 2$	23.404	27.341
$\nu \leq 1$	29.567	33.262
$\nu = 0$	44.118	39.134
	trace-statistic	95% critical values
$\nu \leq 2$	40.493	48.419
$\nu \leq 1$	70.060	69.977
$\nu = 0$	114.178	95.553

Next, we additionally exclude s_t and $il_t^{USA} - il_t^{CH}$ from $\vec{\beta}$. The combined hypothesis is accepted at a significance level of 0.191. Excluding also e_t from $\vec{\beta}$, the new and more restrictive hypothesis is accepted at a significance level of 0.274 and this level decreases to 0.001 if we exclude e_t also from $\vec{\alpha}$. On the other hand, excluding only e_t from $\vec{\alpha}$ and taking $\vec{\beta}$ unrestricted one gets a significance level of 0.037.

The dependence of e_{t+1} on $\tilde{\varepsilon}_t$ will be taken by us as an indirect result of policy rules exercised by the Swiss National Bank and by the Deutsche Bundesbank. We plan some further work on this issue in the future.

4 Some General Remarks about the Swiss franc/U.S.-\$-Rate

While the SNB is mainly concerned with e_t it is not able or not ready to target s_t in the same manner. But if an exchange rate like s_t is not under some control by the national banks there might be an important role to play for private investors[4].

There are two types of private investors in financial markets: "Fundamentalists" who know the work of bringing prices toward fundamentals and "noise traders" who respond to pseudo-signals which do not convey information about future returns in a fully rational model. Fundamentalists, however, are limited as they will not know the fundamental value of an asset exactly, and/or their expected value of an asset might be very different from market prices, while with a finite time horizon, they have to sell or buy at an unknown date in the future. If an asset is for some reason underpriced, there is no riskless hedge for a fundamentalist and his demand for the asset will be limited if he is risk averse. With a finite number of fundamentalists, their combined demand is no longer perfectly elastic.

[4]For the following arguments see A. Shleifer and L. H. Summers (1990)

Noise traders, on the other hand, will only have an influence on market prices if their demand or supply shifts are correlated. But this is very probable for, as one knows from psychological experiments, individuals tend

a) to be overconfident,

b) to extrapolate past time series,

c) to put too much weight on new information.

As noise traders are overconfident they might on average be more aggressive than the fundamentalists and so bear more risk. If risk-taking is somehow rewarded in the market, noise traders can earn higher expected returns although on average they buy at high and sell at low prices. The risk premium earned by them is paid for by national banks as part of the price for trying to target their economies according to e.g. employment goals. But then noise traders as a group will not disappear from the market and shifts in the demand for assets which do not depend on fundamentals will affect prices in the short run and in the long run.

With limited arbitrage and the presence of noise traders, movements in investor sentiments are an important determinant of prices, so that an endogeneous take off of a speculative bubble may appear, see Frankel and Froot (1990). This bubble will mainly be produced by portfolio managers which take positions in the markets by determining exchange rates as weighted averages of the forecasts by arbitrageurs and those by noise traders (chartists). If then e.g. forecasts of depreciation by fundamentalists (based on overshooting models) prove incorrect again and again, portfolio managers will decrease the weight to those forecasts and increase the weights they assign to the forecasts of chartists. Portfolio managers will know that regime switches from an appreciating to a depreciating $ and vice versa happen eventually and they will assign some probability to the possibility of such change and form their forecasts under this assumption.

Additionally, a model for s_t should incorporate what we know about it with some certainty: that its time series structure is similar to that of a random walk.

5 The Model for s_t

According to the arguments from above, we propose to model s_t as a *segmented random walk* (see Engel and Hamilton (1990)), one with a positive (state $1 \doteq x_t = 1$) and one with a negative drift (state $2 \doteq x_t = 2$). At each time period t s_t is in state 1 or state 2 where x_t is not directly observable. With a constant probability of p_{11} it will be in state 1 in period t+1 if it was in state 1 in period t, while it will change to state 2 in t+1 with a probability of $1 - p_{11}$. Correspondingly, it will stay in state 2 in period t+1 with a probability of p_{22} if it was in state 2 during period t, while it will change into state 1 in period t+1 with a probability of $1 - p_{22}$:

$$\begin{aligned} P(x_t = 2|x_{t-1} = 1) &= 1 - p_{11} \\ P(x_t = 1|x_{t-1} = 1) &= p_{11} \\ P(x_t = 2|x_{t-1} = 2) &= p_{22} \\ P(x_t = 1|x_{t-1} = 2) &= 1 - p_{22} \end{aligned} \tag{3}$$

p_{11}, p_{22} and the two drift terms μ_1, μ_2 are unknown and have to be estimated. Moreover, the two states $x_t = 1$, $x_t = 2$ may not only differ with respect to the drift term μ but also with respect to the variance σ^2 which is also unknown. There are therefore six population parameters,

$$\vec{\Theta} = (\mu_1, \mu_2, \sigma_1, \sigma_2, p_{11}, p_{22})$$

They determine together with a corresponding density function the distribution of s_t given x_t and the distribution of x_t given x_{t-1}. We expect $p_{11} > 0.8$, $p_{22} > 0.8$, so that with $\mu_1 > 0$, $\mu_2 < 0$ long swings are implied for s_t.[5] Notice, that the expected length of state i is equal to:

$$(1 - p_{ii})(1 + 2p_{ii} + 3p_{ii}^2 + 4p_{ii}^3 + \ldots) = 1 + p_{ii} + p_{ii}^2 + \ldots = \frac{1}{1 - p_{ii}}$$

Taking e.g. $p_{ii} = 0.95$ the expected length would be 20 months.
If then $s_1^*, \ldots, s_T^*$ is the observed time series and $f(.)$ the chosen density function which describes the joint distribution of $s_1, \ldots, s_T$, $x_1, \ldots, x_T$ given $\vec{\Theta}$, it follows that

$$\begin{aligned} & f(s_1, \ldots, s_T, x_1, \ldots, x_T; \vec{\Theta}) = \\ &= f(s_T, x_T|s_1, \ldots, s_{T-1}, x_1, \ldots, x_{T-1}; \vec{\Theta}) \cdot f(s_1, \ldots, s_{T-1}, x_1, \ldots, x_{T-1}; \vec{\Theta}) \\ &= f(s_T|x_T, s_1, \ldots, x_{T-1}, \vec{\Theta}) \cdot f(x_T|s_1, \ldots, s_{T-1}, x_1, \ldots, x_{T-1}; \vec{\Theta}) \cdot \\ &\quad \cdot f(s_1, \ldots, s_{T-1}, x_1, \ldots, x_{T-1}; \vec{\Theta}) \\ &= f(s_T|x_T; \vec{\Theta}) \cdot f(x_T|x_{T-1}; \vec{\Theta}) \cdot f(s_1, \ldots, s_{T-1}, x_1, \ldots, x_{T-1}; \vec{\Theta}) \end{aligned}$$

---

[5]Considering the data it seems to us that the period 1983.1 – 1992.5 can be devided into a series of subperiods with different regimes (state 1, state 2, state 1, ...), so that by summing over all subperiods a random walk *without a drift* might represent a fairly good model.

As the same arguments can be applied to $f(s_1, \ldots, s_{T-1}, x_1, \ldots, x_{T-1}; \vec{\Theta})$ it follows that

$$
\begin{aligned}
& f(s_1, \ldots, s_T, x_1, \ldots, x_T; \vec{\Theta}) = \\
&= f(s_T|x_T; \vec{\Theta}) \cdot f(x_T|x_{T-1}; \vec{\Theta}) \cdot f(s_{T-1}|x_{T-1}; \vec{\Theta}) \cdot f(x_{T-1}|x_{T-2}; \vec{\Theta}) \cdot \ldots \\
& \quad \ldots \cdot f(s_1|x_1; \vec{\Theta}) \cdot f(x_1; \vec{\Theta})
\end{aligned} \tag{4}
$$

All expressions but $f(x_1; \vec{\Theta})$ on the right hand side of this equation can be estimated. We then get for x_1 because of the implied stationarity of the above Markov chain:

$$
\begin{aligned}
f(x_1 = 1; \vec{\Theta}) &= f(x_1 = 1|x_0 = 1; \vec{\Theta}) f(x_0 = 1; \vec{\Theta}) \\
& \quad + f(x_1 = 1|x_0 = 2; \vec{\Theta}) f(x_0 = 2; \vec{\Theta}) \\
&= f(x_1 = 1|x_0 = 1; \vec{\Theta}) f(x_1 = 1; \vec{\Theta}) \\
& \quad + f(x_1 = 1|x_0 = 2; \vec{\Theta})(1 - f(x_1 = 1; \vec{\Theta}))
\end{aligned}
$$

$$
\begin{aligned}
f(x_1 = 1; \vec{\Theta})((1 - p_{11}) + (1 - p_{22})) &= 1 - p_{22} \qquad \text{so that} \\
f(x_1 = 1; \vec{\Theta}) &= \frac{1 - p_{22}}{(1 - p_{11}) + (1 - p_{22})}
\end{aligned} \tag{5}
$$

Finally, we get the likelihood function of $s_1^*, \ldots, s_T^*$ by the following marginalisation and the succeeding application of eq.(5):

$$
\begin{aligned}
& L(\vec{\Theta}|s_1^*, \ldots, s_T^*) = \\
&= \sum_{x_1=1}^{2} \sum_{x_2=1}^{2} \cdots \sum_{x_T=1}^{2} f(s_1^*, \ldots, s_T^*, x_1, \ldots, x_T; \vec{\Theta}) \\
&= \sum_{x_1=1}^{2} \sum_{x_2=1}^{2} \cdots \sum_{x_T=1}^{2} \prod_{t=2}^{T} f(s_t^*|x_t; \vec{\Theta}) f(x_t|x_{t-1}; \vec{\Theta}) f(s_1^*|x_1; \vec{\Theta}) f(x_1; \vec{\Theta})
\end{aligned}
$$

It remains to apply (5). To get the maximum likelihood estimator of $\vec{\Theta}$, one has to maximise this final expression.

6 The Results for s_t

Notice that the likelihood function which we want to maximise corresponds to a switching regime model. As it is well-known from the literature, these models may have likelihood functions which are unbounded in its parameter space. However, the unboundedness often appears in those "uninteresting parts of the parameter space" in which e.g. a variance $\sigma^2 \longrightarrow 0$. To avoid these problems, Hamilton (1990), Engel and Hamilton (1990), estimate the parameters of the two regimes also in a Bayesian manner. Following them, we choose some Bayesian prior and some starting values for the other parameters and take again monthly data for s_t and the period 1983.1 - 1992.6.[6] The results are contained in the first column of the following table. Estimating the parameters in a non-Bayesian manner changes the results only marginally.

Table 2 The estimates fo the segmented random walk

μ_1	1.19	1.64
	(0.49)	(0.54)
μ_2	-0.73	-0.67
	(0.44)	(0.54)
σ_1^2	4.90	3.80
	(1.51)	(3.08)
σ_2^2	15.83	16.85
	(2.37)	(2.45)
p_{11}	0.98	0.75
	(0.03)	(0.19)
p_{22}	0.99	0.92
	(0.01)	(0.06)

Note: Standard errors are in parantheses. Results are given in percentages.

The second column contains the result for the period 1979.1-1992.6. Again the non-Bayesian results are nearly identical.
Note, that the two regimes are rather different from each other according to both data sets: μ_1 is positive and significantly different from zero while μ_2 is negative but not significantly different from zero, σ_2^2 is much larger than σ_1^2 and p_{11} seems to be somewhat lower than p_{22}.

7 Conclusion

By considering monthly data for the period 1983.1-1992.5 of certain monetary variables including the Swiss franc/U.S.-\$- and the Swiss franc/DM-exchange

[6]The computations were done by working with a Gauss procedure written by Hamilton.

rate, we conclude that only the second rate is part of an error correction model (with one cointegrating relation). While this rate does not belong to the cointegrating vector, it is influenced by it.

On the other hand, the \$-rate follows a segmented random walk with the two states of an increasing and a decreasing \$. The behaviour of this variable is not symmetric with respect to the two states since the variances of the states are distinct.

References

Engel C and Hamilton J D (1990) Long swings in the dollar: Are they in the data and do markets know it? American Economic Review 80, 689 - 713

Fama E F (1984) Forward and spot exchange rate, Journal of Monetary Economics 14, 319 - 338

Frankel J A and Froot K A (1990) Chartists, fundamentalists and the demand for dollars, in Courakis A S and Taylor M P (eds), Private behaviour and government policy in interdependent economies, Oxford, Clarendon Press, 73 - 126

Garbers H (1987) A misspecification analysis of the relationship between spot and forward exchange rates, European Economic Review 31, 1407 - 1417

Garbers H (1991) About the monetary sector of the Swiss economy, Mimeo, Zürich

Garbers H (1992) The relationship between exchange rates and interest rates: The Swiss franc case, Wirtschaftswissenschaftliche Beiträge 60, Ökonometrie und Monetärer Sektor, Physica Verlag, Heidelberg

Hamilton J D (1990) Analysis of time series subject to changes in regime, Journal of Econometrics 45, 39 - 70

Shleifer A and Summers L H (1990) The noise trader approach to finance, Journal of Economic Perspectives 4, 19 - 33

Frequency Domain Analysis of Euromarket Interest Rates[1]

By Gebhard Kirchgässner[2] and Jürgen Wolters[3]

Abstract: We have transformed VAR– and EC–models estimating the linkage between Euromarket 3–month interest rates to the frequency domain. We use models for the EMS countries France, Germany, Italy and the Netherlands as well as models which additionally include Britain and the US. The spectral analysis – especially coherence and gain – enables us to describe the interest rate linkage in much more detail. Moreover, it gives us a further possibility to investigate whether the imposed restrictions are correct. The cointegrating restrictions which can be judged through coherence and gain at the origin are of special interest. We find that the restrictions belonging to these long–run relations seem to be acceptable.

1 Introduction

The European Monetary System (EMS) started in March 1979 and contained the former snake countries Germany, Denmark, the Netherlands, Belgium and Luxemburg as well as France, Italy and Ireland. It was originally intended to be a system of (within certain narrow bands) fixed but adjustable exchange rates within Europe, which should be symmetric with respect to all its participants[4].

In recent years the EMS has been successful in limiting exchange rate volatility. But there are different opinions about how the system has functioned in practice. One hypothesis, put forward by Giavazzi and Giovannini (1987, 1989), is that German monetary policy dominates the whole system, i.e. the EMS works like a Dmark–zone. This hypothesis has been tested on the basis of the developments of interest rates by different authors. As often with empirical research, the results are mixed. There are results in favour of the dominance hypothesis, e.g. Giavazzi and Giovannini (1987,1989), Karfakis and Moschos (1990), and Kirchgässner and Wolters (1991a, 1991b, 1991c),

---

[1] We gratefully acknowlege financial support from the Deutsche Forschungsgemeinschaft by Grant No. 322 147. We would like to thank Herbert S. Buscher, Uwe Hassler, Bernd Lucke, (Freie Universität Berlin) and an anonymous referee for helpful comments

[2] Gebhard Kirchgässner, Hochschule St. Gallen, Dufourstr. 48, CH - 9000 St. Gallen, and ETH Zürich

[3] Jürgen Wolters, Freie Universität Berlin, Institut für Statistik und Ökonometrie, Bolzmannstr. 20, D-14195 Berlin

[4] For the design of the EMS see, e.g., Deutsche Bundesbank (1979).

while e.g. Cohen and Wyplosz (1989), De Grauwe (1989), von Hagen and Fratianni (1990), and Koedijk and Kool (1992) reject this hypothesis. All these papers present empirical evidence in the time domain.

In this paper we will give additional information about the linkage of interest rates in the EMS using frequency domain analysis. Because of the poor estimation properties of multivariate spectra we transform estimated vector autoregressive (VAR) models into the frequency domain. This provides a much more detailed interpretation of the linkage of interest rates. The frequency based method gives us the possibility to analyse the interdependence of interest rates for different cyclical components, as short-run, business-cycle and long-run components. Here we concentrate especially on the analysis of the long-run relationships. For this reason we do not only transform VAR models estimated without any restrictions but also use corresponding error-correction models by Kirchgässner and Wolters (1991c), where cointegrating restrictions as well as restrictions in line with the dominance hypothesis of German interest rates are implemented. This comparison gives additional empirical evidence whether the chosen restrictions are valid or not. In this context cointegrating relations are of special interest.

The paper is organized as follows. In section 2 we present the methodological approach. In section 3 we apply it to different VAR models for three month Euromarket interest rates. In section 4 we draw some conclusions.

2 Methodological Approach

Given a stable vector autoregressive model which can be written without loss of generality as the following first order system[5]

$$y_t = Ay_{t-1} + u_t, E[u_t] = 0, E[u_t u_s] = \begin{cases} \Sigma, & t = s \\ 0, & t \neq s \end{cases} \tag{1}$$

with y_t the $(n, 1)$ vector of the time series considered, A the (n, n) matrix of coefficients, u_t the $(n, 1)$ vector of residuals, assumed to be multivariate white noise.

Using the lag operator L defined as

$$L^k x_t = x_{t-k}, k = \ldots -1, 0, 1, \ldots, \tag{2}$$

one can write (1) as

$$(I - AL)y_t = u_t. \tag{3}$$

[5]Higher order lags can be dealt with by introducing additional variables.

According to the methods presented in, e.g., Wolters (1980) the spectral matrix $F_y(\lambda)$ of (1) is given by

$$F_y(\lambda) = (I - Ae^{-i\lambda})^{-1}\frac{\sum}{2\pi}(I - Ae^{-i\lambda})^{-1'} \;, \; 0 \leq \lambda \leq \pi, \tag{4}$$

where $\sum/2\pi$ is the spectral matrix of the multivariate white noise process u_t. The elements of $F_y(\lambda)$ are the cross spectra $f_{jk}(\lambda)$ between the j–th and the k–th time series. Since these functions have complex values the following real–valued measures are derived[6]. The gain

$$g_{jk}(\lambda) = \frac{|f_{jk}(\lambda)|}{f_{jj}(\lambda)} \tag{5}$$

measures the amplification or attenuation of the components of the j–th time series at the frequencies λ to obtain the corresponding components of the k–th process. Transformation of both variables with the same filter does not affect the gain. As is shown in Wolters (1980, pp. 83–84) the gain at zero frequency $g_{jk}(0)$ is a measure of the absolute value of the long–run influence of time series j on time series k.

The squared coherence

$$K_{jk}(\lambda) = \frac{|f_{jk}(\lambda)|^2}{f_{jj}(\lambda)f_{kk}(\lambda)} \tag{6}$$

is for each frequency λ comparable with a coefficient of determination for the linear relation between corresponding components of the two time series considered. This measure has the advantage of being invariant to linear transformations of the two time series. Moreover, as Granger and Weiss (1983) have mentioned, the squared coherence at frequency zero between two cointegrated I(1)–processes is one[7]. In this case also the interpretation of $g_{jk}(0)$ as a measure of the long–run influence holds. For a formal proof of these two statements see the Appendix.

3 Frequency Domain Representation of Interest Rate Linkages

Using monthly data of three–month Euro–market rates from 1980 to 1988, Kirchgässner and Wolters (1991c) estimated two multivariate error correction

[6]For an introduction to the theory and application of spectral analysis see e.g. König and Wolters (1972) or Koopmans (1974).

[7]A time series is said to be integrated of order one (I(1)) if the first differences of this time series follow a stationary and invertible process, i.e. I(0). A vector of n I (1)-time series is said to be cointegrated if there exists at least one non-trivial linear combination of these time series which is I(0). See e.g. Engle and Granger (1987).

(EC) models. One model contains only the interest rates of the four EMS countries, France (FER), Germany (GER), Italy (IER) and the Netherlands (NER), whereas the other includes Britain (BER) and the US (UER) as well[8].

Applying the multivariate cointegration approach of Johansen (1989), Kirchgässner and Wolters (1991c) found in the four–variable model three cointegrating relations and in the six–variable model five cointegrating relations. This means that all interest rates considered are driven by one stochastic trend and interest rates are pairwise cointegrated. This is a necessary condition for uncovered interest rate parity to hold in levels. In a first step these cointegrating restrictions are implemented. Applying a series of likelihood ratio tests in order to examine causal relations which are implied by the German dominance hypothesis, further zero restrictions were included in the two models. Some of these restrictions were in favour of a long–run German dominance hypothesis. Additional zero restrictions stem from statistical insignificance of estimated parameters.

Here we additionally estimate the corresponding unrestricted VAR models in levels for the four– and the six–variable model denoted as VAR4 and VAR6, respectively. The results are presented in Table 1 together with the resulting point estimates of the restricted error correction models denoted as EC4 and EC6. With the exception of the US interest rate the residuals of the other interest rates show no autocorrelation. Thus the chosen lag order of two seems appropriate to capture the dynamics and the adjustment processes of the Euromarket rates. But, on the other hand, there is indication of ARCH–effects for the German, French and US rates. The residuals for Germany, France, Italy and the US exhibit strong deviations from normality. So one should be cautious in relying on formal test procedures which are based on the normality hypothesis of the residuals. Therefore, with the following frequency domain analysis we perform a more or less descriptive procedure.

The eigenvalues of the matrix A of equation (1) presented in Table 2 give information about the stability and the transient response of the different models. The error correction models which assume three cointegrating relations, EC4, and five, EC6, possess as expected an eigenvalue of one each. This eigenvalue of one corresponds to the stochastic trend in the system. The unrestricted versions exhibit with 0.96 in VAR4 and 0.95 inVAR6 also eigenvalues near one. The other eigenvalues in the corresponding models VAR4 and EC4 as well as VAR6 and EC6 are very similar in magnitude with only a few exceptions.

The evaluation of the spectral matrix in equation (4) has been performed with the programme TRANSF for the frequencies $\lambda_j = j\pi/24$, $j = 0, 1, 2, \ldots, 24$. For A and $\sum$ we substitute the point estimates from the VAR– and EC–models. Since gain and coherence are unaffected by dif-

[8]Britain joined the exchange rate mechanism of the EMS in October 1990, after the sample period for this paper. It is interesting to examine whether Britain behaved like an EMS-country or not.

Table 1 VAR- and EC-Models

	GER				FER			
	VAR4	EC4	VAR6	EC6	VAR4	EC4	VAR6	EC6
Const.	0.28	-0.03	-0.02	-0.12	1.78	2.42	2.09	2.32
GER$_{-1}$	1.18	1.17	0.98	1.12	-0.10	0.22	-0.21	0.26
GER$_{-2}$	-0.12	-0.17	-0.01	-0.19	1.14	0.77	1.16	0.78
FER$_{-1}$	-0.05	-	-0.08	-	0.62	0.70	0.61	0.69
FER$_{-2}$	0.00	-	0.00	-	0.07	-	0.07	-
IER$_{-1}$	-0.00	-	0.03	-	0.37	0.29	0.37	0.28
IER$_{-2}$	0.03	-	0.01	-	-0.31	-0.29	-0.30	-0.28
NER$_{-1}$	-0.08	-	-0.13	-	-0.19	-0.71	-0.18	-0.72
NER$_{-2}$	0.02	-	-0.03	-	-0.59	-	-0.53	-
BER$_{-1}$			0.11	-			-0.00	-
BER$_{-2}$			-0.08	-			-0.06	-
UER$_{-1}$			0.04	0.06			0.09	-
UER$_{-2}$			0.09	-			-0.04	-
SE	0.42	0.43	0.38	0.41	1.64	1.61	1.67	1.61
Q(16)	14.40	14.32	11.26	14.79	26.11*	31.43**	25.54*	31.43**
LM(8)	1.38	1.05	0.87	1.09	1.60	1.11	1.26	1.10
ARCH(4)	9.52**	8.17**	9.24**	13.46**	3.66**	6.11**	4.09**	6.47**
BJ	87.91**	112.73**	9.27**	72.03**	163.13**	127.19**	153.65**	120.11**

	IER				NER			
	VAR4	EC4	VAR6	EC6	VAR4	EC4	VAR6	EC6
Const.	2.03	2.32	1.56	2.12	0.58	0.28	0.39	0.33
GER$_{-1}$	-0.47	-0.39	-0.38	-0.20	0.31	0.22	0.24	0.22
GER$_{-2}$	1.30	1.24	1.23	1.04	-0.04	–	0.02	–
FER$_{-1}$	-0.21	-0.21	-0.20	-0.19	-0.07	-0.04	-0.09	-0.04
FER$_{-2}$	0.26	0.21	0.24	0.19	0.04	0.04	0.05	0.04
IER$_{-1}$	1.23	1.22	1.26	1.22	0.06	0.07	0.07	0.06
IER$_{-2}$	-0.57	-0.55	-0.58	-0.53	-0.06	-0.07	-0.07	-0.06
NER$_{-1}$	0.33	0.11	0.40	0.15	0.62	0.75	0.52	0.74
NER$_{-2}$	-0.66	-0.46	-0.83	-0.49	0.09	–	0.11	–
BER$_{-1}$			-0.17	–			0.21	0.12
BER$_{-2}$			0.25	–			-0.18	-0.12
UER$_{-1}$			-0.21	-0.24			0.04	–
UER$_{-2}$			0.19	0.24			-0.02	–
SE	1.32	1.28	1.31	1.25	0.42	0.42	0.40	1.41
Q(16)	18.27	15.75	22.98	19.71	21.67	26.23*	17.30	25.72*
LM(8)	1.26	1.03	1.48	0.94	3.34**	1.67	2.09*	1.57
ARCH(4)	1.34	1.21	0.85	0.72	2.52*	2.62*	1.78	3.71**
BJ	11.14*	7.65*	10.16**	13.94**	4.62(*)	10.43**	2.19	10.38**

Table 1 cont'd

	BER		UER	
	VAR6	EC6	VAR6	EC6
Const.	1.28	1.05	1.09	0.54
GER_{-1}	0.08	-0.07	0.03	0.44
GER_{-2}	-0.19	–	0.27	–
FER_{-1}	-0.02	–	-0.03	–
FER_{-2}	-0.02	–	-0.10	–
IER_{-1}	0.10	0.08	0.06	–
IER_{-2}	-0.06	-0.08	0.07	–
NER_{-1}	0.01	0.19	-0.02	–
NER_{-2}	0.22	–	0.02	–
BER_{-1}	1.14	1.13	0.11	–
BER_{-2}	-0.35	-0.30	-0.18	–
UER_{-1}	-0.11	-0.10	1.11	1.17
UER_{-2}	0.10	0.10	-0.37	-0.50
SE	0.64	0.62	1.04	1.03
Q(16)	13.71	13.10	37.34**	31.02*
LM(8)	0.45	0.42	2.84**	1.52
ARCH(4)	0.73	0.96	5.34**	4.50**
BJ	4.78(*)	7.45(*)	142.12**	149.62**

ARCH(4) ... test for fourth order autoregressive conditional hetero-scedasticity (F–type test)
BJ ... Bera and Jarque test for normality
LM(8) ... Lagrange multiplier test for serial correlation up to order 8
Q(16) ... Box–Pierce test for serial correlation up to order 16
SE ... standard error of regression
(*) , * , ** ... means that the null hypothesis is rejected at the 10, 5, and 1 per cent level, respectively.

ferencing all variables we transform the equations in levels.

In Figures 1a and 1b the squared coherence according to (6) and the gain according to (5) between Germany and France are plotted. Squared coherence and gain between Germany and Italy, Germany and the Netherlands, Germany and Britain and the US and Germany are given in Figures 2a, 2b, 3a, 3b, 4a, 4b and 5a, 5b respectively. Squared coherence and gain are plotted for France, Italy and the Netherlands vis á vis Germany for all four versions and for Britain and the US vis á vis Germany for the versions VAR6 and EC6[9].

From this frequency domain analysis we can draw conclusions about the influence of two different information sets, about the effects of the imposed restrictions and about the linkage of interest rates for different components. The two information sets are given through the models with four variables and the models with six variables.

[9]All other bivariate relations are available on request. The frequencies 0.52, 1.57 and 3.14 correspond to cycles with periods of one year, 4 months and 2 months, respectively.

Table 2 (Eigenvalues of VAR- and EC-Models)

VAR4		EC4		VAR6		EC6	
roots	mod.	roots	mod.	roots	mod.	roots	mod.
0.96	0.96	1.00	1.00	0.95	0.95	1.00	1.00
0.83	0.83	0.75	0.75	$0.80 \pm 0.08i$	0.80	$0.79 \pm 0.11i$	0.80
$0.59 \pm 0.40i$	0.71	$0.56 \pm 0.38i$	0.68	$0.59 \pm 0.49i$	0.77	$0.60 \pm 0.35i$	0.70
0.65	0.65	0.64	0.64	$0.65 \pm 0.10i$	0.66	$0.54 \pm 0.41i$	0.68
0.20	0.20	0.25	0.25	$0.44 \pm 0.42i$	0.61	0.57	0.57
-0.17	0.17	0.17	0.17	$-0.18 \pm 0.11i$	0.21	$0.27 \pm 0.13i$	0.30
0.01	0.01	-0.10	0.10	0.07	0.07	0.21	0.21
						-0.10	0.10

From Figures 1 to 3 it is very clear to see that the additional inclusion of the interest rates of Britain and the US does not change the relations of France, Italy, and the Netherlands to Germany respectively.

Looking at Figures 1a to 5a we find that the squared coherences for the restricted versions EC4 and EC6 all have the value one at zero frequency. As we have shown in the Appendix, we get this value if a bivariate cointegration relation exists. But also in the unrestricted versions VAR4 and VAR6 the squared coherences at frequency zero are very close to the theoretical value of one. We get the lowest value with 0.82 for the relation between Germany and Britain. So, all in all, despite the deviation from normality for the residuals of the VAR- and EC-models we strengthen the existence of three bivariate cointegration relations with the squared coherences at zero frequency from the VAR4-model and to a smaller extent from the VAR6-model the existence of five bivariate cointegration relations[10].

As we have seen before, the gain at zero frequency corresponds to the long-run coefficient of the two variables considered. In Figures 1b to 5b the gain at zero for the versions VAR4 and VAR6 gives the long-run values estimated without any restrictions whereas the gain at zero for the versions EC4 and EC6 represent the long-run values imposed by the Johansen procedure. In all cases these values are very similar in magnitude.

From the results with respect to coherences and gains at zero frequency we can conclude that the restrictions belonging to the long-run relations seem to be correct.

Figures 1a and 1b show that there are minor deviations for the range $0 < \lambda \leq \pi$ between the restricted and unrestricted versions for the relation between Germany and France. Such minor deviations also exist for the gains of Germany and Italy (Figure 2b) as well as Germany and Britain (Figure 4b). This may be a hint that not all imposed zero restrictions may be quite correct. But for all other relations there are nearly no differences. This holds especially for the connection between Germany and the Netherlands.

[10]Performing the Johansen tests in Kirchgässner and Wolters (1991c) the cointegrating relation for Britain is only significant at the 10 % level.

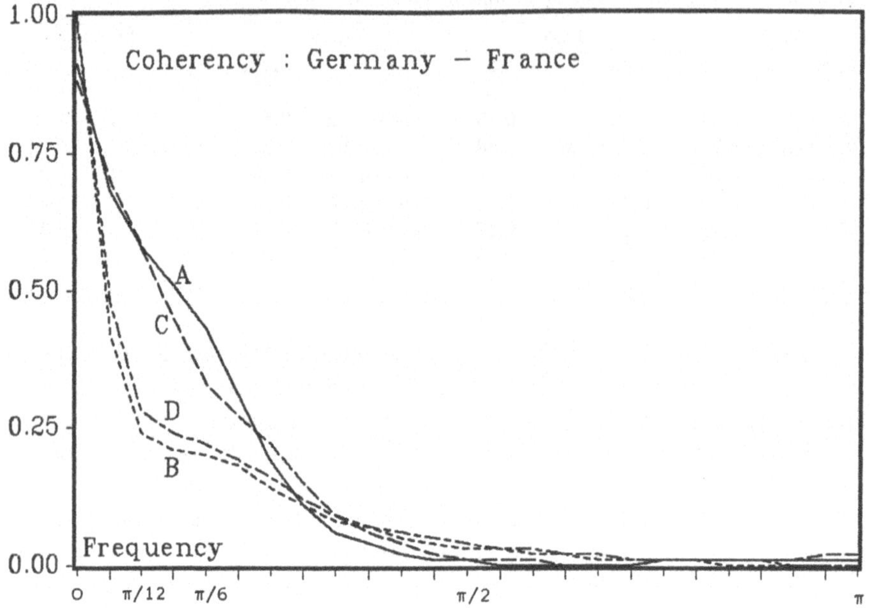

Figure 1a Squared Coherence: Germany – France

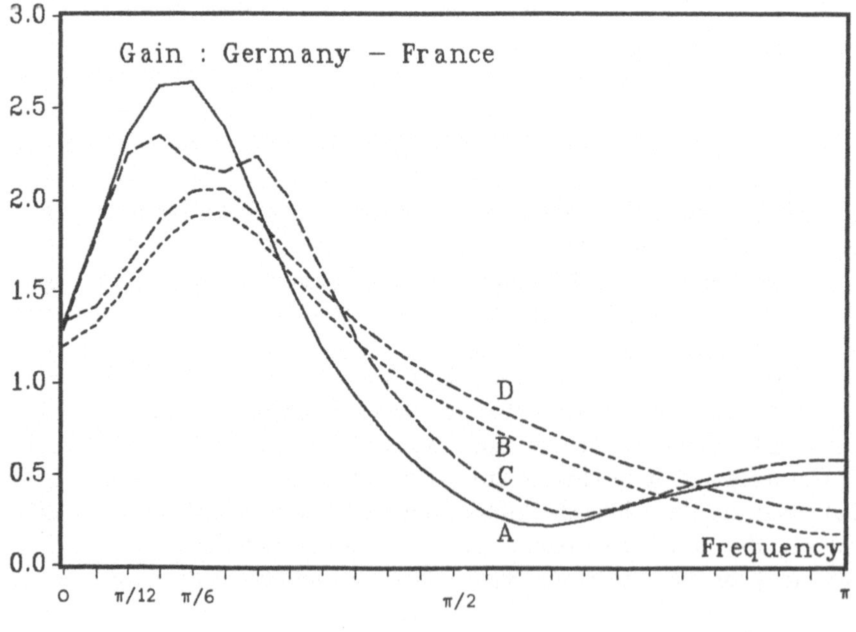

Figure 1b Gain: Germany – France

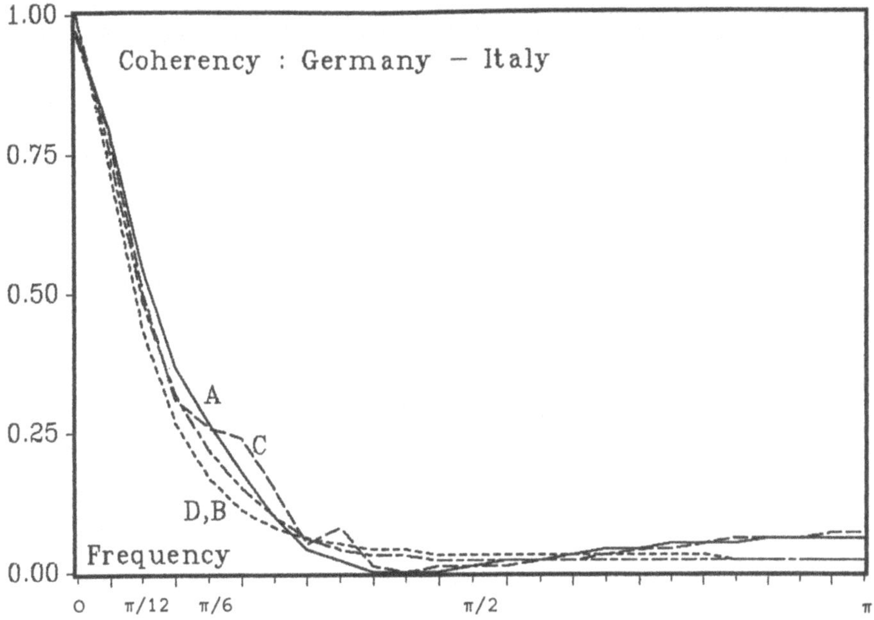

Figure 2a Squared Coherence: Germany – Italy

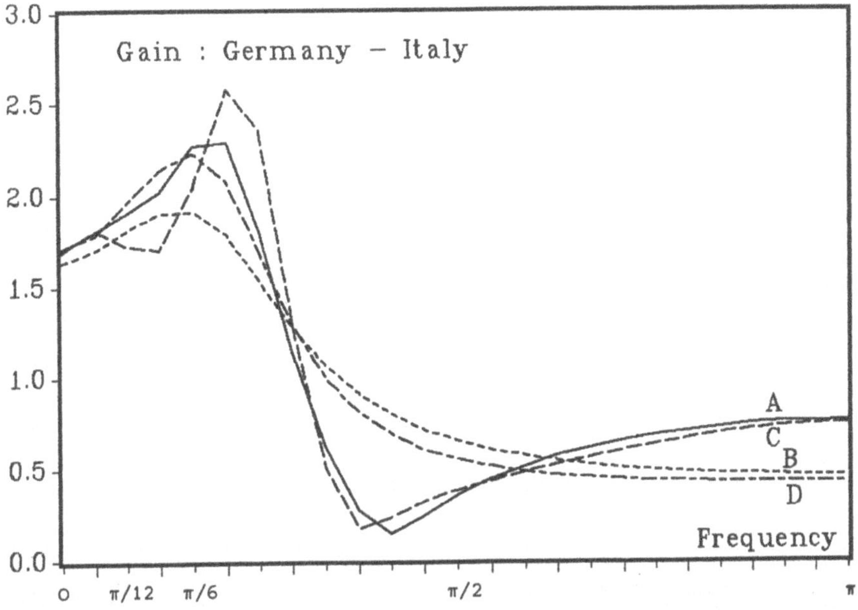

Figure 2b Gain: Germany – Italy

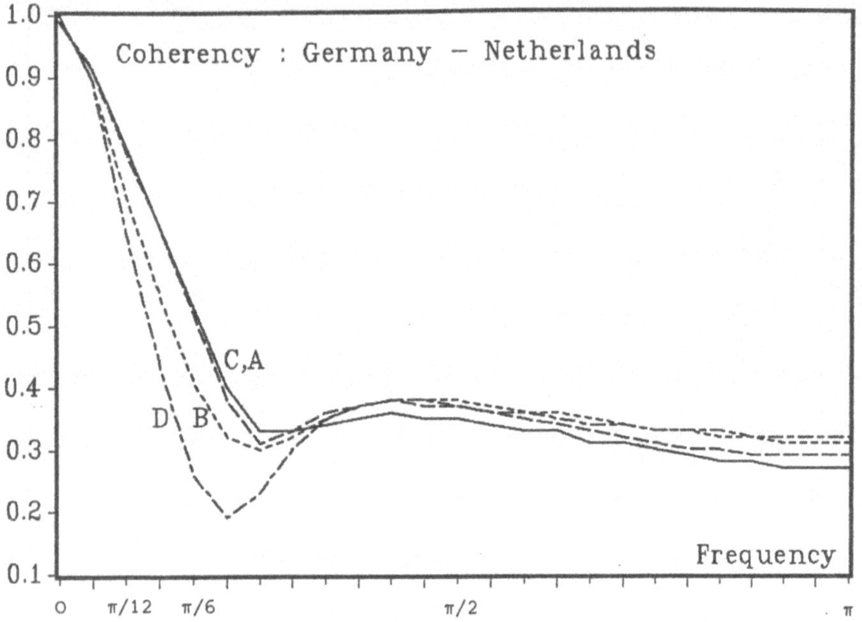

Figure 3a Squared Coherence: Germany – Netherlands

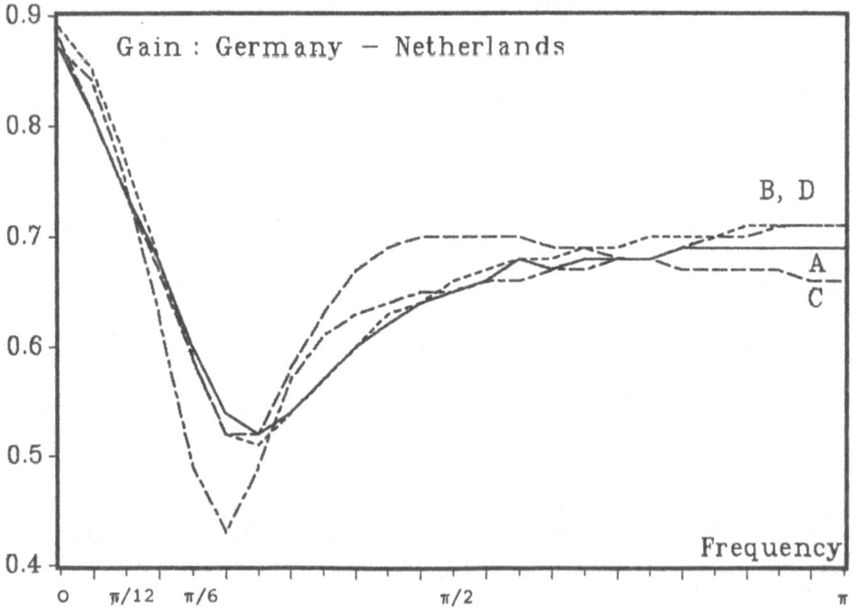

Figure 3b Gain: Germany – Netherlands

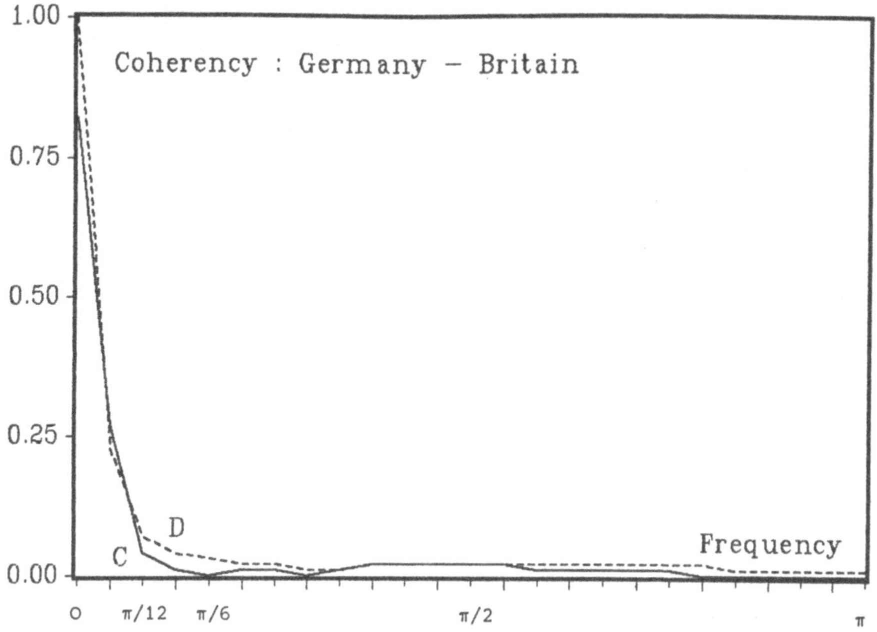

Figure 4a Squared Coherence: Germany - Britain

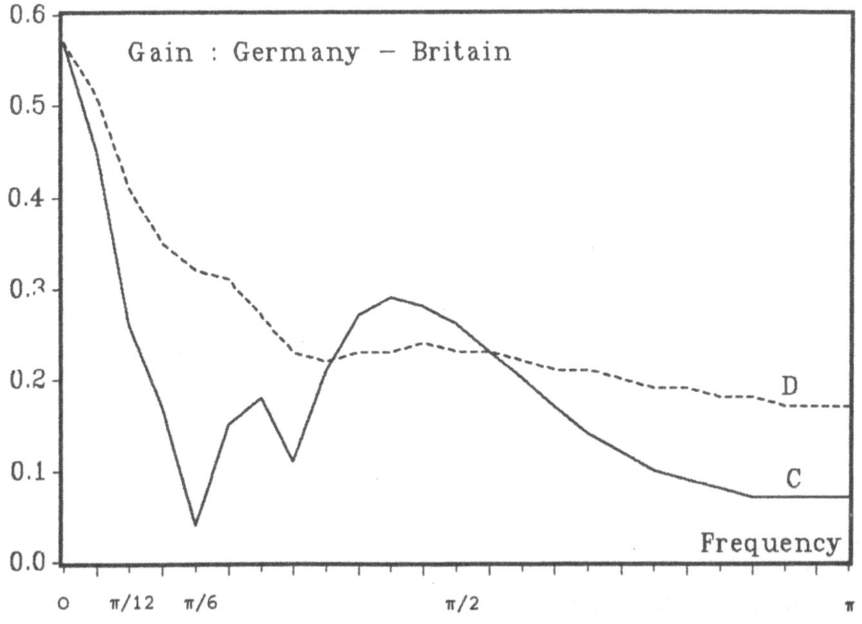

Figure 4b Gain: Germany - Britain

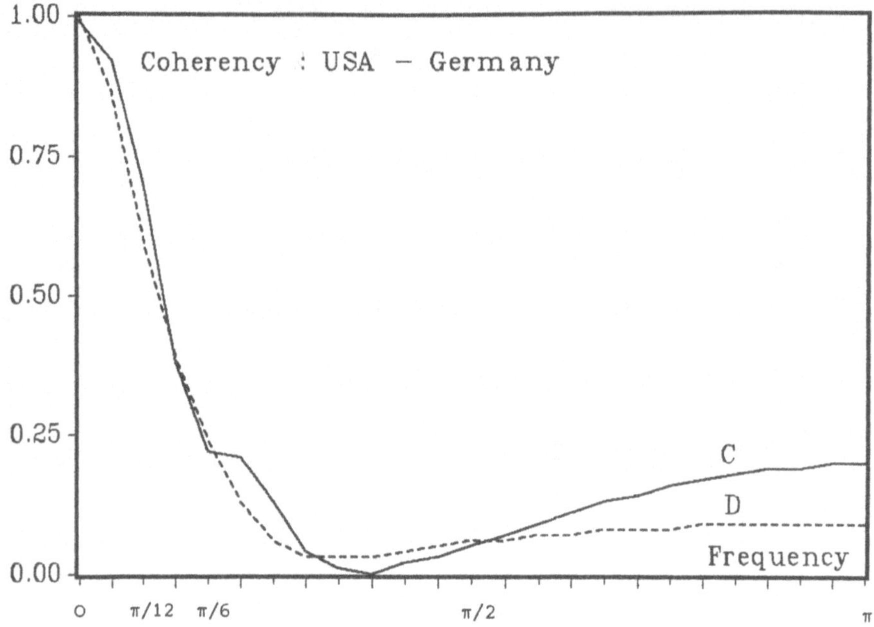

Figure 5a Squared Coherence: USA – Germany

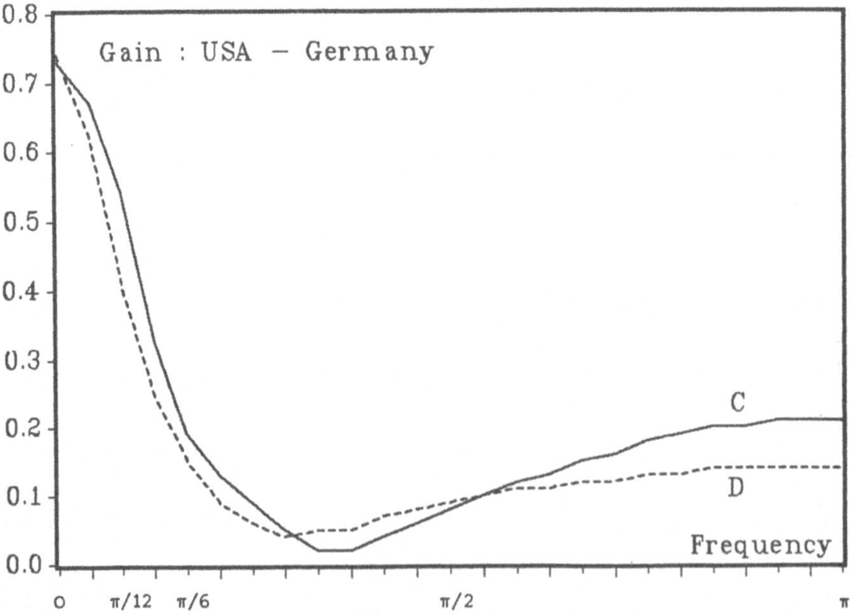

Figure 5b Gain: USA – Germany

Regarding the interest rate linkage for the different cyclical components, we see that we have close relations – i.e. coherences larger than zero – only for the components with periods larger than one year. This holds for the relationships between Germany and France, Germany and Italy as well as US and Germany. We have two exceptions from this picture. The one is Britain, not formally belonging to the exchange rate mechanism of the EMS, which is linked to the German development only in the very long-run components. The other exception is the Netherlands. Here we have significant relations for the whole frequency range. So we have a very strong linkage (also for the very short-run components we find a gain of about 0.7) between German and Dutch interest rates. This can be interpreted as a currency union between Germany and the Netherlands[11].

4 Conclusion

In this paper we have transformed VAR- and EC-models estimating the linkage between Euromarket interest rates to the frequency domain. The spectral analysis enables us to describe this linkage in much more detail as well as to investigate whether the imposed restrictions are correct. The cointegrating restrictions are of special interest.

The relations of the EMS countries France, Italy, and the Netherlands to Germany are not influenced by the inclusion of the non EMS countries Britain and the US. The relation of Germany to the EMS countries as well as to the US are relatively strong for all cycles with periods longer than one year. Moreover, this strong relation holds for the Netherlands also for all short-run components. This may be an indication of a currency union between Germany and the Netherlands. Britain, not belonging to the EMS and principally able to perform its own monetary policy, is connected to the German development only with respect to very long-run relations.

5 Appendix

Given x_t and y_t are two cointegrated I(1)-variables with the long-run relation

$$y_t = \beta x_t + z_t \,,\; z_t \sim I(0),$$

then it holds (see e.g. Stock and Watson (1988))

$$\begin{aligned} x_t &= w_t + \tilde{x}_t \\ y_t &= \beta w_t + \tilde{y}_t \end{aligned}$$

[11]See also the results of Koedijk and Kool (1992).

with $w_t = w_{t-1} + \varepsilon_t$ the common stochastic trend and $\tilde{x}_t$ and $\tilde{y}_t$ are stationary time series. ε_t is a white noise process with mean zero and constant variance σ^2. For the differenced series, which are stationary, we can write

$$\begin{aligned}\Delta x_t &= \varepsilon_t + \Delta\tilde{x}_t\\ \Delta y_t &= \beta\varepsilon_t + \Delta\tilde{y}_t.\end{aligned}$$

For the power-spectra and cross-spectra holds (see e.g. Koopmans (1974, p. 143)

$$\begin{aligned}f_{\Delta x\Delta x}(\lambda) &= \sigma^2/2\pi + f_{\Delta\tilde{x}\Delta\tilde{x}}(\lambda) + 2C_{\varepsilon\Delta\tilde{x}}(\lambda)\\ f_{\Delta y\Delta y}(\lambda) &= \beta^2\sigma^2/2\pi + f_{\Delta\tilde{y}\Delta\tilde{y}}(\lambda) + 2C_{\varepsilon\Delta\tilde{y}}(\lambda)\\ f_{\Delta x\Delta y}(\lambda) &= \beta\sigma^2/2\pi + f_{\varepsilon\Delta\tilde{y}}(\lambda) + \beta f_{\varepsilon\Delta\tilde{x}}(\lambda) + f_{\Delta\tilde{x}\Delta\tilde{y}}(\lambda)\end{aligned}$$

with C denoting the cospectrum.

From equation (5) the gain between Δx_t and Δy_t can be written as

$$g_{\Delta x\Delta y}(\lambda) = \frac{|\beta\sigma^2/2\pi + f_{\varepsilon\Delta\tilde{y}}(\lambda) + \beta f_{\varepsilon\Delta\tilde{x}}(\lambda) + f_{\Delta\tilde{x}\Delta\tilde{y}}(\lambda)|}{\sigma^2/2\pi + f_{\Delta\tilde{x}\Delta\tilde{x}}(\lambda) + 2C_{\varepsilon\Delta\tilde{x}}(\lambda)}.$$

The squared coherence between Δx_t and Δy_t is according to (6) given as

$$K_{\Delta y\Delta x}(\lambda) = \frac{|\beta\sigma^2/2\pi + f_{\varepsilon\Delta\tilde{y}}(\lambda) + \beta f_{\varepsilon\Delta\tilde{x}}(\lambda) + f_{\Delta\tilde{x}\Delta\tilde{y}}(\lambda)|^2}{(\sigma^2/2\pi + f_{\Delta\tilde{x}\Delta\tilde{x}}(\lambda) + 2C_{\varepsilon\Delta\tilde{x}}(\lambda))\,(\beta^2\sigma^2/2\pi + f_{\Delta\tilde{y}\Delta\tilde{y}}(\lambda) + 2C_{\varepsilon\Delta\tilde{y}}(\lambda))}$$

Since $\Delta\tilde{x}_t$ and $\Delta\tilde{y}_t$ are noninvertible processes their power spectra, cross-spectra and cospectra vanish at the origin. Therefore we have

$$g_{\Delta x\Delta y}(0) = \frac{|\beta\sigma^2/2\pi|}{\sigma^2/2\pi} = |\beta|$$

and

$$K_{\Delta y\Delta x}(0) = \frac{\beta^2\sigma^4/4\pi^2}{\beta^2\sigma^4/4\pi^2} = 1.$$

Thus the first differences of two cointegrated I(1)-processes have a coherence of one at the origin and a gain at zero frequency, which measures the absolute value of the long-run relation between the two series. These results also hold in a system with n I(1)-variables which are pairwise cointegrated, since we have $n-1$ independent bivariate cointegrating relations and only one stochastic trend driving the system.

References

Cohen D, Wyplocz Ch (1989) The European Monetary System – An Agnostic Evaluation, in: R C Bryant et al. (eds.) Macroeconomic Policies in an Interdependent World, International Monetary Fund, Washington D.C.

De Grauwe P (1989) Is the European Monetary System a DM–Zone? Discussion Paper No. 297, Centre for Economic Policy Research

Deutsche Bundesbank (1979) Das Europäische Währungssystem: Aufbau und Arbeitsweise, Monatsberichte der Deutschen Bundesbank, März 1979, 11 – 18

Engle R F, Granger C W J (1987) Co–Integration and Error Correction: Representation, Estimation and Testing, Econometrica 55, 143 – 159

Giavazzi F, Giovannini A (1987) Models of the EMS: Is Europe a Greater Deutschmark Area? In: R C Bryant and R Portes (eds.), Global Macroeconomics, St. Martin's Press, New York, 237 – 265

Giavazzi F, Giovannini A (1989) Limiting Exchange Rate Flexibility, The European Monetary System, MIT Press, Cambridge (Mass.)

Granger C W J, Weiss A A (1983) Time Series Analysis of Error Correction Models, in: S Karlin et al. (eds.) Studies in Econometrics, Time Series and Multivariate Statistics, Academic Press, 255 – 278

Hagen J von, Fratianni M (1990) German Dominance in the EMS: Evidence from Interest Rates, Journal of International Money and Finance 9, 358 – 375

Johansen S (1989) Likelihood Based Inference on Cointegration. Theory and Application, Centro Interuniversitario di Econometria, Bologna

Karfakis C J, Moschos D M (1990) Interest Rate Linkages within the European Monetary System: A Time Series Analysis, Journal of Money, Credit, and Banking 22, 388 – 394

Kirchgässner G, Wolters J (1991a) Gibt es eine DM–Zone in Europa? In: J Siebke (ed.), Monetäre Konfliktfelder der Weltwirtschaft, Duncker und Humblot, Berlin, 503 – 516

Kirchgässner G, Wolters J (1991b) Interest Rate Linkages in Europe before and after the Introduction of the European Monetary System, Discussion Paper, Fachbereich Wirtschaftswissenschaften University of Osnabrück, July 1991

Kirchgässner G, Wolters J (1991c) Does the DM dominate the Euro Market? An Empirical Investigation, mimeo

Koedijk K G, Kool C J M (1992) Dominant Interest and Inflation Differentials within the EMS, European Economic Review 36, 925 – 943

König H, Wolters J (1972) Einführung in die Spektralanalyse ökonomischer Zeitreihen, Meisenheim/Glan

Koopmans L H (1974) The Spectral Analysis of Time Series, New York

Stock J H, Watson M W (1988) Variable Trends in Economic Time Series, Journal of Economic Perspectives 2, 147 – 174

Wolters J (1980) Stochastic Dynamic Properties of Linear Econometric Models, Springer Verlag, Berlin

Structuring Volatile Swiss Interest Rates: Some Evidence on the Present Value Model and a VAR-VARCH Approach[1]

By Robert M. Kunst[2] and Wolfgang Polasek[3]

Abstract: We establish some characteristics about daily Swiss interest rates in a bivariate model consisting of a short-term and a long-term rate. Implications of the present-value model are checked on the basis of vector autoregressions. On the whole, the evidence agrees with the theory. The two rates are shown to be cointegrated. In vector autoregressions with daily data, multiples of the weekly lag play a key role. The obvious clusters of high volatility suggest modelling the whole system as a bivariate cointegrated VAR-VARCH model. Yet, under the conventional assumption of conditional normality, this VAR-VARCH model still fails to explain the leptokurtosis of the interest rates completely.

1 Introduction

This paper is concerned with an investigation into the joint properties of daily data on a long-term and a short-term Swiss interest rate. At first, it is checked whether these properties can be reconciled with the implications of the present-value model.

In the original form used by Campbell and Shiller (1987, hereafter C&S), the present-value model (PVM) states that a long-term interest rate RL_t - theoretically an infinitely-termed consol yield - is a linear function of the discounted value of an expected future short-term interest rate RS_t whose maturity matches the sampling frequency:

$$RL_t = (1-\delta)\sum_{i=0}^{\infty} \delta^i E_t RS_{t+i} \ + c \tag{1}$$

This conforms to a Koyck distributed lag model for the future. The constant δ is a discount factor[4], c is a term premium, and E_t denotes stochastic

[1]This work was partially funded by the WWZ-grant E4 of the Universität Basel. Helpful comments from Robert Engle, from the participants in a seminar at the Institute for Advanced Studies, in particular from George Tiao and Andreas Woergoetter, and from an anonymous referee, are gratefully acknowledged.

[2]Robert M. Kunst, Institute for Advanced Studies, 56 Stumpergasse, Vienna, Austria

[3]Wolfgang Polasek, Universität Basel, 51 Petersgraben, CH-4051 Basel, Switzerland

[4]The exact specification for δ suggested by C&S is given in Section 4.2.

expectation, conditional on a sufficiently complete information set which at least includes the history of RS_t and RL_t. Expectations are commonly assumed to be linear. With regard to the conditional means of the variables, this assumption will be retained. With regard to the conditional expectations of squares and variances, it will be relaxed later. No complete parameterization, however, is prescribed by (1) and, in particular, the time series structure of RS_t and the formation of expectations are not determined.

In strict accordance with the theory, RL corresponds to an infinite term and RS to a term exactly matching the sampling frequency. Even for this case, some authors stress the fact that (1) is a *linearized* version of the true PVM not the PVM as such (see Shea (1992)). If the maturity of RL is finite, the sum changes to a finite sum of discounted short-term rates. If the sampling frequency is only a fraction of the shorter maturity, the weighting of future expected RS changes to more complicated or general patterns. Campbell and Shiller (1991) present a revised formula which, however, builds on the assumption that economic agents do not use any discounting if they assess yields related to finite maturities. This appears to be a rather strong assumption, hence the following formula reflects the most general formulation of the PVM which the present investigation builds on:

$$RL_t = (\sum_{i=0}^{\infty} \delta_i)^{-1} \sum_{i=0}^{\infty} \delta_i E_t RS_{t+i} \ + c \tag{2}$$

A more restricted generalization of (1) would assign zero weights to all expected rates except those occurring at a chain sequence. For instance, the observation of a one-year rate on a certain day would only depend on expected one-month rates at one month ahead, two months ahead etc., with the chain sequence ending at exactly one year ahead. The assumption that the expected trajectory of the interest rates between these dates is ignored in expectation formation appears rather strong, hence we do not want to further specify the weight sequence δ_i, though we may expect larger weights at the time points corresponding to the restricted formula.

Repeatedly, testable hypotheses have been derived from the PVM and statistical tests have been conducted. The test of linear restrictions by C&S heavily depends on the geometric weighting imposed in (1). This weighting as such appears to be doubtful for theoretical reasons, particularly in the light of the heteroskedasticity described in Section 5. Rational subjects should use stronger discounting of the future during volatile phases and less discounting in calm phases. Moreover, even if (1) exactly holds for consols and a monthly sampled monthly rate, say, the weighting scheme for more general pairs in (2) can be very different. Yet, testable hypotheses can be found which are only necessary (not sufficient) for the PVM and are rather robust at the same time.

Firstly, if either RS or RL is a first-order integrated process (I(1)), the other variable must also be I(1) while the "spread" $SP = RL - RS$ must be stationary (I(0)). In other words, RL and RS should be cointegrated. Alternatively, both rates could be stationary. This question is unsettled in the literature. C&S, Shea (1992), Hall et al. (1992), and others support the I(1) hypothesis for all interest rates while e.g. Fama and Bliss (1987) present evidence for their stationarity. The hypothesis of the cointegrating yield spread will be denoted by H1.

Secondly, the model implies that, in a bivariate model consisting of the spread and ΔRS_t, SP_t should Granger-cause ΔRS_t (Hypothesis H2). Theory does not suggest any restriction on the reverse direction. Tests on H2 are more interesting in the case of the shorter term matching the sampling frequency. Hence, H2 was tested on the daily series as well as on re-constructed layers of monthly series.

Thirdly, the PVM implies that the innovation in RL_t, $RX_t = RL_t - E_{t-1}RL_t$, obeys the formula

$$RX_t = SP_t - \delta^{-1} SP_{t-1} + \Delta RS_t \tag{3}$$

A necessary condition for the model to hold is thus that the right hand side is unpredictable from any past information (Hypothesis H3). Unlike H1 and H2, H3 depends on δ and on the geometric decay and therefore the re-constructed monthly layers were used exclusively for evaluating H3. In any case, test results on H3 are less reliable than those for the other two hypotheses.

In sections 2 and 3, we show that the assumed time series properties, i.e. integratedness of the series and cointegration of the spread (Hypothesis H1), can be reconciled with our data set. Section 4 considers hypotheses H2 and H3. It is demonstrated that both H2 and H3 are generally encouraged by the data.

Using the cointegrating relation, a vector autoregression for ΔRS_t and ΔRL_t is established. The residuals from this model, though close to white noise with respect to their means, show strong autocorrelation in their squares. These effects are modelled according to the ARCH (autoregressive conditional heteroskedastic) methodology. In Section 5, we show that the ARCH patterns of the two series are strongly interrelated. Section 6 concludes.

2 Univariate Properties of the Interest Rates

We use daily data from January 1, 1974, to April 12, 1989, on the Swiss 1-month and 1-year Euromarket interest rates. This data has been kindly provided by the Swiss National Bank. We have adjusted the raw series for public holidays by interpolation, in order not to lose evidence on cycles which are multiples of a week (i.e. 5 days).

This data set was selected primarily in order to enable a closer approximation to the true data-generating process (DGP) by exploiting the additional information contained in high-frequency data. Even mere tests of the PVM hypotheses H1-H3, however, should benefit from this high-frequency information. Once one should succeed in identifying the true DGP of the interest rates, the problem of testing the PVM has been solved *a fortiori*. A referee has pointed out that the Swiss National Bank changed its monetary policy several times during the sampling interval. Though it is conceivable that such policy changes affect the DGP, their effects on the PVM are unclear and critically hinge on assumptions about whether they have been anticipated by market expectations or not.

Figure 1 shows the data series (3986 observations each) and Figure 2 shows the first differences. Visual inspection of Figure 2 insinuates that the differenced series do have constant means but time-changing volatility. As long as this heteroskedasticity can be explained by conditional distributions and the long-run variance can be assumed as constant, the differenced series are still second-order stationary. At first, we want to test by statistical methods whether RL and RS are indeed first-order integrated.

2.1 Trend and Seasons

Non-augmented Dickey-Fuller (DF) tests are t-tests on the coefficient b in regressions of the form

$$\Delta X_t = a + bX_{t-1} + u_t \tag{4}$$

If X_t is integrated ("has a unit root"), the coefficient b should be zero. If X_t is stationary ("the unit root hypothesis is rejected"), b is negative. The significance of b is tested by its t-statistic t_b which obeys a non-standard law under the null of a unit root. Fuller (1976) gives appropriate significance points.

The results of the DF test for RS and RL are reported in Table 1A. t_b is significant (at 1%) for RS but insignificant for RL. In both equations, Durbin-Watson statistics (not reported) are close to 2.0 but some autocorrelation is found at higher lags. The autocorrelation structure of RS deserves attention, as the null hypothesis of integration was rejected for this variable. The autocorrelation function of ΔRS reveals marginally significant values at lags 3 to 5 and 8 to 11. These could point to an influence of weekly or biweekly cycles. Autocorrelation is absent at monthly intervals (20 to 25 days).

An estimation of the "augmented" equation

$$\Delta X_t = a + bX_{t-1} + \sum_{i=1}^{p} c_i \Delta X_{t-i} + u_t \qquad (5)$$

with the order $p = 11$ fixed by AIC (Akaike's Information Criterion) again resulted in a value of t_b significant at the 1% level. Consequently, statistical criteria would suggest viewing RS as a stationary series and RL as non-stationary which is not acceptable for theoretical reasons.

Table 1 Testing for unit roots and univariate statistics

Series	a	t_a	b	t_b	R^2	# lags
A. Dickey-Fuller test						
RL	0.0100	2.000	-0.0023	-2.37	0.0010	
RS	0.0270	3.100	-0.0068	-3.86	0.0040	
ΔRL	-0.0008	-0.373	-1.1010	-69.80	0.5510	
ΔRS	-0.0018	-0.396	-0.9820	-62.90	0.4980	
B. Augmented Dickey-Fuller test						
RL	0.010	2.04	-0.0023	-2.44	0.016	10
RS	0.026	3.16	-0.0070	-4.07	0.019	11

C. Summary statistics

C1. Moments

Series	mean	variance	skewness	kurtosis
ΔRL	-0.0007	0.0183	-0.1550	13.61
ΔRS	-0.0011	0.0892	-0.7918	23.15

C2. Koutrouvelis estimates

Series	α	β	c	d
ΔRL	1.54	-0.04	0.06	0.0001
ΔRS	1.14	-0.02	0.96	-0.0031

Note: Throughout the paper, "kurtosis", in accordance with the RATS software output, refers to what is otherwise known as "excess kurtosis" and hence is 0 for the normal distribution.

In order to cope with any eventually remaining residual autocorrelation, an optimum subset autoregressive representation was specified for RS on the basis of AIC, using an intricate search algorithm. The selected subset contained, among other lags, the lags 130, 195, 260, 261, which correspond to two, three, and four quarters of a year. This autoregressive subset model displays a sum of regression coefficient estimates of 0.993736. According to the DF-statistic t_b of -3.82, this is still significantly different from 1. We will assume, however, that it is close enough to keep the unit root as a working hypothesis for RS.

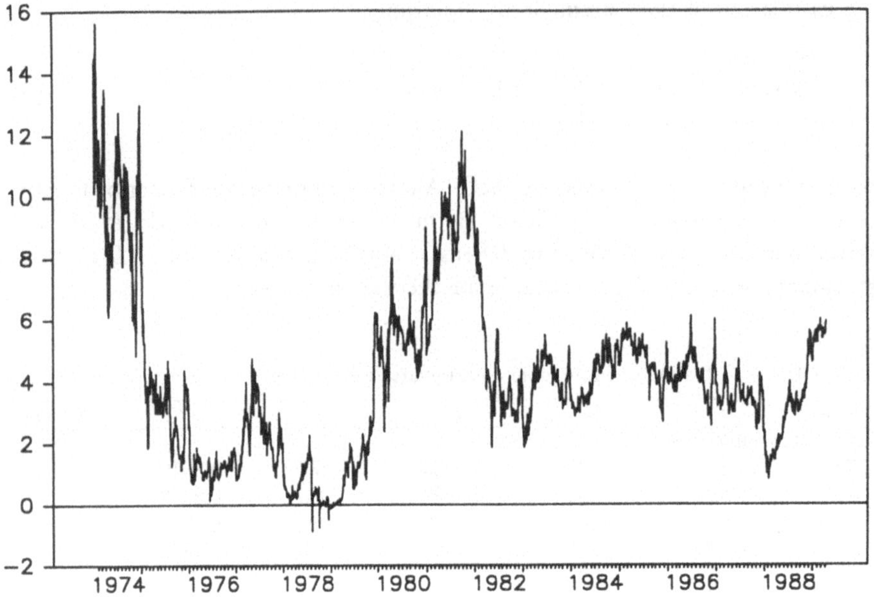

Figure 1a Swiss 1-month interest rate

Figure 1b Swiss 1-year interest rate

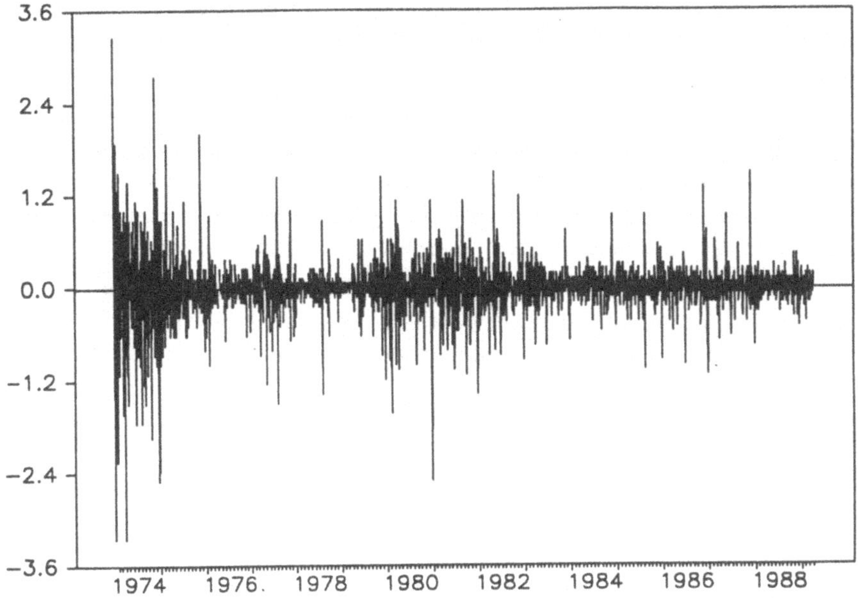

Figure 2a First differences of 1-month rate *RS*

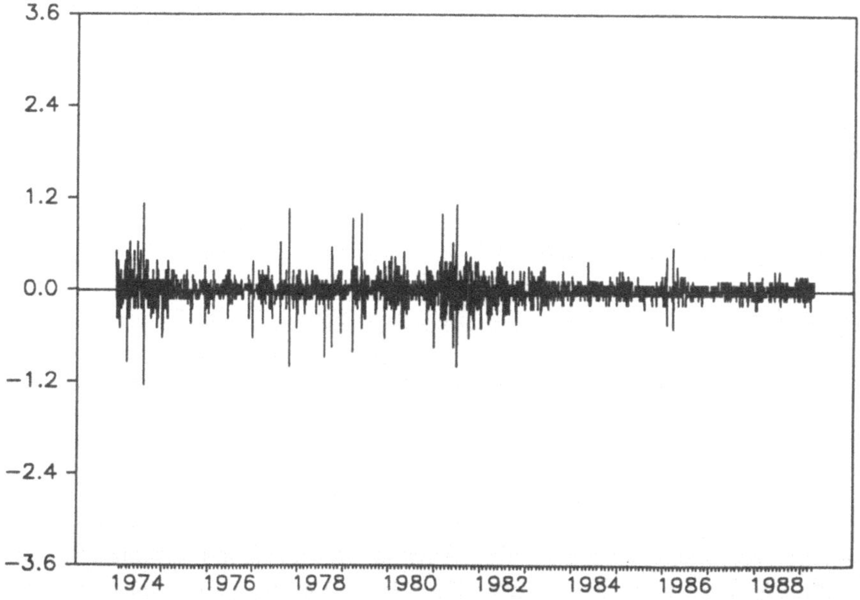

Figure 2b First differences of 1-year rate *RL*

Three key arguments should support this point of view: evidence from multivariate models, the behaviour of the DF statistics in its evolution through time, the distortion stemming from ARCH effects.

In the bivariate model (see Section 3), the method by Johansen (1988, 1991) points to integration of the system (RS, RL). At the 5% risk level, a stationary system is suggested, i.e. stationary short-term *and* long-term rates. At the 1% risk level, the spread RL-RS evolves as a cointegrating variable and RL as well as RS are regarded as non-stationary.

The evolution of test statistics through time is commonly used as an indicator of structural breaks in the data. In "moving regressions" on "rolling samples", statistics DF_{td} are estimated from samples of fixed size $[t, t+d-1]$ for $t = 1, ..., T-d+1$.

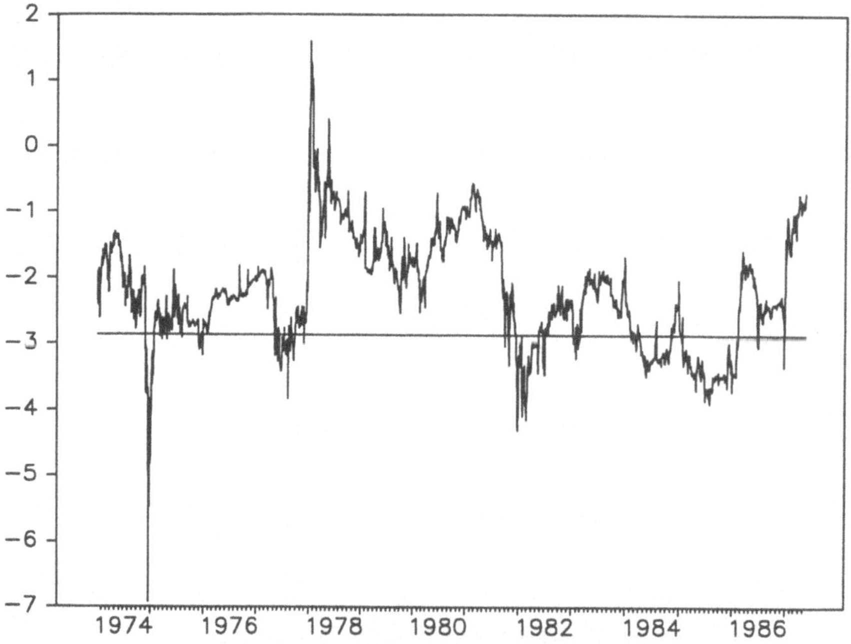

Figure 3 DF test statistic for shortened ("rolling") samples

Note: Corresponding samples start at time indicated on the x-axis and have 500 observations each. The horizontal line gives the 5% significance point.

Figure 3 gives a time plot of the non-augmented DF_{td}, calculated from moving regressions with $d = 500$. During 1974-1977, DF_{td} remains close to the 5% significance bound, except for an extraordinary influence of some extreme observations near the end of 1976, which generates curious peaks for time points t in the end of 1974. During 1978-1980, DF_{td} tends to be insignificant and thus to support the unit root hypothesis. Subsequently, it moves back down to the boundary. The last few observations, however, again fail to provide any evidence against the unit root hypothesis. In summary, even though the data could be grouped into several regimes or phases, the plot rather strengthens the validity of the unit root hypothesis and points at the same time to an increased probability of rejection due to leptokurtosis or heteroskedasticity.

Asymptotically, the distribution of the DF statistic remains unchanged even in the cases of heteroskedastic or fat-tailed errors, as long as finite moment conditions are satisfied[5]. This can be contrasted with the asymptotic properties of the t-test in a stationary environment which is affected by heteroskedasticity (compare Weiss (1984)). In finite samples, DF significance points can be quite distorted. To demonstrate this effect, we simulated random walks with increments following stable distributions, each of the sample having 4000 observations. A tail index of $\alpha = 1.97$ approximately replicates the kurtosis observed in the interest rates sample [6]. The empirical fractiles shifted considerably to the left: the 5% point was -4.5 and the 10% point -4.1. Similar distortions can be obtained from ARCH models if the conditional distribution fully accounts for the observed excess kurtosis. Hence, positive dependence among variances, particularly in conjunction with additional leptokurtosis, can induce a size bias. The differenced series raise little suspicion on their stationarity. DF statistics are much larger in absolute values and clearly reject eventual second unit roots.

2.2 Volatility and Distributional Results

Panel C1 of Table 1 provides some summary statistics based on the first four empirical moments of the two series. It is evident that the first differences of both RL and RS show substantial skewness as well as leptokurtosis. According to the usual approximate quantiles of higher moments tests, the null hypotheses of zero skewness and normal kurtosis can be rejected at extreme risk levels.

Panel C2 gives the coefficients from Koutrouvelis regressions. These regressions are based on fitting the empirical characteristic functions to those of the stable Paretian (in short, "stable") distributions (see Koutrouvelis (1980)). The class of stable distributions can be described by four parameters, the most important one being the "tail index" α, which is 2 for the Gaussian and 1 for the Cauchy law. Distributions become more leptokurtic if α moves away from 2, with finite moments only existing for orders less than α. β represents the skewness of the distribution while c and d measure scale and location. The estimates point to extremely non-normal distributions with

---

[5]If the assumption of finite moments is violated, a widely different class of processes must be considered, which was analyzed recently by Phillips (1990).

[6]The theoretical fourth and even second moments do not exist but the median of the finite-sample empirical distribution coincides with the measurements from the data.

infinite variances but with negligible skewness. The fit of the Koutrouvelis regressions is rather high with R^2 values around 0.98.

Leptokurtosis in financial data has been the subject of much controversy. Following Mandelbrot (1963) and Fama (1965), many investigators have retained the assumption of, at least approximately [7], independent price changes and tried to describe their distributions by parametric families, preferably the stable Paretian family. The Koutrouvelis procedure is related to this strand of research. In contrast, the ARCH model by Engle (1982) explains leptokurtosis by serial dependence in variances and - at least in its original version - retains the assumption of normal conditional distributions. The marginal distributions imposed by ARCH models do not have closed forms and can have any amount of leptokurtosis, depending on the parameters of the ARCH equations. Even if second moments become infinite, however, these marginal distributions are not stable laws. So far, little is known about which stable parameter estimates are obtained from ARCH models in finite samples. A related simulation study has been conducted by Kunst (1993).

3 Cointegration in the Bivariate System

Seeing both interest rates *RS* and *RL* as first-order integrated component processes of a bivariate vector autoregression (VAR) motivates a search for possible cointegration. The PVM gives the yield spread $SP = RL - RS$ as a cointegrating vector. This can be regarded as a testable hypothesis implied by the theory. We first turn to the properties of the spread and then check whether the prescribed relation is confirmed by direct estimation from the data.

3.1 The Spread

Table 2 reports the application of the DF test to the spread. In its augmented as well as in its original form, the null hypothesis of a unit root is rejected at the level of 1% and even at more rigid levels. This corroborates the assumption that *RS* and *RL* are cointegrated. Any augmentation has hardly any effect on the test statistic. The AIC criterion produces local minima at 10 and 22 lags, the latter specification indicating monthly cycles in daily data. Tentative insertion of selected higher lags into the DF regression did not affect the results substantially either, increasing the t-statistic to -5.8 in the worst case which still falls short of the corresponding values from the interest rates (compare Table 1).

Panel B of Table 2 shows that, although the third and fourth moments are still highly non-normal, the kurtosis appears greatly reduced relative to

[7] Fama (1965,p.87), in fact, was conscious of the possibility of conditional heteroskedasticity but judged it as "not too important".

the differenced interest rates. It follows that the cointegrating relation not only removes nonstationarity but also a substantial part of the non-normality of the original series. This phenomenon is supported by the coefficient estimates of the stable distributions estimates according to Koutrouvelis (1980). Whereas the differenced interest rate series give rise to α estimates of less than 1.6, the α estimate of the spread is close to 1.8.

Table 2 The spread

A. Dickey-Fuller test

a	t_a	b	t_b	res. σ^2	ser. σ^2	# lags
0.027	5.28	-0.0402	-9.07	0.0692	0.0706	0
0.021	4.31	-0.0306	-6.76	0.0625	0.0706	10
0.021	4.20	-0.0301	-6.31	0.0597	0.0706	22

Note: "res.σ^2" and "ser.σ^2" refer to the sample variance of the residual series from the DF regression and that of ΔSP, respectively; "# lags" gives the number of augmenting lags of ΔSP used in the DF test.

B. Summary statistics

mean	variance	skewness	kurtosis
0.6608	0.8862	-0.1677	2.6817

As mentioned above, the last result should not be taken as evidence that the data have been generated by stable laws or that their variance does not exist. It is known that non-stable distributions with finite variance entail Koutrouvelis estimates which are sometimes considerably less than 2 (compare Akgiray and Booth (1988) or Kunst (1993)). In any case, these estimates demonstrate the non-normality of the original data and the reduction of this non-normality in the spread. Presumably, unusual observations in both RS and RL come together and these outliers are eliminated by considering their difference.

3.2 Estimating Cointegrating Vectors

The descriptive results on the spread indicate that RS and RL are indeed cointegrated with the cointegrating vector (1 -1) imposed by theory. To check on the coefficient restriction, one could also be interested in estimating such a vector.

Tentative estimation by direct regression methods as suggested by Engle and Granger (1987) resulted in a variety of different parameter estimates that partly came close to the spread vector (1 -1). The most dependable estimates, however, were probably found by the efficient multivariate maximum likelihood estimation procedure according to Johansen (1988, 1991). Unlike regression, this method does not attach special preference to certain directions in the coordinate space as it uses eigenvectors and canonical analysis. The algorithm calculates the canonical correlations between differenced and level data, conditioned on a "short-run structure" of lagged differences. As the algorithm uses a VAR, a short-run lag structure had to be explicitly specified. As a good compromise between the goals of parsimony and of whitening all error series, the following lags were selected: all lags from 1 to 22, 44 for two months, 65 for a quarter of a year, 130 for half a year, 195 for three quarters, and the yearly lags of 260 and 261, the latter two reflecting the fact that a year has between 260 and 261 trading days (including holidays but excluding weekends) on average. In the following, this selection of lags will be referred to as the "seasonal lags set" (SLS).

The resulting eigenvalues were 0.0025 and 0.0094 and the corresponding statistics were 9.62 and 35.06. The smaller eigenvalue was significant at 5% while the larger one was significant at extreme risk levels. Ruling out the possibility of a stationary system, this suggests exactly one cointegrating vector[8]. Its corresponding estimate is $RS - 1.086RL$ which is very close to the spread. The chi-square test for the null hypothesis that the coefficient is one (see Johansen [1991]) is unable to reject this restriction. The "error correction" imposed by the spread exerts its influence on ΔRS rather than on the long-term rate but the influence of ΔRL is strong enough to ensure that the vector estimated from the full system is much closer to 1. The canonical problem maximizes the correlation between a linear combination of RS and RL and another one of ΔRS and ΔRL, whereas regression maximizes the correlation simply between ΔRS and a linear combination of the levels.

4 Testing the Causality Hypotheses

4.1 The Spread as a Leading Indicator

Testable hypothesis H2 tells that the spread must be a "leading indicator" for changes in the short-term interest rate in the sense of Granger causation in a bivariate model. A variable $X1$ is said to Granger cause another variable $X2$ if $X2$ is predicted better by taking the joint history of both variables into account than by the univariate history alone. Starting from the cointegrated VAR model, this can be formally transformed into a VAR for the stationary variates SP and ΔRS. Upon this model, an F-test for causality can be based.

A straightforward analysis of successive daily observations yields strong indication of causality in both directions, with tests rejecting at extreme risk

---

[8]With leptokurtic distributions, the finite-sample significance points for the Johansen test change. Tentative simulations suggest that the modifications support the existence of exactly one cointegrating vector.

levels, even if short-run ARCH features (see Section 5) are accounted for.

A causality test based on re-constructed series of monthly observations proved to be more sensitive. Such monthly data were constructed in the following way. A first data series consists of the first observation in January 1974, the first one in February, then in March etc. A second data series comprises the second available observations in each month. This same pattern is followed until the twentieth observations are reached which exhaust all observations in the Februaries. Similarly, one could have started from the ends of the months and the procedure has some inherent arbitrariness but this can probably be neglected as the raw data contain some uncertainty with respect to the end of terms, i.e. same date of next month versus 30 calendar days, and some averaging.

The Granger test for causality requires a good specification of the lag structure. The optimum AIC specification for the VAR varied among the layers but, on the whole, an order of three evolved as the preference of the data.

Table 3 Granger causality tests of the present value model

Causality hypothesis	average F	# rejections
from SP to SP	36.39	20
from ΔRS to SP	1.68	2
from SP to ΔRS	6.74	20
from ΔRS to ΔRS	1.77	2

Table 3 reports the results of F-tests in all directions, including those for the influence on a variable by its own history. Reported numbers are two for each hypothesis: the average of the 20 F-statistics and the number of cases of rejection at the conventional 5% level. The dynamic influence from SP to ΔRS, suggested by H2, is clearly supported. Moreover, the spread even accounts for all but the whole of the dynamics of ΔRS and feedback is low. Note that two rejections out of 20 hardly exceed the one rejection prescribed statistically by the risk level.

4.2 The Excess Return

Testable hypothesis H3 relies on the formula (3)

$$RL_t - E_{t-1}RL_t = SP_t - (1/\delta)SP_{t-1} + \Delta RS_t \tag{6}$$

which tells that the right-hand side variable RX_t must be unpredictable from past information. In accordance with C&S, δ is set equal to $1/(1+R_0)$, with

R_0 being an average monthly rate derived from the sample mean $\overline{R}$ of RL_t via

$$R_0 = (1 + \overline{R})^{1/12} - 1 \tag{7}$$

where, unlike in the remaining paper, R_0 and $\overline{R}$ are in percentages to ease notation. This δ is necessarily close to one (exact estimate 0.996163) and the behavior of RX is similar to that of ΔRL. Table 1 shows that a unit root in ΔRL is rejected strongly and hence the excess return can be regarded as stationary. Shea (1992) has pointed out that defining δ via (7) or similar formulae is contradictory in principle as C&S assume that RL is I(1) and hence does not have a population mean. However, as long as δ is varied in a range of values close to 1, our basic empirical results remain unaffected, hence they appear to be rather robust toward eventual violations of (7).

A key problem arises, however, as the PVM assumes that the sampling frequency matches the term of the shorter rate. Here, these do not match and the excess return relative to the daily frequency can have properties different from those derived from the model. Hence, H3 was tested exclusively on the monthly strata outlined in Section 4.1.

The results given in Table 4 consist of averages of the F-statistics over the whole sample of twenty series and frequencies of rejection with respect to the conventional 5%-level and the F-distribution. Because of an uncertain degree of dependence among the series and eventual serial dependence of the second moments to be analyzed below, these results yield a summary picture rather than a statistically accurate test.

Table 4 The excess return $RX_t = SP_t - \frac{1}{\delta}SP_{t-1} + \Delta RS_t$

Regressor	average $F(3,173)$	# rejections
A. Regression of RX on past values of ΔRS and the spread SP		
SP	1.28	0
ΔRS	1.10	0
B. Regression of RX on past values of RS and RL		
RS	3.07	13
RL	3.63	19

Firstly, a causality test is evaluated on the basis of regressing the excess return on past values of ΔRS and the spread, exactly the kind of test used by C&S. On the average, three lags of both regressors were found to suffice for clean residuals. Panel A of Table 4 demonstrates that there is no evidence for a rejection of the non-predictability hypothesis. In contrast, Panel B shows that non-predictability ceases to hold if the original series RS and RL are used as regressors. These statistics could deviate, however, from the F-distribution because of the non-stationarity of the regressors.

Rejection of the non-predictability hypothesis is primarily caused by a linear combination of RS and RL at the 3-months lag with opposite signs which is, however, slightly different from the spread vector (1 -1). This is at odds with the fact that cointegration analysis tells that the spread is the *only* stationary combination and hence the only candidate for a non-zero correlation with the assumedly stationary excess return. Taking the remaining lags into account, the causing source comes closer to the spread.

In summary, the spread appears to be of some use for predicting the excess return. This influence is at the borderline of significance and becomes even less significant if conditional heteroskedasticity is accounted for.

5 ARCH Effects

In this section, we use the VAR for the two variables ΔRS and ΔRL as a starting point, assuming RS and RL to be cointegrated with cointegrating vector $RS - RL$, the spread:

$$\begin{bmatrix} \Delta RS_t \\ \Delta RL_t \end{bmatrix} = \sum_{i \in I} \Phi_i \begin{bmatrix} \Delta RS_{t-i} \\ \Delta RL_{t-i} \end{bmatrix} + \alpha sp_{t-1} + \begin{bmatrix} r_{1t} \\ r_{2t} \end{bmatrix} \tag{8}$$

The index set I contains the SLS. sp stands for the centred variable $SP = RL - RS$. r_{1t} and r_{2t} denote white noise errors. The matrices Φ_i are estimated without any restriction on the coefficients. Apart from the restriction on the error-correction variable to be the spread and a restriction on the constants, this is the system known from the Johansen procedure in Section 3.2. Recall that the spread influences significantly the short-term, but not the long-term rate. The goodness of fit statistics remain unaffected (significances of individual portmanteau Q statistics are 2.2% and 5.8%, R^2 values are 0.088 and 0.057).

The modelling of constant terms by adjusting the spread to its mean and dropping constants elsewhere is useful as this prevents the model from explosive behaviour caused by linear time trends. Linear trends would separate RS and RL in the longer run which is counterintuitive.

The residuals from the system show noteworthy clusters of increased and of reduced volatility. This observation raises suspicion on whether there are ARCH (conditional heteroskedasticity) effects in the data. This suspicion is corroborated by the autocorrelation function (ACF) of the squared residuals[9].

[9]This ACF is very similar to the cross correlation function (CCF) plotted in Figure 4 and therefore not shown, as ΔRL and ΔRS are close to white noise.

Following the introduction of the ARCH model for white noise processes and for the regression design, two different ARCH versions have been developed if the model for the conditional mean is a general autoregressive or ARMA process. The first concept, which seems more attractive from a statistical perspective and has been applied more widely, was suggested by Bollerslev (1986) who assumes that conditional variances h_t of the innovations from the linear model e_t depend on past conditional variances and on past squared errors:

$$h_t = \alpha_0 + \sum_{i=1}^{p} \alpha_i e_{t-i}^2 + \sum_{i=1}^{q} \beta_i h_{t-i} \tag{9}$$

This so-called GARCH model resembles the common ARMA model for means and can be shown to replicate some of its properties. Its drawback is that, unlike the ARMA model, it imposes the main structure on the unobserved series h_t and thus its parameters can only be estimated via nonlinear optimization.

In contrast, the alternative offered by Weiss (1984) expresses h_t as a linear combination of past squares of directly observed variables like the (centred) process y_t itself or at least indirectly observed ones like e_t:

$$h_t = \alpha_0 + \sum_{i=1}^{p} \alpha_i (y_{t-1} - \overline{y})^2 + \sum_{i=1}^{q} \beta_i e_{t-i}^2 \qquad \overline{y} = E(y_t) \tag{10}$$

These models, which will be used here, are called ARMA-ARCH models. To prevent the possible generation of negative conditional variances, all coefficients must be restricted to be non-negative, with the constant α_0 being strictly positive.

Preliminary estimation and lag specification of the ARMA-ARCH models is usually performed via two OLS regression steps, the first one for estimating the ARMA structure for the means and the second one for the ARCH parameters. As Weiss (1984) points out, non-linear ML estimation is not necessarily more efficient than OLS, as long as conditional normality is not guaranteed. Nevertheless, it is suggested to finally rely on, at least approximate, non-linear ML optimization rather than on the least squares estimates. ML estimates are preferred for two reasons: firstly, they better take into account the information in the process by estimating the linear and the ARCH part jointly; secondly, they require weaker moment restrictions for results like consistency and asymptotic normality to hold.

In our case, with the relevant variables so close to white noise processes, the squared centred process and its squared innovations should not be inserted at the same time. Therefore, here $p = 0$ and the α_i are estimated from a regression of the squared residuals from the vector autoregression on past squared variables. Among the past variables to be squared, we considered lags

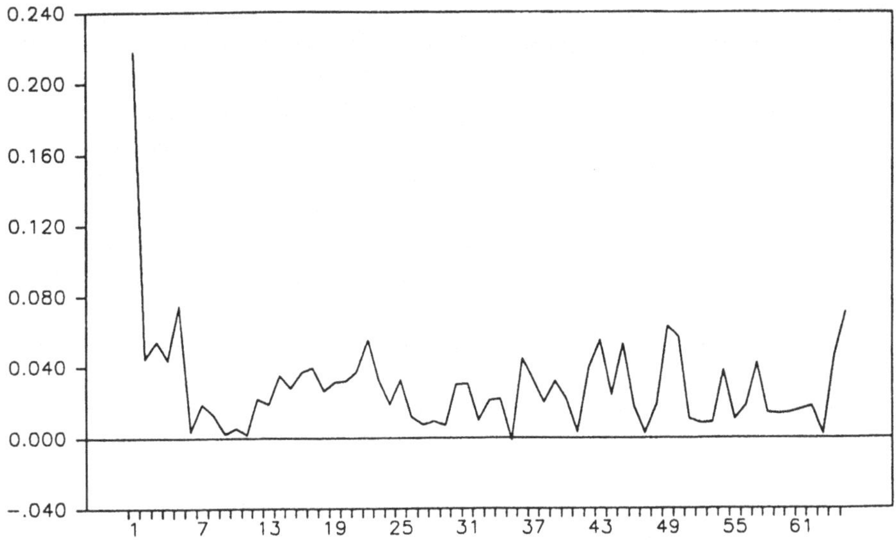

Figure 4a *RS*: Cross correlations (r_1^2, lags of $(\Delta RS)^2$)

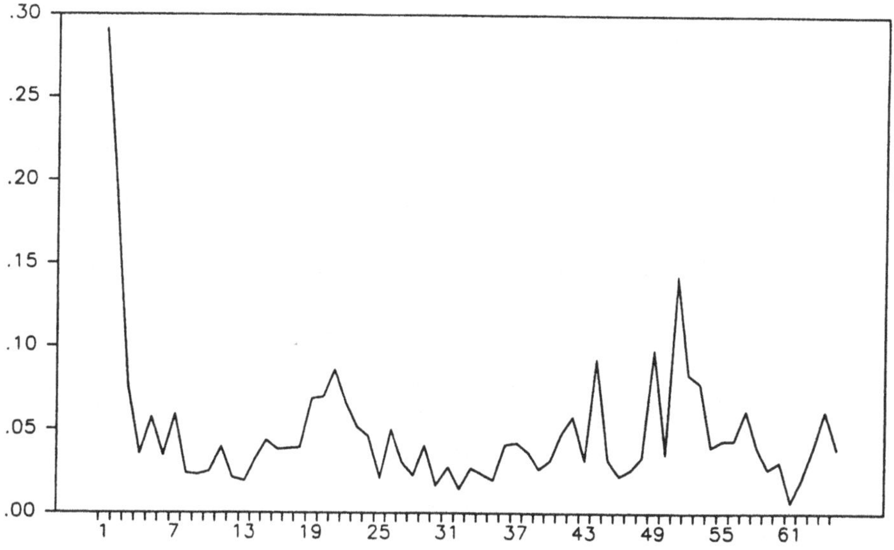

Figure 4b *RL*: Cross correlations (r_2^2, lags of $(\Delta RL)^2$)

of both ΔRS and ΔRL as well as lags of the spread. In concordance with the established acronyms, such a model can be called a cointegrated VAR-VARCH model, as both the linear and the ARCH parts are vector models[10].

The insertion of the squared explanatory terms deserves some explanation. It is straightforward to include influences from lagged differences ΔRS and ΔRL. In theory, both differenced series have mean zero and therefore we did not subtract an empirical mean. In contrast, if the squared spread is allowed to enter into the regression, it has to be centred to conform with the ARMA-ARCH structure. To this end, the sample mean 0.6608 was subtracted. In principle, the spread could enter in the form of several lags as the representation restrictions of the mean-VAR do not apply to the VARCH model. All lags but the first one, however, proved to be very small and thus the VARCH model basically resembles the mean-VAR.

Some specification search and subset modelling had to be performed for the VARCH system because of the non-negativity restriction on the coefficients. Useful tools are higher-order CCF graphs like those of Figure 4 which show the cross-correlations for the squared residuals and the lagged squared differences. Only CCFs of the residuals with the corresponding left-hand side variable in the VAR are shown, the other CCFs have somewhat weaker patterns. In all cases, there is substantial cross-correlation at the first few lags. For r_2 and RL, an interesting peak around lag 50 appears which plays a role in the VARCH model below.

The general structure of the equations of the VARCH models is

$$r_{lt}^2 = \mu + \sum_{i \in I} \alpha_i (\Delta RS_{t-i})^2 + \sum_{j \in J} \beta_j (\Delta R_{t-j})^2 + \sum_{k \in K} \gamma_k (sp_{t-k})^2 \tag{11}$$

with I,J,K being appropriate index sets and $l = 1,2$.

Starting from larger index sets and eliminating insignificant lags and also those with negative signs led to a rather parsimonious representation of the residuals from the ΔRS equation (with the non-normal error series and the index t being suppressed):

$$\begin{aligned} r_1^2 &= 0.013 + 0.141(\Delta RS_{-1})^2 + 0.024(\Delta RS_{-3})^2 + \\ &\quad + 0.034(\Delta RS_{-5})^2 + 0.019(\Delta RS_{-22})^2 + \\ &\quad + 0.369(\Delta RL_{-1})^2 + 0.024(SP_{-1} - 0.6608)^2 \\ &\quad (R^2 = 0.101, \text{ p-value of } Q(181) \text{ is } 18\%) \end{aligned} \tag{12}$$

The size of the portmanteau Q tends to be biased in such a relation as the residuals are certainly highly non-normal even if no ARCH effects are

[10]Note that "cointegration" does not apply to the VARCH part of the model, as the rather small coefficients do not entail integration in variance.

present. In this case, the residual distribution is a centred chi-square with one degree of freedom. Some simulation reveals, however, that the 5% significance points of Q on the basis of centered chi-square(1) variables are hardly any different from the chi-square points on the basis of normal variables. There are larger differences in the tails, e.g. for 1% significance points.

Specifying a satisfactory ARCH model for the ΔRL residuals turned out to be more difficult. In all specifications, the "second-order" residuals appeared correlated at unusual and rather high lags. The best reasonable model is

$$\begin{aligned} r_2^2 &= 0.005 + 0.010(\Delta RS_{-6})^2 + 0.008(\Delta RS_{-52})^2 + \\ &+ 0.213(\Delta RL_{-1})^2 + 0.071(\Delta RL_{-2})^2 + 0.027(\Delta RL_{-5})^2 + \\ &+ 0.034(\Delta RL_{-19})^2 + 0.043(\Delta RL_{-21})^2 + 0.105(\Delta RL_{-51}) + \\ &+ 0.002(SP_{-1} - 0.6608)^2 \\ &(R^2 = 0.122, Q(183) \text{ highly significant}) \end{aligned} \tag{13}$$

The residual correlation is disconcerting but, as it can only be properly accounted for by insertion of very long lags without obvious interpretation, it seems that nothing can be done about it. It is possible that such behaviour is due to few isolated outliers in the sample and that the above parsimonious model should be generally preferred.

If the original residuals r_1 and r_2 are adjusted for their conditional variances, the resulting series are still highly non-normal with the kurtosis falling from around 11 to 7.6 (r_1) and 8.8 (r_2). Extreme non-normality should not really affect the estimation of the vector autoregression as least squares are known to perform quite well in autoregressions with fat-tailed residuals but the performance of the VARCH estimates in this case is unknown.

Both VARCH equations show that, although the main weight of the coefficients is on the past of the "own" lags, there are significant cross-effects among the conditional variances, particularly from ΔRL to the short-term residual r_1. The coefficients are in general rather small and thus it is reasonable to expect that the model is asymptotically stable and stationary, though this is difficult to assess analytically, particularly because of the influence of the error correction on the stochastic difference equation system[11]. To corroborate this conjecture, we performed a little simulation experiment.

Figure 5 shows a display of the simulated series. The simulation was started from real data during 1986. 780 values were generated on the basis of conditional normal random numbers, approximately corresponding to three years of trading days. The simulated series mirror most of the characteristics of the data series: phases of high and low volatility, occasional phases of

[11]For a simple VAR-VARCH model, stability conditions are analyzed in Kunst (1991).

negative spread (inverse term structure), and a general co-movement of the two series. Due to the normality assumption in the experiment, however, the frequency of outliers appears reduced in comparison to the actual data. In particular, the kurtosis values for real ΔRS and ΔRL are around 23 and 14, respectively, whereas the simulated series only attain kurtosis of 10.9 and 3.6.

To check the influence of the least squares estimation procedure, an approximation step in the direction of non-linear ML was performed. Optimization of the overall likelihood of the bivariate system turned out to be impossible for numerical reasons. We therefore took up the suggestion of Engle (1982) to use the method of scoring iteratively.

Engle (1982, p.995-998) showed that the ML estimate can be approximated by iterative steps of weighted least squares regressions for the linear part and the ARCH part. Take $\Theta^{(i)}$ as the estimate obtained from the i-th iteration. Then $\Theta^{(i+1)}$ is obtained from the scoring formula

$$\Theta^{(i+1)} = \Theta^{(i)} + (I^{(i)})^{-1} \sum s^i / T \tag{14}$$

where $I^{(i)}$ and $s^{(i)}$ are the estimated information matrix and the vector of first derivatives of the likelihood with respect to Θ, both from step i. The iterative algorithm is based on the fact that the information matrix is block diagonal [12]. Engle demonstrated that the scoring step of the ARCH equation boils down to a weighted least squares regression, with the weights being the squares of the previously estimated conditional variances for each observation. In our model, the differences between the squared residuals from the linear model and the estimated conditional variances are regressed on specified squares of lagged variables. The coefficient estimates are then added to the previous estimates for α_j, β_j, γ_j.

The scoring step for the coefficients of the linear part is, in fact, easier than in Engle's procedure as here the conditional variances do not depend on lagged errors. Again, weighted least squares is the solution, this time the weights are simply the estimated conditional variances. The linear errors are regressed on the specified past variables, and the resulting coefficients are again added to the old ones[13].

Table 5 summarizes the observed movements of the ARCH coefficients during three iteration steps. Most coefficients turned out to be fairly stable during iterations, with the difference between least-squares and the first scoring step being the largest one. The overall picture appears to support a slight shift of explanatory power from the squared spread to squared lags of the corresponding left-hand side variable. A similar effect is found for the linear coefficients (not shown).

---

[12]In fact, it is block diagonal for all "regular" ARCH problems. It is easily shown that ours is a regular one.

[13]A RATS code for this scoring algorithm can be obtained from the first author upon request.

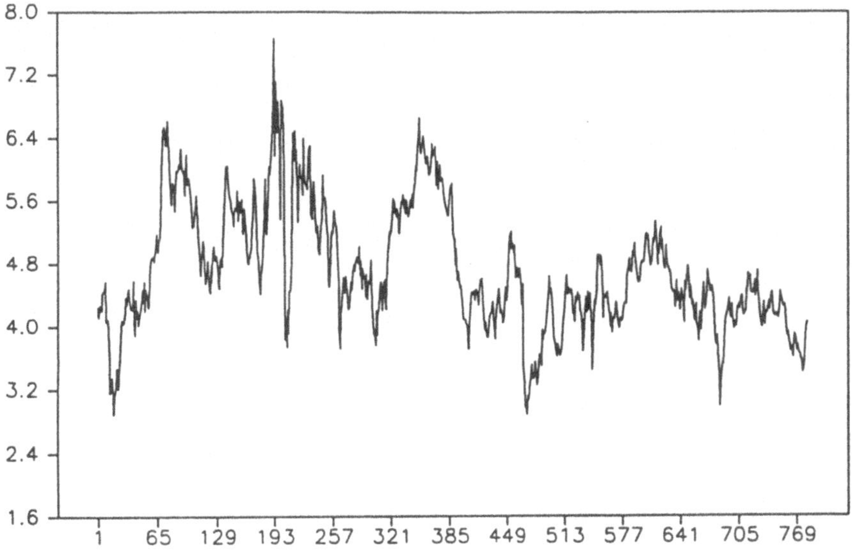

Figure 5a 780 simulated data of *RS*

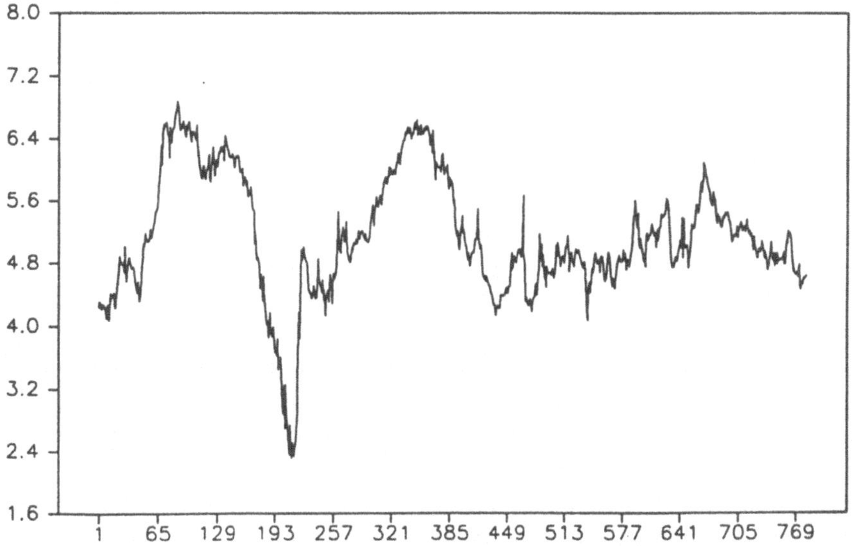

Figure 5b 780 simulated data of *RL*

Table 5 Scoring iterations of the VAR-VARCH model; estimates of the ARCH parameters

variable	iteration 0	1	2	3
a) variance of the RS equation				
constant	0.013	0.015	0.014	0.014
$(\Delta RS[-1])^2$	0.141	0.241	0.257	0.263
$(\Delta RS[-3])^2$	0.024	0.036	0.032	0.031
$(\Delta RS[-5])^2$	0.035	0.039	0.044	0.048
$(\Delta RS[-22])^2$	0.019	0.031	0.038	0.042
$(\Delta RL[-1])^2$	0.369	0.365	0.381	0.383
$(sp[-1])^2$	0.024	0.016	0.015	0.015
b) variance of the RL equation				
constant	0.005	0.004	0.004	0.004
$(\Delta RS[-6])^2$	0.010	0.008	0.008	0.008
$(\Delta RS[-52])^2$	0.008	0.005	0.005	0.005
$(\Delta RL[-1])^2$	0.213	0.199	0.199	0.198
$(\Delta RL[-2])^2$	0.071	0.150	0.165	0.166
$(\Delta RL[-5])^2$	0.027	0.053	0.080	0.101
$(\Delta RL[-19])^2$	0.034	0.034	0.033	0.030
$(\Delta RL[-21])^2$	0.043	0.075	0.092	0.097
$(\Delta RL[-51])^2$	0.105	0.100	0.096	0.091
$(sp[-1])^2$	0.002	0.001	0.001	0.001

6 Conclusions

This paper establishes some important characteristics about daily Swiss interest rates. Firstly, evidence in favor of the PVM is rather stronger than in the investigation of C&S for monthly U.S. data. In accordance with theory, the spread $RL - RS$ can be regarded as stationary whereas both RL and RS are both integrated of first order, which makes $RL - RS$ a cointegrating vector. The PVM also holds as far as it claims that the spread Granger-causes the short-term interest rate without feedback. Some doubt is cast on the restriction of non-predictability of the "excess return", too weak however to allow a persuasive rejection of the theory.

Secondly, we find noteworthy conditional heteroskedasticity in the data. We show that the DGP can, to a certain degree, be approximated by a bivariate VAR-VARCH model. The variance of the residuals of the linear part of the model turns out to depend on past seasonal events in both interest rates as well as on the lagged squared spread. The influence of the corresponding series dominates, however, and the explanatory power of both parts of the VAR-VARCH model remains small.

Thirdly, the model diagnosis by simulation mimics reality at least partially. The VAR-VARCH model replicates well the behavior of the actual series, except for the frequency of outlying observations which is apparently too low. Thus, the VARCH part of the simulated model with normal errors does not succeed in explaining the excessive kurtosis of the original series and the VAR residuals.

In the light of the identified ARCH effects, the results about the linear part may deserve some re-consideration. As the linear lags become less significant on the whole by accounting for ARCH, heteroskedasticity weakens any remaining evidence against the hypothesis of non-predictability H3 but also weakens the evidence in favor of the causality hypothesis H2. In the latter case, however, heteroskedasticity does not succeed in invalidating the PVM.

Possible further research could be developed into several directions. More sophisticated economic models of the term structure could be developed and tested directly. Also, more elaborate VAR-VARCH models could be developed to capture the interest volatility. It is worth noting that seasonal influences, though important for the modelling of the mean and variance of daily and weekly interest rates, are not strong enough to justify seasonal (co)integration models. Hence, future work should attach greater weight to modeling outliers and volatility.

No attempt was made to work on refined deterministics in the system, such as structural breaks, non-linear trend curves, or effects specific to certain calendar days. Such modeling attempts were avoided deliberately as we wanted to restrict ourselves to a purely stochastic approximation to the data-generating process.

References

Akgiray V and Booth G G (1988) The stable-law model of stock returns, Journal of Business & Economic Statistics 6, 51 - 57

Bollerslev T (1986) Generalized autoregressive conditional heteroskedasticity, Journal of Econometrics 31, 307 - 327

Campbell J Y and Shiller R J (1987) Cointegration and tests of present value models, Journal of Political Economy 95, 1062 - 1088

Campbell J Y and Shiller R J (1991) Yield spreads and interest rate movements: a bird's eye view, Review of Economic Studies 58, 495 - 514

Engle R F (1982) Autoregressive conditional heteroscedasticity with estimates of the variance of United Kingdom inflation, Econometrica 50, 987 - 1007

Engle R F and Granger C W J (1987) Cointegration and error-correction: representation, estimation and testing, Econometrica 55, 251 - 276

Fama E F (1965) The behavior of stock market prices, Journal of Business 38, 34 - 105

Fama E F and Bliss R P (1987) The information in long-maturity forward rates, The American Economic Review 77, 680 - 692

Fuller W A (1976) Introduction to statistical time series, Wiley, New York

Hall A D, Anderson H M, Granger C W J (1992) A cointegration analysis of treasury bill yields, Review of Economics and Statistics LXXIV, 116 - 126

Johansen S (1988) Statistical analysis of cointegration vectors, Journal of Economic Dynamics and Control 12, 231 - 254

Johansen S (1991) Estimation and hypothesis testing of cointegration vectors in Gaussian vector autoregressive models, Econometrica 59, 1551 - 1580

Koutrouvelis I A (1980) Regression-type estimation of the parameters of stable laws, Journal of the American Statistical Association 75, 918 - 928

Kunst R M (1991) Stability conditions for a bivariate ARCH system which is cointegrated in mean, Institute for Advanced Studies, Vienna, mimeo

Kunst R M (1993) Apparently stable increments in finance data: could ARCH effects be the cause, Journal of Statistical Computation and Simulation 45, 121 - 127

Mandelbrot B (1963) The variation of certain speculative prices, Journal of Business 36, 394 - 419

Phillips P C B (1990) Time series regressions with a unit root and infinite-variance errors, Econometric Theory 6, 44 - 62

Shea G S (1992) Benchmarking the expectations hypothesis of the interest-rate term structure: an analysis of cointegration vectors, Journal of Business & Economic Statistics 10, 347 - 366

Weiss A A (1984) ARMA models with ARCH errors, Journal of Time Series Analysis 5, 129 - 143

The Expectation Hypothesis and Interest Rate Volatility on the Euromarket: Some Empirical Results[1]

By Peter Kugler[2]

Abstract: This paper estimates the predictive power of the spread for short rate changes in a regression framework allowing for ARCH-M effects, which should take into account time variation in the term premium. Monthly data for one and three months Euro interest rates covering nine currencies and the period 1979/11 - 91/2 indicate that the spread has clearly predictive power for one-months interest rates as implied by the expectations theory, but the parametric restriction of the expectations theory has to be rejected in a statistical test in most cases.

1 Introduction

There is a lot of empirical evidence showing that the expectations theory of the term structure of interest rates does not hold under the assumption of a time invariant term premium. This is well established for the USA for the short and long end of the maturity spectrum (e.g. Campbell and Shiller (1987;1991), Mankiw (1984), Mankiw and Miron (1986), Shiller (1990)) but it also holds true for the short end of the maturity spectrum for Eurointerest rates for some European currencies (Campbell and Clarida (1987), Hakkio and Leiderman (1986), Kugler (1990), Kugler and Borutta (1993)). Usually this failure of the expectations theory is attributed to time variations of the term premium[3]. The term premium is motivated by expectations errors with respect to future short rates.

Interest rates, like many other financial market prices exhibit non-linear dependence in the sense that large (small) changes are followed by large

[1]Earlier versions of this paper were presented at the Conference on Financial Market Econometrics, Mannheim, February 1992 and the Annual Congress of the European Economic Association, Dublin, August 1992. Helpful comments of participants of both meetings are gratefully acknowledged.

[2]Peter Kugler, Institut für Wirtschaftswissenschaften, Universität Wien, Hohenstaufengasse 9, A-1010 Wien, Austria.

[3]The commitment of the central bank to stabilize short-term interest rates is an alternative explanation for the empirical finding at the short end of the maturity spectrum (Mankiw and Miron (1986)). This hypothesis is supported by an analysis of Swiss and German interest rates (Kugler 1990), but it is not confirmed by the data of a couple of other countries (Kugler and Borutta 1993).

(small) changes of either sign. This empirical regularity seems to be well accounted for by the Autoregressive Conditional Heteroscedastic (ARCH) model introduced by Engle (1982) and extended by Bollerslev (1986). Thus we expect expectations errors for short rates to have a changing conditional variance, which in turn might cause time variations of the term premium. This leads us to the so called ARCH in Mean (ARCH-M) model, which was developed and successfully applied to US-treasury bills by Engle, Lilien and Robins (1987).

The primary aim of this paper consists of an empirical application of the ARCH-M model in the framework of a regression test of the expectations theory. I consider monthly data from November 1979 to February 1991 covering one and three months Eurointerest rates for nine major currencies.The remainder of this paper is organized as follows. In the second section the theoretical underpinnings and the corresponding regression model are briefly outlined. The empirical results are given in Section 3 and conclusions are given in Section 4.

2 An ARCH-M Regression Test of the Expectation Hypothesis

Consider the linearized term-structure equation which relates the N-period interest rate R_t to the one-period interest rate r_t

$$R_t = \frac{1}{N}(r_t + r^e_{t+1} + \ldots + r^e_{t+N-1}) + \theta_t \tag{1}$$

where r^e_{t+j} is the expected value of r_{t+j} given the information available at period t and θ_t is a term premium. Under rational expectations $r^e_{t+j} = E(r_{t+j} \mid I_t)$ where I_t denotes the information available at period t. This equation can be written after some arithmetic as

$$S_t = R_t - r_t = \sum_{j=1}^{N-1} \frac{N-j}{N} \Delta r^e_{t+j} + \theta_t \tag{2}$$

This equation says that the spread S_t is the sum of a weighted average of expected future short rate changes and the term premium. Replacing Δr^e_{t+j} by $\Delta r_{t+j} + \eta^j_{t+j}$ where η^j_t is the error of j-period ahead expectations formed at time t, we can rewrite (2) for N equal to 3 and get[4]:

$$\Delta r_{t+2} + 2\Delta r_{t+1} = -3\theta_t + 3(R_t - r_t) + \xi_{t+2} \tag{3a}$$

[4]This regression framework is used to test the expectations theory by Mankiw and Miron (1986), Campbell and Shiller (1991), and Kugler (1988). They assume that θ_t is constant, run a simple OLS regression and test the hypothesis that the slope coefficient is 3.

with

$$\xi_{t+2} = -(2\eta^1_{t+1} + \eta^2_{t+2}) \tag{3b}$$

or

$$\xi_{t+2} = b\varepsilon_{t+1} + \varepsilon_{t+2} \tag{3c}$$

If we impose rational expectations $E(\eta^j_{t+j} \mid I_t) = 0$ holds. Therefore η_{t+2} follows a MA(1) process, driven by the one and two period ahead forecasting errors for Δr_t. The univariate innovation of this process is denoted by ε_t. Alternatively, we could formulate a corresponding equation for the excess return of three months deposits over the sum of one month deposits. Replacing Δr_{t+j} by its definition in (3a) yields after some rearrangements

$$R_t - \frac{1}{3}(r_{t+2} + r_{t+1} + r_t) = \theta_t - \frac{1}{3}\xi_{t+2} \tag{4}$$

This equation has essentially the same error term as (3a). If we assume $\theta_t = \theta$ we may run a simple regression of the excess return on the spread and test the hypothesis that the slope coefficient is zero. This procedure yields obviously the same result as the test of a slope coefficient value of 3 in the former regression model. Of course in both models one has to account for the MA(1) error when computing the test statistic. This excess return procedure is used, among others, by Engle, Lilien and Robins (1987).

Now ε_t is likely to exhibit ARCH behaviour. Thus, we may proceed on the assumption that ε_t is $N(0, h_t)$–distributed where h_t is given by the usual ARCH - formula

$$h_t = \omega + \alpha \sum_{\tau=1}^{m} w_\tau \varepsilon^2_{t-\tau}, \qquad \text{with} \qquad w_\tau = \frac{2(m+1-\tau)}{m(m+1)} \tag{5}$$

or the GARCH - formula

$$h_t = \omega + \alpha\varepsilon^2_{t-1} + \beta h_{t-1} \tag{6}$$

If we adopt such a specification for the error term of equation (3a), our intuition and a simple asset pricing model outlined in Engle, Lilien and Robins (1987) suggest that θ_t is positively related to $\sqrt{h_{t+1}}$. Remember that h_{t+1} depends only on *lagged* information and belongs, therefore, to I_t . Thus we arrive at the following ARCH-M regression equation which is written for a time t left hand variable:

$$\Delta r_t + 2\Delta r_{t-1} = a_0 + a_1(R_{t-2} - r_{t-2}) + a_2\sqrt{h_{t-1}} + b\varepsilon_{t-1} + \varepsilon_t \tag{7}$$

where

$$\theta_{t-2} = -\frac{1}{3}(a_0 + a_2\sqrt{h_{t-1}})$$

according to the expectations theory, a_1 should be equated to 3 and a_2 should be smaller than zero.

In order to test these hypotheses, we estimate (7) subject to (5) or (6) using iterative Maximum Likelihood Methods. In particular the Bernd/Hall/Hall/Hausman algorithm along with numerical first order derivatives of the likelihood function is applied. Of course this is a limited information maximum likelihood procedure, as we proceed with a given lagged spread. It may also be worthwhile to note that our application of the ARCH-M model differs from the original work of Engle, Lilien and Robins in two respects. First, the long rate is of two period maturity in their paper. Thus, no MA(1) error structure has to be accounted for. Second, Engle, Lilien and Robins used the excess return formulation (4) of the term structure model and then tested for the significance of omitted variables like the spread using an Lagrange-multiplier-framework.

3 Empirical Results

The model outlined in the last section was estimated using monthly Euromarket data covering the period 1979/11 to 1991/2 and nine currencies. The countries, whose interest rates were analyzed, are Canada, France, Germany, Italy, Japan, Netherlands, Switzerland, UK and USA[5]. The sample period is motivated by the major change in US monetary policy in October 1979, which probably had effects on the interest rate of all currencies considered. Before turning to the estimation results for our ARCH-M model we will briefly present some results on the integration or stationarity property of the relevant series and on the performance of the "constant term premium" expectations theory. Table 1 reports the results of the Phillips-Perron unit-root test. This approach was used since we expect conditional heteroscedasticity in the interest rate series. The unit root hypothesis has clearly to be rejected for all cases irrespective of the order of autocorrelation correction adopted. Thus, we can safely conclude that the series we use in our analysis are integrated of order zero.

Next, let us turn to Table 2 which contains the results of the standard regression test (assuming a constant term premium) of the term structure. The standard errors of the OLS estimates are consistently estimated using the Hansen-White approach, which, in addition to autocorrelation, accounts

[5]The series are middle rates collected on the last working day of the week. The data were kindly supplied by BAK (Basler Arbeitsgruppe fr Konjunktur-forschung). The data source is the WEFA INTLINE Bank.

Table 1 Phillips-Perron Unit-Root Test for Changes in the Short Rate and Spread 1979/11-91/2
p: Lags in autocorrelation correction

p		3	6	9	12
Canada	Δr_t	-8.76	-8.65	-8.65	-8.65
	$R_t - r_t$	-7.41	-7.58	-7.50	-7.49
France	Δr_t	-16.56	-17.92	-19.03	-19.50
	$R_t - r_t$	-9.10	-9.31	-9.63	-9.92
Germany	Δr_t	-15.04	-14.66	-14.49	-14.35
	$R_t - r_t$	-8.57	-8.50	-8.28	-8.22
Italy	Δr_t	-15.69	-16.49	-17.55	-19.50
	$R_t - r_t$	-11.43	-11.49	-11.46	-11.47
Japan	Δr_t	-14.99	-14.81	-14.93	-15.15
	$R_t - r_t$	-7.41	-7.41	-7.38	-7.33
Netherlands	Δr_t	-14.75	-14.48	-14.52	-14.51
	$R_t - r_t$	-8.09	-7.98	-7.92	-7.84
Switzerland	Δr_t	-13.12	-13.00	-12.97	-12.97
	$R_t - r_t$	-6.80	-6.77	-6.73	-6.73
UK	Δr_t	-11.79	-11.93	-11.98	-11.99
	$R_t - r_t$	-6.92	-6.89	-6.86	-6.85
USA	Δr_t	-10.33	-10.69	-11.19	-11.29
	$R_t - r_t$	-7.66	-7.66	-7.60	-7.60

Critical values are -2.57 (10%), -2.87 (5%), -3.41 (1%).

for heteroscedasticity. The results obtained correspond to those of earlier papers (Kugler (1988), Kugler and Borutta (1991)) with slightly different samples. In five out of nine cases (Canada, France, Italy, Japan, UK) the spread has clearly highly significant predictive power for future short rate changes and the estimate of a_1 is not statistically significantly different from its theoretical value of 3. For the remaining countries, namely Germany, Netherlands, Switzerland, and USA, the results obtained are less favorable to the expectations theory.

How are these results affected by taking into account ARCH residuals and a time varying term premium? Table 3 reports the results for our corresponding ARCH-M regression model, using a linearly declining lag structure for the ARCH-mechanism. A GARCH variant of this model was also estimated, but it did not pass the residual diagnostic tests (Q-statistics for the standardized residuals $(Q-x)$ and for the squared standardized residuals (Q_{xx})) in many cases. However, as a rule, the results of the GARCH-M model are essentially equal to those reported in Table 3. The only notable exception is Italy, where the GARCH variant pointed to a much stronger mean-effect

Table 2 Predictive Power of the Spread for One-Month Interest Rate Changes 1979/11 - 91/2

$\Delta r_{t+2} + 2\Delta r_{t+1} = a_0 + a_1(R_t - r_t) + \xi_{t+2}$

	a_0	a_1	R^2
Canada	-0.37	2.64	0.18
	(-1.37)	(4.73)	
France	-1.06	3.24	0.30
	(-1.42)	(3.35)	
Germany	-0.20	2.05	0.10
	(-1.23)	(3.22)	
Italy	-0.62	3.05	0.25
	(-0.84)	(4.00)	
Japan	-0.21	2.55	0.29
	(-1.76)	(5.90)	
Netherlands	-0.23	2.01	0.08
	(-1.29)	(1.72)	
Switzerland	-0.042	0.75	0.022
	(-0.22)	(1.25)	
UK	-0.60	2.71	0.22
	(-0.33)	(5.44)	
USA	-0.28	1.21	0.029
	(-0.91)	(1.38)	

Asymptotic t-values, based on estimated Hansen (1982) standard errors, are given in brackets.

of the conditional standard deviation[6].

For all models considered we find estimates of the ARCH parameter α which are significantly different from zero. In four cases (France, Italy, Japan, USA) $\hat{\alpha}$ is even greater than one, which indicates instability of the conditional variance process. In most cases the ARCH-M parameter a_2 is significantly (at the 5% level) lower than zero, as we would expect (recall that the term premium is equal to $-\frac{1}{3}(a_0 + a_2\sqrt{h_t})$). The exceptions are UK and USA, where there seems to be no influence of the conditional standard deviation on the mean. For all countries the spread coefficient estimate $\hat{a_1}$ is highly significant and it is between 1.58 and 3.46 , but the hypothesis $\hat{a_1} = 3$ has to be rejected at conventional significance levels except for the Japanese data. Thus the qualitative implication of the expectations theory that the spread has predictive power for short rate changes is confirmed by the data but the spread moves too much to be justified by subsequent short rate changes since

[6]The estimated model is

$$\Delta r_t + 2\Delta r_{t-1} = \underset{(3.99)}{1.83} + \underset{(30.8)}{3.40}\,(R_t - r_{t-1}) - \underset{(-5.15)}{1.05}\,\sqrt{h_t} + 1.05\epsilon_{t-1}$$

$$h_t = \underset{(3.81)}{1.53} + \underset{(5.07)}{0.41\epsilon_{t-1}^2} + \underset{(5.72)}{0.46\,h_{t-1}}$$

$\hat{a}_1$ is smaller than 3 for most countries.

Table 3 ARCH-M Model and the Relationship Between One Month Rate Change and Spread 1979/11 - 91/2

$\Delta r_{t+2} + 2\Delta r_{t+1} = a_0 + a_1(R_t - r_t) + a_2\sqrt{h_t} + b\varepsilon_{t+1} + \varepsilon_{t+2}$

$\varepsilon_t \sim N(0, h_t); h_t = \omega + \alpha \sum_{\tau=1}^{4} w_\tau \varepsilon_{t-\tau}^2$

p	a_0	a_1	a_2	b	ω	α	$Q_x(12)$[2]	$Q_x(24)$	$Q_{xx}(12)$	$Q_{xx}(24)$
Canada	0.87	1.58	-0.86	0.51	0.85	0.73	9.78	15.79	3.20	9.35
	(1.85)[1]	(4.09)	(-2.57)	(5.30)	(6.11)	(3.71)				
France	-0.019	2.03	-0.43	0.46	0.45	1.71	10.19	21.39	3.59	17.63
	(-0.072)	(7.66)	(-2.55)	(5.55)	(2.16)	(10.1)				
Germany	0.71	1.86	-0.81	0.43	0.53	0.83	12.56	26.16	0.76	8.41
	(1.63)	(3.78)	(-2.04)	(3.12)	(3.91)	(3.57)				
Italy	-0.008	3.46	-0.39	0.82	2.34	1.22	13.72	20.68	4.51	9.20
	(-0.012)	(20.68)	(-1.77)	(19.47)	(4.41)	(7.02)				
Japan	-0.004	2.99	-0.31	0.41	0.095	1.33	17.11	27.67	10.34	17.27
	(-0.034)	(41.99)	(-2.29)	(3.88)	(2.58)	(6.64)				
Netherlands	0.87	1.58	-0.86	0.51	0.85	0.73	9.78	19.80	3.20	9.35
	(1.85)	(4.09)	(-2.57)	(5.30)	(6.11)	(3.71)				
Switzerland	0.76	2.21	-0.74	0.66	1.10	0.53	8.06	14.99	6.87	31.26
	(1.14)	(7.55)	(-1.65)	(9.03)	(5.70)	(3.65)				
UK	-0.044	1.86	-0.056	0.46	1.26	0.52	7.19	15.54	9.33	14.88
	(-0.061)	(4.91)	(-0.15)	(5.38)	(5.27)	(3.10)				
USA	-0.090	1.63	0.060	0.60	0.74	1.15	6.38	14.72	1.98	2.51
	(-0.28)	(5.52)	(0.27)	(7.04)	(6.38)	(6.33)				

1) Asymptotic t-values in brackets.

2) Q-statistics for residuals and squared residuals. $Q(m)$ is χ^2_{m-1} distributed under the hypothesis of nonlinear or quadratic dependence, respectively.

A comparison with Table 2 indicates that the expectations theory, in its strict quantitative sense, has to be rejected in more cases in the framework of the model allowing for a time variant term premium than in the simple constant term premium approach. This result is surprising and deserves some discussion. There are two main reasons for this finding. First, the standard errors of the a_1 estimates are clearly smaller in the ARCH-M model than in the simple OLS regression. Second, for a first group of five countries (Canada, France, Germany, Netherlands, UK) the OLS a - estimate is greater than the ARCH-M a_1 - estimate. This fact leads to OLS-estimates which are more favorable to the expectations theory. For a second group (Italy, Japan, Switzerland and USA) the estimated spread coefficient is greater in the ARCH-M framework than in the OLS model. How can we explain these results differing across countries? Of course, the correlation of the spread and the term premium is crucial for these results. For the second group of countries there seems to exist a positive correlation between the spread and the term premium. This implies a negative correlation between the right hand side variable and the error term of the constant term premium regression, which results in a negative OLS bias. According to equation (2) this situation is brought about when the spread and expected short rate changes are not negatively correlated. The same argument implies that a positive asymptotic OLS bias for a_1 is brought about by *negative* correlation of expected short rate changes and the term premium. Thus, in the first group of countries, namely Canada, France, Germany, Netherlands and UK, high interest rate volatility and low (perhaps negative) expected short rate changes occurred jointly during the time span considered.

4 Conclusion

This paper estimates the predictive power of the spread for short rate changes in a regression framework allowing for ARCH- M effects, which should take into account time variation in the term premium. Monthly data for one and three months Euro interest rates covering nine currencies and the period 1979/11 - 91/2 indicate that the spread has clearly predictive power for one-months interest rates as implied by the expectations theory. In addition ARCH-M effects are statistically significant in most cases. However, the expectations theory has to be rejected in a statistical test in most cases. More specifically, the spread moves too much compared to future short rate changes for most cases considered. This finding may be brought about by non-rational expectations or by a misspecification of the term premium in our model. The latter possibility deserves attention, as we only used a two asset framework which may result in a misspecification of the non- diversifiable risk component.

References

Bollerslev T (1986) Generalized Autoregressive Conditional Heteroskedasticity, Journal of Econometrics 31: 307-327

Campbell J Y, Clarida R H (1987) The Term Structure of Euromarket Interest Rates: An Empirical Investigation, Journal of Monetary Economics 19: 25-44

Campbell J Y, Shiller R J (1987) Cointegration and Tests of Present Value Models, Journal of Political Economy 95: 1062-1088

Campbell J Y, Shiller R J (1991) Yield Spreads and Interest Rate Movements: A Bird's Eye View, Review of Economic Studies 58:495-514

Engle R F (1982) Autoregressive Conditional Heteroscedasticity With Estimates of the Variance of UK Inflations, Econometrica 50: 987-1007

Engle R F, Lilien D M,Robins R P (1987) Estimating Time Varying Risk Premia in the Term Structure: The ARCH-M Model, Econometrica 55: 381-408

Hakkio C S, Leiderman L (1986) Intertemporal Asset Pricing and the Term Structure of Exchange Rates and Interest Rates: The Eurocurrency Market, European Economic Review 30: 325-344

Hansen L P (1982) Large Sample Properties of the Generalized Method of Moments, Econometrica 50: 1029-54

Kugler P (1988) An Empirical Note on Term Structure and Interest Rate Stabilization Policies, Quarterly Journal of Economics 53: 689-692

Kugler P (1990) The Term Structure of Euro Interest Rates and Rational Expectations, Journal of International Money and Finance 9: 234-244

Kugler P, Borutta H J (1993) An Empirical Note on Euro Market Interest Rates, Domestic Interest Rates and the Expectations Theory of the Term Structure, Empirical Economics 18: 95-101

Mankiw G N (1986) The Term Structure of Interest Rates Revisited, Brookings Papers on Economic Activity 1: 61- 110

Mankiw G N, Miron J A (1986) The Changing Behaviour of the Term Structure of Interest Rates, Quarterly Journal of Economics 51: 211-228

Phillips P C B, Perron P (1988) Testing for a Unit Root in Time Series Regression, Biometrika 75: 335-346

Shiller R J (1990) The Term Structure of Interest Rates, in: B M Friedman and F H Hahn (eds.), Handbook of Monetary Econometrics Vol 1 (North Holland): 627-722

An Investigation of the Effect of Funding on the Slope of the Yield Curve[1]

By Don M. Egginton[2] and Stephen G. Hall[3]

Abstract: Market practitioners often have a firm view that funding operation clearly affect the slope of the yield curve. The standard theory of the expectations model of the yield curve determination contradicts this view, as does much of the empirical academic literature. This paper addresses the empirical determination of the yield curve using a new, high frequency, data set and modern econometric techniques. It is argued here that evidence can be found for direct effects from the authorities funding policy on the slope of the yield curve and that this effect conforms well with practitioners views on what happens.

1 Introduction

The determination of the yield curve is of interest from a number of viewpoints. Macroeconomists and policy makers for example are interested in the yield curve because they often believe that direct influence over interest rates can only be exercised at the short term end of the spectrum while long rates have the most powerful effects on the economy (through investment, for example). Market traders and portfolio managers believe the determination of the yield curve to be a central question due to the link between yields and asset prices and the profit opportunities which may be created by a better understanding of yield curve changes. A central bank may be interested for both of these reasons, but may also be interested in the question of the behaviour of monetary aggregates, which may be affected by the slope of the yield curve. A further consideration may be the cost of servicing the national debt and whether changing the structure of the debt can reduce servicing costs.

Earlier studies in the Bank of England (most notably Taylor(1990)), have

---

[1]This work was undertaken while the authors were associated with the economics division of the Bank of England. The views expressed in this paper are those of the authors and not necessarily those of the Bank of England, the TSB or the LBS. We would like to thank an anonymous referee and Juergen Kaehler for helpful comments.

[2]Don M. Egginton, TSB Group plc., P.O. Box 33,25 Milk St., London EC2V 8LU, Great Britain.

[3]Stephen G. Hall, London Business School, Regents Park, London NW1 4SA, Great Britain.

outlined the basic theories of yield curve determination and have suggested that there is some evidence that the expectations theory of the yield curve is not a complete explanation. This paper is intended to pursue this line of empirical research further by developing a more comprehensive data set than has hitherto been used and by focusing more tightly on the specific question, 'does the composition of the stock of government bonds affect the slope of the yield curve?'

Below we will present a brief description of the various theories of yield curve determination, a more detailed exposition may be found in Melino(1988) or Shiller and McCulloch(1987).

The dominant theory for many years within the academic literature has been the expectations theory, stemming from early work by Keynes(1930), Fisher(1930), Lutz(1940) and Hicks(1946). This simply formalises the notion that, if agents are risk neutral profit maximizers with uniform expectations, a perfectly efficient market will set a long rate as a simple function of the expected future short rates so that expected profits will be equalised between holdings of either a long bond or a sequence of short bonds.

We may define the yield to maturity for a bond with n periods to maturity (R_t^n) as the solution to the following formula,

$$P_t^n = \sum_{i=t}^{t+n} \frac{C_i}{(1+R_t)^{i-t-1}} + \frac{V}{(1+R_t)^n} \tag{1}$$

where P^n is the price of the bond, C_i is the coupon paid on the bond in period i and V is the par value. This formula simply makes the yield to maturity the rate which equates the present value of the bond and its current price. So if a bond with n periods to maturity gives an overall return of $(1+R_t^n)^n$ then the expectations model would suggest that this should be equal to the expected product of short rates over the next n periods. That is,

$$(1+R_t^n)^n = (1+R_t^1)\,(1+E_t(R_{t+1}^1))\ldots(1+E_t(R_{t+n}^1)) \tag{2}$$

where $E_t(R_{t+i}^1)$ is the expectation formed at period t of the one period ahead yield in period $t+i$. If this relationship does not hold it suggests that some market participants could expect to make profits simply by moving funds between bonds of differing maturity. The consequence of this model is rather strong in that it suggests that the only factor which affects the slope of the yield curve is expectations and hence funding, or any other form of market intervention, can have no direct effect.

Another long standing model is the liquidity preference model of Hicks (1946). This may be thought of as a minor generalisation of the pure expectations model to allow for the possibility that agents are risk averse. So when an agent buys a six month bond he is uncertain of its value three months into the future while a sequence of two three month bonds would give complete capital certainty at three and six months (although the income over the whole period would then be uncertain). It is then argued that an agent will require a premium to give up the capital certainty of the three month bond in favour of holding the six month bond and thus the yield curve would be expected to slope upwards. One way to motivate this model is in terms of the term premium; if we define the holding period return to be,

$$H_t^n = \frac{P_{t+1} - P_t + C_t}{P_t} \tag{3}$$

That is the total return earned by the bond between period t and $t+1$ expressed as a rate, then we may define the term premium as,

$$T_t^n = E(H_t^n) - R_t^1 \quad . \tag{4}$$

So, the term premium is the difference between the expected gain to holding a bond with n years to maturity over the next period and the gain to holding a one period bond over that period. Under the full expectations model the term premia should be zero, whereas the liquidity preference model suggests that the term premia should be an increasing function of n. The liquidity preference model is, however, still just a generalisation of the expectations model and thus there is no scope for other factors such as funding to enter the determination of the yield curve.

The only theory which offers a real scope for the positive manipulation of the yield curve by market participants is the market segmentation (or preferred habitat) model. This model sees the market for government debt as being made up of quite separate areas of operation with little or no overlap in market operators between different areas of the market. Under this condition it is possible that profit opportunities between different sectors could go unexploited and so there would be a real scope for effects from funding and other government policies on the yield curve.

Empirical work [Kessel (1965), Shiller, Campbell and Schoenholtz (1983), Fama (1984a, 1984b), Pesando (1978, 1983), Mankiw (1986), Modigliani and Shiller (1973), Sargent (1979), Hansen and Sargent (1981), Cox et al (1981, 1985), Shiller (1981), MacDonald and Speight (1988) and Mills (1991)] has established that in its simplest form the expectations model is not completely adequate. It is generally agreed that the term premium increases with maturity for example. The notion that the market segmentation model may hold so that the outstanding amount of government bonds may actually affect the slope of the yield curve is, however, not widely accepted. Market participants often believe that the yield curve changes as they operate in the market, but academic studies have found it hard to substantiate this belief. 'Despite the fact that in a world of disparate expectations and risk aversion debt management operations ought to affect the yield curve, we could find no evidence from our studies on UK data that it has done so.' (Goodhart and Gowland(1978)). A good statement of the current academic view may be found in the conclusion of Shiller and McCulloch's(1987) survey paper 'Empirical work on the term structure has produced consensus on little more than that the rational expectations model, while containing an element of truth, can be rejected. There is no consensus on why term premia vary.'

In this study we attempt to answer this question by taking a rather different line of empirical research to that normally followed:

- First we derive a high frequency (daily) data base on the yield curve of government bonds and the outstanding stock of bonds with various periods to maturity over the period 2nd January 1979 to 21st August 1990. The use of daily data is very important as one possible explanation of the lack of firm results in previous studies is that market segmentation effects may be important in the very short run but monthly or quarterly data may obscure these effects. This data set is new to the Bank of England and we will spend some time describing both the method of its construction and the data set itself in this paper. Using very high frequency data for estimation has a number of advantages. It obviously makes estimates much more reliable in a general sense simply because of the increase in degrees of freedom, but in this case there is another very strong reason for using a very high frequency data set. If we begin, as we do, from the premise that to characterise the yield curve we need more than the simple expectations theory, then we have to accept that some of the variables which may be important to test more elaborate models are simply not available. In particular, figures of the outstanding amount of non-government bonds are very hard to obtain as are those for foreign government and non-government bonds. However, at a daily level it would be very surprising if there was a strong correlation between government bonds for which we have measures, and the other factors for which we do not. On the not unreasonable assumption that at this frequency the correlation is low (or zero) then omitting such factors from our analysis should not induce biased coefficients but simply more complex dynamics. Another factor in choosing high frequency data is to deal with the criticisms that government bonds may be affected by changes in the yield curve and so estimation results may be biased. This may be true at the quarterly level but it is less obvious to propose that bonds respond at daily frequency to yield curve changes. Hence using high frequency data simplifies issues of causality.

- The second important aspect of this study is the use of principal components to produce a direct measure of the slope of the yield curve (a technique proposed by Steeley(1989)). Thus we are able to focus directly on the question – does government funding policy affect the *slope* of the yield curve? This is important because changes in the slope of the yield curve account for only a very small part of the variation in yields so the chances of finding this effect must be much reduced.

- The final important feature concerns the time-varying nature of volatility in yield curve behaviour. This is now a widely accepted property of financial data in general. Here we adopt an estimation strategy which is specifically designed to deal with this feature, the details of which are given below.

The plan of this paper is then to begin in Section 2 by describing the data set in terms of its construction. In Section 3 we will apply a decomposition of the set of derived bond yield data using principal components to allow the estimation of a series which represents, as purely as possible, the slope of the yield curve. In Section 4 we model this estimate of the slope of the yield curve, testing for stationarity and for a time-varying covariance structure, and finally building a model which incorporates all these properties and allows a formal test of the effect of funding on the slope of the yield curve. Finally Section 5 will draw some conclusions.

2 The Data

We have two rather different data sets, the yield to maturity on government bonds and the outstanding stock of government bonds. We will describe each in turn.

2.1 The Yield Data

Data Construction

Gross prices on British Government bonds were collected for each working day between 2nd January 1979 and 21st August 1990 from "Mullens' Blues" which are now published by Warburg Securities. The yield to maturity for each bond was calculated. For those bonds with dual redemption dates which were still traded after the 21 August 1990 it was assumed that they would be redeemed at their last redemption date (this may introduce some small bias into the yield curve but it was considered better to do this than to exclude these bonds entirely). From this data set a more homogeneous set of Gilts were derived by excluding index linked, undated and conversion bonds. Partly-paid bonds were also excluded until the first coupon payment after they became fully paid. To minimise possible tax effects, any bond with a coupon rate well below the general yield was also excluded from the sample. After these exclusions 96 gilts remained of which 22 existed for the entire sample period. The longest maturity was the Exchequer 12% 2017 whilst the shortest maturity was the Treasury 9 1/2% 1980.

The estimated yields to redemption and the maturity for each bond were used to calculate a yield curve for each working day using a cubic spline function. This was achieved using a version of the Bank of England's yield curve program (see Bank of England(1990)) in which the tax rates had been constrained to be equivalent for each of the gilts. The special tax calculations which are available within the yield curve program were unnecessary as those bonds which were affected were removed from our sample.

Data Description

Having derived the spline function for the yield curve for each day over our sample (1979-1990) it is then possible to read off a consistent set of rates for any maturity band. These are the yields to maturity for an n-year bond. We have done this for maturities of 2, 4, 6, 8, 10, 12, 14, 16, 18, 20, 22 and 24 years. A maximum maturity of 24 years was chosen because this was the longest date which always allowed the existence of some actual bond beyond this horizon. The two year ahead yield is shown in Figure 1 and the spread between the 2 and 24 year yield is shown in Figure 2 (graphs of all the data are available in the Discussion paper version of this paper from the Bank of England). In very broad terms we could characterise the period from 1979 to around 1985 (observation 1500) as being one of a fairly flat yield curve, 1985 to 1987 was a period of moderate downward slope, 1987 to 1989 was one of a moderate upward slope and the period since 1989 as a fairly strong downward slope in the yield curve. Without prejudging the complex questions to be addressed later it is perhaps worth noting that this pattern accords fairly well with the expectations model. 1985 to 1987 could well be viewed as a period when expectations were looking forward to lower short term interest rates and so we would have expected a falling yield curve. 1987-1989 was a period of increasing concern about inflation rates and hence future interest rates and so we might expect the yield curve to rise and finally the most recent period would be seen as one where short term rates were above their expected long term level and so again we would expect the yield curve to be downward sloping.

2.2 The Outstanding Debt Data

Data Construction

Two sources of data were used to construct the outstanding amount of government bonds; one source for bonds without a redemption date and another for all other bonds. In the case of all bonds with an announced redemption date we obtained details of government transactions on any bonds which were outstanding over our data periods. This consists of the original quantity issued, the exact date of issue, the date and quantity of subsequent government trading in the gilt and the final redemption date (there were 725 market op-

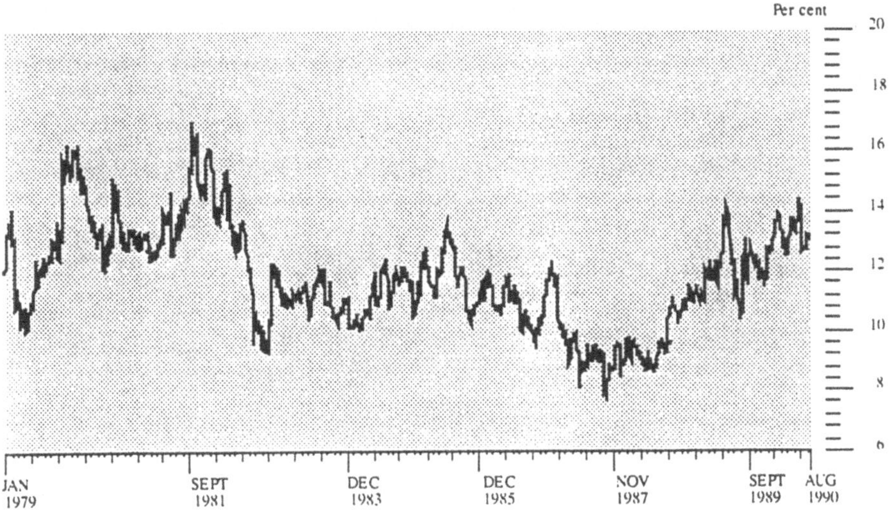

Figure 1 The Two Year Ahead Yield

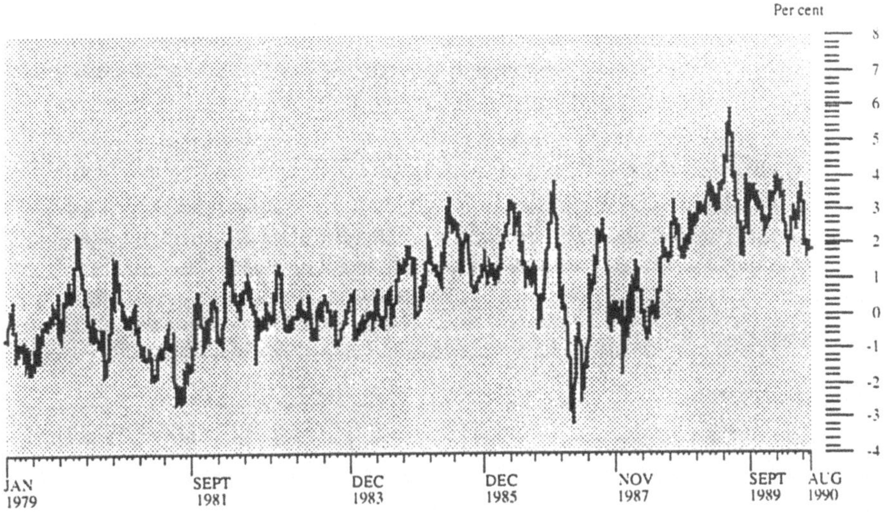

Figure 2 The Spread between 2 and 24 Year Yields

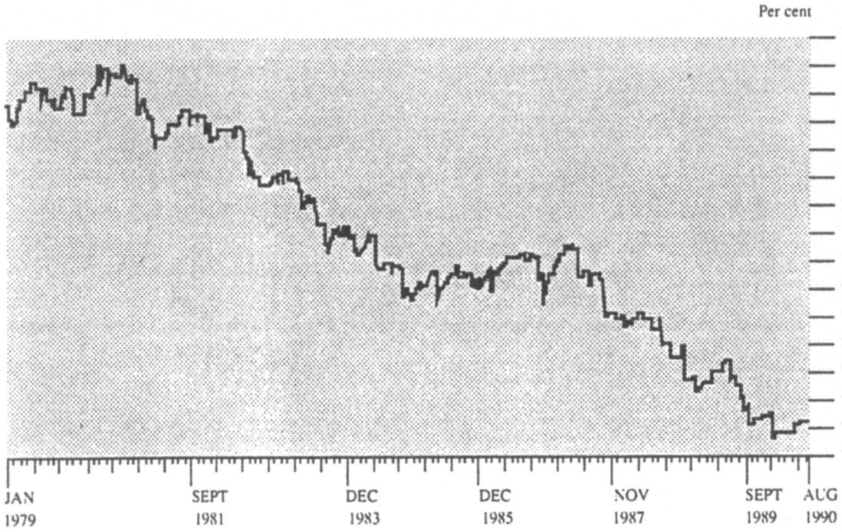

Figure 3 The Proportion of Bonds with More than 10 Years to Maturity

erations which affected the quantity of bonds over our data period). For each day of the sample period it was then possible to construct the total *face* value (not the market value) of bonds outstanding which would mature within any given period of that date. The chosen categories were bonds with less than one year to maturity, bonds with one to five years to maturity, bonds with five to ten years to maturity, bonds with ten to fifteen years to maturity and bonds with more than fifteen years to maturity. The data for irredeemable gilts were calculated in a slightly different way. In this case we had quantity data for total undated bonds on 5 July 1990 and a record of exact transactions (again amounts and dates) going back into the past. The construction of the outstanding debt series then consisted of deriving the time series from this transaction series.

Data Description

Because of its importance to the later analysis we show, in Figure 3, the data for the proportion of government bonds with a maturity over 10 years, the detailed maturity bands will not be shown here for space reasons. The most striking feature of this data is simply how different the maturity bands are from each other - the composition of debt has been varying quite markedly over the period. The stock of bonds with less than ten years to maturity has clearly been rising quite rapidly, bonds between ten and fifteen years to maturity rose during the early part of the 1980s in line with shorter term debt but the rise stopped in about 1985 and since 1988 a fairly steady reduction in debt has taken place. But perhaps the most striking feature is the behaviour of outstanding debt with more than fifteen years to maturity which has shown very marked fluctuations, rising rapidly in the 1979-1981 period then falling sharply until 1985, rising again until 1988 and finally falling dramatically until the end of the period. The undated gilts fall consistently over the period and their actual quantity is much less than that of the other bonds.

3 A Decomposition of the Yield Data

3.1 Introduction

In this section we will take the yield to maturity data and decompose it using principal components. A common practice is simply to take the spread between a short rate and a long rate as a measure of the slope of the yield curve. This practice builds a number of assumptions into the data; two actual data points are chosen, and this choice may affect the results. Also it is not clear how important this spread is in determining the yield at different maturities. Finally, it is not clear how this measure will respond to twists and changes in the shape of the yield curve. Principal components analysis circumvents having to choose just two arbitrary points and it also allows a systematic investigation of how important the slope (and other measures of the shape of the yield curve) are in determining yield levels. We could equally as well have used factor analysis as principal components as the two techniques would give identical results up to a normalisation factor. The qualitative nature of the following results in the paper would therefore have been completely unaffected.

We begin by giving a brief intuitive account of principal components, we then describe the application of this technique to our data.

3.2 Principal Components

As with many statistical techniques principal components can be derived in a number of ways depending on the motivation and framework used. One of the most common approaches is to motivate it as a way of dealing with multicollinearity. Taking an extreme assumption, if there are two variables which are perfectly collinear then obviously they cannot both be included in a regression model. Principal components will take these two variables and construct a variable which contains all the information in the two collinear variables. In the case of perfect collinearity it will need to construct only one variable which will contain all the explanatory power of the two collinear variables. In the case of less than perfect collinearity it is always possible to get the explanatory power of the original two variables with two new variables. But because principal components puts the variability of the two variables into the first principal component most of the explanatory power of the original two variables will be 'concentrated' in this one variable.

In a more formal way consider k variables $X_1 \dots X_k$ and define a linear function of these variables as

$$l_1 = a_1X_1 + a_2X_2 + \dots + a_kX_k \tag{5}$$

Now choose the a's so that the variance of l_1 is maximized subject to the condition that $\sum a_i^2 = 1$ (a normalization condition which simply prevents giving l an infinite variance by making the a's infinitely large); l_1 is then the first principal component. It will contain the largest proportion of explanatory power possible by combining all the X's together in one variable; in other words, it is the linear function of the X's which has the highest possible variance.

Now consider another linear function

$$l_2 = b_1X_1 + b_2X_2 + \dots + b_kX_k \tag{6}$$

and this time choose the b's to maximize the variance of l_2 subject to the condition that l_1 and l_2 are uncorrelated and subject to the normalization condition $\sum b_i^2 = 1$. l_2 will then be the second principal component. This procedure can be repeated up to k times, giving $l_1 \dots l_k$ mutually orthogonal variables which will be the full set of principal components. Furthermore it is possible to show that,

$$\sum var(l_i) = \sum var(X_i) \tag{7}$$

ie., the total variability of the two sets of series will be the same. However, the l_i variables are uncorrelated with each other as opposed to the X_i variables which may potentially be highly correlated.

In the case of the yield curve we have a set of time series observations of points on the yield curve but these observations will tend to be highly collinear as the whole yield curve can be expected to broadly rise and fall with the overall level of interest rates. Our interest is largely focused on questions about changes in the shape of the yield curve rather than the more straightforward question of the determination of its overall level. But an investigation of these effects is rendered extremely difficult by the collinearity between points on the yield curve. That is to say, we can explain ten year rates very well by movements in five year rates but what we are interested in is the relatively small changes which occur in the relationship between ten and five year rates. Principal components can be used in this context to isolate the different types of movement which take place in interest rates. The first principal component should capture all the movements which the term structure has in common across all maturities. We would expect this to explain most of the variation in all the rates. The higher principal components would then be associated with the various twists in the yield curve.

The number of points from the yield curve we feed into the principal component procedure will obviously affect the answer we get out. If we simply put two series in (a short maturity and a long one) then we could only derive two principal components, the first would have to be the level of interest rates while the second would have to be the slope of the yield curve. As we increase the number of series we input we can begin to allow for more complex twisting in the shape of the yield curve. Experimentation over the number of input series will allow us to judge how sensitive the results are to this choice. One small caveat to this procedure is that as we are dealing with stochastic variables (as they are taken from an estimate of the yield curve) the full unbiased properties of principal components is not applicable. The large sample however means that consistency becomes the more relevent concept.

3.3 Decomposing the Yield Curve

One of the major advantages of using principal components is that we can select a varying number of points on the yield curve and apply the technique to assess how sensitive it is to this choice. We have chosen to investigate 12 points (every two years from two to twenty four years), 6 points and three points. This means that for the first case up to 12 principal components can be generated, for the second up to six and for the third up to three. A number of features are of interest in these results; we can look at the cumulative R^2 to see how much explanatory power lies in each of the principal components. We can look to see how similar the estimate of the principal components are when different numbers of points are used and finally we can look at the 'factor loadings' which show how each component affects each point on the original yield curve.

The estimates of the second principal components from the 12 point case is presented in Figure 4, a figure of the first principal component is not presented here as it looked very similar to the level of interest rates in Figure 1. The estimates for the first two principal components from the six and three point cases were virtually identical to these. The third principal component varied markedly between the three cases as one might expect. The first principal component very clearly reproduces the pattern of the level of interest rates and it is interesting to note that the principal component is actually smoother than any of the yield observations. So by extracting an overall measure of the level of yield rates we are able to filter out much of the noise which seems to affect individual bonds. The second principal component is also very similar in overall movement to the spread between short and long rates so it is clearly capturing the basic notion of the 'slope' of the yield curve although again it is clearly filtering out some of the noise associated with choosing individual points. We will not attempt any firm interpretation of the third component except to say that it seems to represent a tendency for a 'kink' to develop in the yield curve around 16 years maturity (this is

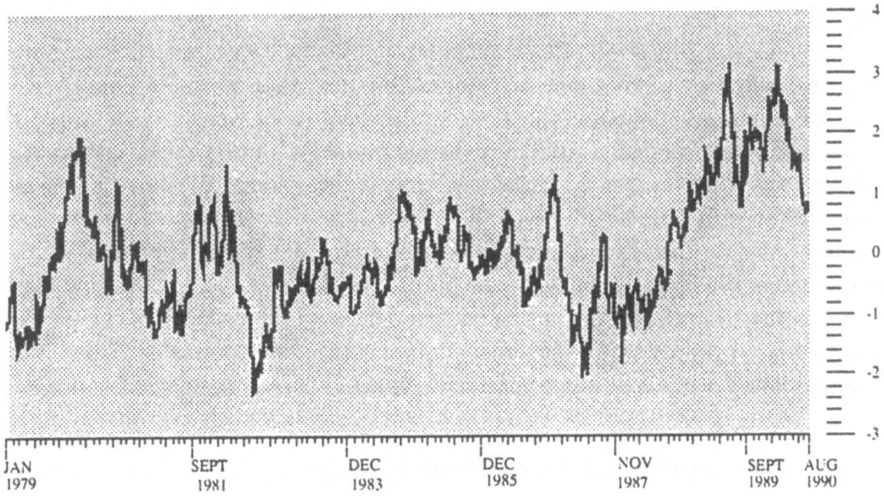

Figure 4 The Second Principal Component

shown in the factor loading tables below).

Now consider the cumulative R^2 for the three cases, Table 1 shows this.

Table 1 Cumulative R^2 for 12, 6 and 3 Points from the Yield Curve

principal component No.	12 point case	6 point case	3 point case
1	0.85	0.86	0.88
2	0.90	0.93	0.97
3	0.93	0.95	1.0
4	0.94	0.97	-
5	0.96	0.99	-
6	0.97	1.0	-

The interpretation of this table is that the general level of interest rates (the first principal component) explains over 85% of the variation in all individual rates. In the 12 component case the second principal component (the 'slope') explains about another 5% while in the 6 component case it explains about another 7% and in the three component case it explains a further 9% of the variation in the individual rates. Higher components each explain only a very small part (1 or 2%) of interest rate variation. This justifies focusing primarily on the two first components as the major explanation of yield rate variation.

Table 2 gives the factor loadings for the 12 component case. The factor loading show the correlation between each principal component and the original data.

Table 2 The Factor Loadings for the 12 Component Case

Maturity of Bond(years)	first comp.	second comp.	third comp.	fourth comp.
2	0.82	0.49	0.03	0.16
4	0.91	0.31	0.01	-0.09
6	0.95	0.11	0.04	-0.02
8	0.93	0.06	0.17	0.10
10	0.97	-0.07	0.12	-0.02
12	0.96	0.05	0.03	-0.13
14	0.93	0.01	-0.13	-0.28
16	0.88	-0.04	-0.44	0.06
18	0.92	-0.18	-0.14	0.19
20	0.91	-0.24	0.29	0.00
22	0.92	-0.29	0.03	0.03
24	0.95	-0.17	-0.03	0.02

The factor loadings on the first principal component are interesting in that they are all around 0.9 except for the loading on the very short term yield. The interpretation of this is that for bonds of four years maturity and beyond a change in the general level of interest rates is reflected fairly uniformly amongst all rates but the short term rate does not follow this simple relationship. Instead the second component loading factor shows that there is a high loading on the 2 year maturity yield relative to all the other maturities, so a large part of changes in the slope are reflected purely at the shortest end of the yield curve. Another point to note about the loading factors for the second component is the sign pattern – the effect of maturities of two to eight years is clearly positive, the loadings for maturities from 10 to 16 years are very small and for practical purposes zero while the loadings for maturities from eighteen to twenty-four years are clearly negative. This means that, for example, when the yield curve tilts so as to slope downwards more steeply we expect short term rates to rise a lot, there will be a general increase in rates up to eight years in maturity, we expect no change in rates between ten and sixteen years maturity and we expect rates beyond eighteen years to fall. In other words *the yield curve generally tends to pivot around a point in the ten to sixteen year maturity band.* The higher principal components loading factors do not seem to be of great interest. The set of factors for the third component seems to indicate the presence of an occasional kink which develops around sixteen years maturity and most of the loadings for the fourth component are small. We do not report the loadings for the other components.

To confirm the strong link between the spread between short, two year, rates and long term, 24 year, yields and the second principal component (SPC) we performed the following simple regression of the second principal component on the spread.

$$\begin{array}{lcccl} \text{spread} & = & \underset{(70.5)}{0.711} & + & \underset{(139.9)}{1.410}\ \text{SPC} \qquad R^2 = 0.87 \end{array} \tag{8}$$

where spread = two year rate minus 24 year rate.

This indeed confirms that there is a very close correlation between the second component and the spread.

The next section will investigate the time series properties of the second principal component and it will introduce the data on bonds into a formal model of slope determination.

4 Testing for the Effects of Changing the Debt Structure

4.1 Introduction

This section will analyze the second principal component (SPC) derived above as a measure of the slope of the yield curve, by examining the univariate properties of the series and investigating the effects of changing government debt on the slope of the yield curve. Much recent work on financial data has stressed the presence of time varying volatility, as periods of high volatility seem to come in waves with intermittent periods of relative calm. It is important to recognise this property of financial data when carrying out formal tests as to ignore these effects when they are in fact present can completely invalidate the test procedure. We will proceed by first estimating a univariate model of the SPC and then estimating a model which allows for this changing volatility. This second model will demonstrate the important presence of time varying volatility and so the formal tests of the effects of bonds on the SPC can then be conducted within this framework. The specific model we use to deal with the time varying volatility is a member of the class of ARCH models. The next section will outline these models before giving the formal tests.

4.2 ARCH Models

Engle, Lilien and Robins (1987) suggest an extension of Engle's (1982) ARCH model whereby the conditional first moment of a time series itself becomes a function of the conditional second moment, which follows an ARCH process:

$$y_t = \alpha' x_t + \delta h_t^2 + \epsilon_t \tag{9}$$

$$\epsilon_t | \Omega_{t-1} \sim N(0, h_t^2) \tag{10}$$

$$h_t^2 = \gamma_0 + \sum_{i=1}^{n} \gamma_i \epsilon_{t-i}^2 \tag{11}$$

where x_t is a vector of conditioning variables, weakly exogenous for all parameters of (9) and (11). Engle Lilien and Robins(1987) term this kind of model ARCH-in-mean or ARCH-M. Note the h_t^2 is the conditional variance of ϵ_t formed at period t based on the set (σ-field) of all information, Ω, up to period $t-1$.

A further extension of the ARCH formulation, which imposes smoother behaviour on the conditional second moments, has been suggested by Bollerslev (1986). In Bollerslev's GARCH formulation, the conditional second moments are functions of their own lagged values as well as the squares of the lagged forecast errors. Bollerslev did not consider the GARCH-M extension although this is a fairly obvious one which was subsequently used in Bollerslev, Engle and Wooldridge(1988). Thus, for example, the GARCH-M (n, p) formulation of the above model would consist of (9), (10) and

$$h_t^2 = A_0 + \sum_{i=1}^{n} A_i \epsilon_{t-i}^2 + \sum_{i=1}^{p} B_i h_{t-i}^2 \tag{12}$$

where the B_i and A_i are coefficients.

Stacking all of the parameters of the system into a single vector

$$\mu = (\alpha, \delta, A_0, A_1, \ldots, A_n, B_1, \ldots, B_p) \tag{13}$$

and applying Schweppe's (1965) prediction error decomposition form of the likelihood function, the log-likelihood for a sample of T observations (conditional on initial values) is proportional to

$$L(\mu) = \sum_{t=1}^{T} (-\log |h_t^2| - \epsilon_t^2 / h_t^2) \tag{14}$$

(where we have assumed normality of the forecast errors).

Although the analytic derivatives of (14) can be computed (see Engle, Lilien and Robins, 1987) variable-metric algorithms which employ numerical derivatives are simpler to use and easily allow changes in specification. Under suitable regularity conditions (Crowder, 1976), maximization of (14) will yield maximum likelihood estimates with the usual properties.

4.3 Testing for the Effects of Bonds on the Slope of the Yield Curve

We begin by presenting conventional tests of stationarity for the first and second principal components. These tests are of considerable relevance to the policy question as, in this context, we can associate the notion of stationarity with that of persistence. If a shock hits the level of the yield curve and the level is a non-stationary process we will, in general, expect that shock to persist indefinitely (that is to say the level will be permanently higher). If the level of the yield curve is a stationary process then the shock will be expected to persist for only a short time and the overall effect will be reversed. We may asses this question of non-stationarity in a number of ways, by using formal tests for stationarity (the augmented Dickey-Fuller test will be used) as well as informal descriptive statistics (the autocorrelation and partial autocorrelation function).

For completeness we begin by considering the first principal component.

Table 3 Time Series Properties of the First Principal Component

Augmented Dickey-Fuller test = -1.67					
1	2	3	4	5	6
Autocorrelation function.					
0.998	0.997	0.995	0.993	0.991	0.989
Partial Autocorrelation function.					
0.998	-0.060	0.018	-0.038	-0.004	-0.004
Autocorrelation function for Squares.					
0.995	0.990	0.984	0.978	0.972	0.965
Partial Autocorrelation function for Squares.					
0.995	-0.084	-0.006	-0.053	0.004	-0.067

Note: The Dickey-Fuller test was augmented by four lags, this was sufficient to whiten the error process, although the broad conclusions were not affected by using other dynamic structures.

The Dickey-Fuller test does not allow us to reject the hypothesis that the first principal component is non-stationary and all the evidence from the descriptive statistics strongly supports the view that the first principal component (the level of rates) is non-stationary and shocks would be expected to persist.

We now turn to the second principal component.

In this case we can decisively reject the hypothesis of non-stationarity in the Dickey-Fuller test and the descriptive statistics give a clear picture (bearing in mind that this is daily data) of a stationary process. So we can reach a

Table 4 Time Series Properties of the Second Principal Component

Augmented Dickey-Fuller test = -4.0					
1	2	3	4	5	6
Autocorrelation function.					
0.991	0.981	0.970	0.960	0.949	0.939
Partial Autocorrelation function.					
0.991	-0.035	-0.022	-0.015	-0.005	-0.008
Autocorrelation function for Squares.					
0.973	0.944	0.916	0.890	0.865	0.838
Partial Autocorrelation function for Squares.					
0.973	-0.040	-0.006	0.022	-0.001	-0.053

fairly robust conclusion that the second principal component is a stationary time series. This means that over time any shock which hits the slope of the yield curve will tend to reverse itself. In view of the work presented below it is also worth noting that the partial autocorrelation function for the SPC suggests a fairly low order autoregressive process would be adequate as a time series representation of this series. Also the partial autocorrelation function for the squares of the series suggests that a low order GARCH model of the variance process would also probably be appropriate.

Before testing directly for the effects of bonds on the SPC it is important to establish a reasonably adequate time series model, so next we report in Table 5 a univariate model of the SPC estimated both by OLS and as a GARCH-M(1,1) model over the full daily data set. The regressions reported in the following tables use the second principal component using three points from the yield curve. The conclusions are unaltered if the second principal component using twelve points from the yield curve are used.

In terms of serial correlation both models are reasonably satisfactory, the GARCH-M model does not have a highly significant role for the effect of volatility on the SPC, so it seems that periods of high volatility do not systematically change the shape of the yield curve. There are, however, very strong signs of ARCH effects in the residuals as shown by the highly significant coefficients A_1 and B_1. This suggests that proper tests of the market segmentation hypothesis should be conducted within a GARCH-M framework.

Having established this basic framework we can proceed to introduce a variable to capture the effects of changes in the composition of government bonds. Given the profile of bonds outlined a sensible split seems to exist between bonds with less than ten years to maturity, which have generally been trending upwards, and bonds of over ten years to maturity which have been falling in recent years. So as the simplest measure of bond movements

Table 5 A Time Series Model of the SPC

	OLS	GARCH-M
constant	0.00063 (0.1)	-0.004 (1.6)
SPC_{t-1}	0.846 (46.6)	0.671 (82.9)
SPC_{t-2}	0.093 (3.9)	0.186 (8.4)
SPC_{t-3}	0.033 (1.8)	0.097 (4.9)
δ	-	-0.765 (1.7)
A_0	-	0.002 (3.6)
A_1	-	0.185 (3.5)
B_1	-	0.454 (71.5)
COR1	-0.0001	0.056
COR2	-0.0007	0.042
COR4	-0.0077	0.035
COR8	0.0161	0.046

(*t* statistics in parenthesis, CORi is the i-th point on the correlogram of the residuals, demonstrating their serial correlation properties)

we use the proportion of bonds with a maturity of over ten years (PB10), this proportion is shown in Figure 3. This variable may then be entered into the model outlined above as a test of the market segmentation hypothesis, and under the expectations hypothesis it should have a zero coefficient. According to the market segmentation hypothesis we would expect an increase in this proportion to lower the price of long bonds thus raising their yield. As SPC is essentially the short yield minus the long yield, we would expect the SPC to go down giving a negative relationship between PB10 and SPC.

We report in Table 6 both the OLS and the GARCH-M results, even though the OLS assumptions are violated, mainly for completeness and to demonstrate that the test conclusions are not reliant solely on using this sophisticated estimation methodology. In both estimation exercises PB10 is negative and significant. The conclusion is therefore that the composition of governemt debt does affect the shape of the yield curve. This suggests that the expectations hypothesis cannot be seen as a complete explanation of yield curve behaviour as this would give no role for such effects. It also provides evidence in favour of the market segmentation view of the determination of the yield. Changing the composition of government debt does appear to change the shape of the yield curve.

4.4 Some Subsidiary Hypotheses

We will now consider a number of alternative hypotheses which might reconcile our findings with the simple expectations theory. The first of these is

Table 6 Testing the Market Segmentation Hypothesis

	OLS	GARCH-M
constant	0.09 (2.8)	0.164 (9.5)
SPC_{t-1}	0.84 (46.4)	0.80 (34.9)
SPC_{t-2}	0.09 (3.9)	0.15 (14.0)
SPC_{t-3}	0.03 (1.7)	-0.03 (1.8)
PB10	-0.19 (2.9)	-0.377 (10.7)
δ	-	-0.59 (0.74)
A_0	-	0.0003 (2.9)
A_1	-	0.03 (2.8)
B_1	-	0.46 (64.9)
COR1	0.0000	0.03
COR2	-0.0003	0.04
COR4	-0.0053	0.07
COR8	0.0178	0.07

(t statistics in parenthesis, CORi is the i-th point on the correlogram of the residuals)

the idea, put forward by Goodhart and Gowland(1978), that the expectations theory may hold in the longer run but that market segmentation may exist for a short period. The results presented above suggest a long run effect from bonds but in fairness this is presupposed by our choice of functional form. That is, by using the level of the percentage of government bonds we impose the result that, if this variable is significant, it will have a long run effect. We can test this by including both the change in the variable as well as the level, so if there is only a temporary effect, only the difference term will be significant but if the effect is permanent the level term will also be significant.

The result in Table 7 is quite striking in that the inclusion of the change in bonds is clearly insignificant in both the GARCH and OLS estimates. The conclusion then seems to be quite strong, the effect of bonds on the yield curve is permanent rather than transitory. Of course we must make a slight caveat to this, as with daily data it is very hard to be confident about very long run properties. It is always possible that the effect of bonds fades out over a period of years, and we cannot rule out this possibility. But the evidence we report points strongly towards a long lasting effect.

Another area in which our choice of model structure has been arbitrary has been the specific way we have proxied bonds. The choice of using the proportion of bonds with over 10 years to maturity was made partly on account of how bond stocks had changed over the sample and partly with a view to other principal component evidence which suggested that the yield curve had tended to pivot at a maturity around ten to sixteen years. But this is clearly something that warrants further investigation. So we produced

Table 7 Testing for Dynamic Effects

	OLS	GARCH-M
constant	0.089 (2.8)	0.151 (8.7)
SPC_{t-1}	0.843 (46.4)	0.702 (90.9)
SPC_{t-2}	0.092 (3.9)	0.188 (8.8)
SPC_{t-3}	0.031 (1.7)	0.052 (4.6)
PB10	-0.185 (2.8)	-0.322 (9.2)
ΔPB10	-0.293 (0.1)	0.026 (0.02)
δ	-	-0.812 (1.4)
A_0	-	0.002 (3.0)
A_1	-	0.162 (2.9)
B_1	-	0.453 (64.8)
COR1	0.0000	0.054
COR2	-0.0003	0.042
COR4	-0.0053	0.051
COR8	0.0178	0.059

(t statistics in parenthesis, CORi is the i-th point on the correlogram of the residuals)

a disaggregation of our single bond measure by defining the proportion of bonds with maturities between five and ten years (PB5-10), the proportion of bonds with between ten and fifteen years to maturity (PB10-15) and the proportion of bonds with over fifteen years to maturity (PB15+). Table 8 gives the results of investigating this disaggregation.

In both sets of estimates the proportion of bonds between 5 and ten years is insignificant, in the OLS results it is negative while the GARCH results actually find an insignificant but positive effect. This suggests that the choice of a break between under and over ten years to maturity was a correct one. The category between ten and fifteen years to maturity has a more powerful and significant effect than the very long maturity group, although both are correctly signed. This may reflect the fact that the change in this group has been numerically much larger than in any of the others. On the whole we would judge that these results conform well with our initial aggregation choices.

5 Conclusions

In this paper we have addressed the very specific question of whether the composition of government debt affects the slope of the yield curve. We have generated a high quality data set consisting of something over three thousand daily observations of both the yield curve, and the stock and composition of government debt. Using principal component analysis we have derived a

Table 8 Testing More Disaggregated Bond Measures

	OLS	GARCH-M
constant	0.240 (1.6)	0.197 (2.5)
SPC_{t-1}	0.842 (46.3)	0.811 (94.1)
SPC_{t-2}	0.092 (3.9)	0.128 (5.2)
SPC_{t-3}	0.030 (1.65)	-0.023 (1.1)
PB5-10	-0.168 (0.8)	0.140 (1.2)
PB10-15	-0.554 (2.1)	-0.818 (5.5)
PB15+	-0.345 (1.6)	-0.283 (2.6)
δ	-	-0.453 (0.9)
A_0	-	0.001 (2.6)
A_1	-	0.062 (2.6)
B_1	-	0.465 (57.4)
COR1	0.0000	0.04
COR2	-0.0002	0.05
COR4	-0.0047	0.08
COR8	0.0182	0.08

(t statistics in parenthesis, CORi is the i-th point on the correlogram of the residuals)

measure of the slope of the yield curve which is thus separately identified from the general level of interest rates. We then model this slope measure using both standard OLS techniques and more appropriate GARCH estimation.

We find very significant effects from the composition of government debt on the slope of the yield curve. The effect seems to be long lasting, and it is not simply a transitory effect while expectations adjust over some short period. There seems to be a division at around ten years to maturity, so that increasing the stock of bonds over this maturity tends to make the yield curve slope upwards while increasing bonds with a maturity of less than ten years tends to make it slope downwards.

Given our estimated model we can work backwards through the principal components to calculate the expected effect of a change in debt composition on the shape of the yield curve. Let us ask the question, *what would be the effect of raising the proportion of debt with more than ten years to maturity by ten percentage points (eg from 40% to 50%)*? The impact effect would be an increase in the long rate relative to the short rate by around 0.05 (eg from 1% to 1.05%) on the actual day of the effect. This would then be expected to grow over time as the market adjusted to produce a long run effect of almost 0.7 (eg from 1% to 1.7%).

These findings refute the simple expectations model of the yield curve in favour of a richer model which would undoubtedly fall within the general area covered by the market segmentation model. These results open up the possibility of policy makers actively manipulating the yield curve, something which is not possible if the expectations model holds in its simple form.

References

Bank of England (1990) A New Yield Curve Model, Bank of England Quarterly Bulletin 30, 84-85

Bollerslev T (1986) Generalized Autoregressive Conditional Heteroscedasticity, Journal of Econometrics 31, 307-327

Bollerslev T, Engle R F and Wooldridge J M (1988) A Capital Asset Pricing Model with Time-Varying Covariances, Journal of Political Economy 96, 116-131

Cox J C, Ingersoll J E and Ross S A (1981) A Reexamination of Traditional Hypotheses about the Term Structure of Interest Rates, Journal of Finance 36, 769-799

Cox J C, Ingersoll J E and Ross S A (1985) A Theory of the Term Structure of Interest Rates, Econometrica 53, 363-384

Crowder M J (1976) Maximum Likelihood Estimation for Dependent Observations, Journal of the Royal Statistical Society, Series B, 38, 45-53

Engle R F (1982) Autoregressive Conditional Heteroscedasticity with Estimates of the Variance of United Kingdom Inflation, Econometrica 50, 987-1007

Engle R F, Lilien D M and Robins R P (1987) Estimating Time Varying Risk Premia in the Term Structure: The ARCH-M Model, Econometrica 55, 391-407

Fama E F (1976) Forward Rates as Predictors of Future Spot Rates, Journal of Financial Economics 3, 361-377

Fama E F (1984a) The Information in the Term Structure of Interest Rates, Journal of Financial Economics 13, 509-528

Fama E F (1984b) Term Premiums in Bond Returns, Journal of Financial Economics 13, 529-546

Fisher I (1930) Theory of Interest, New York, Macmillan

Goodhart C A E and Gowland D H (1978) The Relationship between Long Dated Gilt Yields and Other Variables, Bulletin of Economic Research 30, 59-69

Hall S G (1990) A Note on the Estimation of GARCH-M Models Using the Kalman Filter, Bank of England Discussion Paper No. 32

Hansen L P and Sargent T J (1981) Exact Linear Rational Expectations Models: Specification and Estimation, Staff Report, Federal Reserve Bank of Minneapolis

Hicks J R (1946) Value and Capital, Oxford University Press

Keynes J M (1930) A Treatise on Money, New York, Macmillan

Kessel R A (1965) The Cyclical Behaviour of the Term Structure of Interest Rates, NBER, New York

Lutz F (1940) The Structure of Interest Rates, Quarterly Journal of Economics 55, 36-63

MacDonald R and Speight A E H (1988) The Term Structure of Interest Rates in the UK, Bulletin of Economic Research 40, 287-299

Mankiw N G (1986) The Term Structure of Interest Rates Revisited, Brookings Papers on Economic Activity I, 61-110

Melino A (1988) The Term Structure of Interest Rates: Evidence and Theory, Journal of Economic Surveys 2, 335-361

Mills T C (1991) The Term Structure of UK Interest Rates: Tests of the Expectations Hypothesis, Applied Economics 23, 599-606

Modigliani F and Shiller R J (1973) Inflation, Rational Expectations and the Term Structure of Interest Rates, Economica 40, 12-43

Pesando J E (1978) On the Efficiency of the Bond Market: Some Canadian Evidence, Journal of Political Economy 86, 1057-1076

Pesando J E (1983) On Expectations, Term Premiums and the Volatility of Long Term Interest Rates, Journal of Monetary Economics 12, 467-474

Sargent T J (1979) A Note on the Estimation of the Rational Expectations Model of the Term Structure, Journal of Monetary Economics 5, 133-143

Schweppe F (1965) Evaluation of Likelihood Functions for Gaussian Signals, IEEE Transactions on Information 11, 61-70

Shiller R J (1981) Alternative Tests of Rational Expectations Models; the Case of the Term Structure, Journal of Econometrics 16, 17-87

Shiller R J, Campbell J Y and Schoenholtz K L (1983) Forward Rates and Future Policy: Interpreting the Term Structure of Interest Rates, Brookings Papers on Economic Activity, 173-217

Shiller R J and McCulloch J H (1987) The Term Structure of Interest Rates, in B M Friedman and F H Hahn (eds.), Handbook of Monetary Economics 1, Amsterdam, North-Holland, 627-722

Steeley J M (1989) The Effects of the Big Bang on the Gilt-Edged Market: Term Structure Movements and Market Efficiency, PhD thesis submitted to Warwick University

Taylor M P (1990) The Term Structure of Interest Rates: Theory and Evidence, Bank of England, mimeo

Stylized Facts, Realignments and Investment Strategies in the EMS[1]

By Kees G. Koedijk[2], Philip A. Stork and Casper G. de Vries[3]

Abstract: A discrete time approximation is derived from the standard continuous time target zone model which possesses all the key features of the continuous time version. The model allows for explicit incorporation of the stylized facts on intra-EMS exchange rate behaviour, as well as the mean-reversion effect. Realignment probabilities of the exchange rates versus the Deutsch mark of the six initial members of the EMS are calculated. The strength of the method is evaluated by comparing the realignment probabilities to the opinion of the news media around realignment days. As a second means of evaluation a number of investment strategies is run which use the realignment probabilities as a decision rule to get in and out of the EMS money market. It is shown that the investment strategy relying on the model with conditional heteroskedasticity renders higher excess returns than the model with a constant variance assumption.

1 Introduction

In recent years researcher's and practitioner's interest in target zones for exchange rates has risen dramatically. The interest in policy circles for target zones seems to be motivated by the perceived negative effects of large swings in the value of the dollar during the early eighties. As a consequence monetary authorities have attempted in the second part of the decade to limit the rate of exchange rate variation. Efforts to limit variation in dollar exchange rates have led to the Louvre and Plaza arrangements to keep the exchange rates within target zones. Among the European countries, efforts to limit exchange rate variations resulted in establishing the European Monetary Systems (EMS) in March 1979. The aim of this paper is to contribute

---

[1]Previous drafts of this paper have been presented in seminars at Erasmus Universiteit Rotterdam, Rijksuniversiteit Limburg, K.U. Leuven, CORE, the ESEM in Cambridge 1991, CentER, ZEW, and the Kniedag. We are grateful for comments and suggestions by Roel Beetsma, Harris Dellas, Paul De Grauwe, Frank de Jong, Theo Nijman, Peter Schotman, Peter Vlaar and an anonymous referee. Work by the second author was supported through grant 450-229-006 by the Dutch NWO and the third author benefitted from grant IUAP26 of the Belgian Government.

[2]Kees G. Koedijk, Rijksuniversiteit Limburg, Department of Finance, P.O. Box 616, 6200 MD Maastricht, The Netherlands

[3]Philip A. Stork and Casper G. de Vries, Tinbergen Institute, Oostmaaslaan 950-952, 3063 DM Rotterdam, The Netherlands

to the analysis of this specific target zone both theoretically and empirically.

At the level of economic theory two important developments have taken place which allow us to rigorously analyze the EMS. The description of exchange rate behaviour within a target zone and during a speculative attack has been formalized over the past few years. For the analysis of the EMS the former literature is relevant as long as exchange rates stay within the EMS band, while the latter literature applies during times of realignments. The contribution of our paper is best motivated by a review of the available literature on the two subjects.

The seminal theoretical work on speculative attacks is Flood and Garber (1984) which employs the monetary model of exchange rates. With a one way biased money growth rate they derive the timing of the speculative attack and the switch from a fixed to a flexible rate regime. Blanco and Garber (1986) implement this empirically to calculate one-period-ahead probabilities on devaluation of the Mexican Peso. To do this the reduced form exchange rate equation is appended with a first-order autoregressive stochastic process cum normal innovations, the structural parameters are estimated, and the probabilities on devaluation are calculated from the solution of the stochastic difference equation.

Inherent to the use of purely structural exchange rate models is, at the very best, the dependence on monthly, or quarterly data. This is in contrast to the situation in the EMS where events often occur very suddenly and may lead to a realignment in a matter of weeks or days. Henceforth, structural models seem less equipped to capture all short-term movements of intra-EMS exchange rates. Moreover, due to arbitrage simple martingale models dominate structural models on high frequency data. In the currently available literature on speculative attacks, relatively little attention has been given to this specification of the stochastic process. Moreover, incorporation of all well-known stylized facts in the innovation variables is lacking.

Blanco and Garber (1986) already warn against interpreting the results of their autoregressive model as a test of its empirical validity, because first "a considerable amount of effort needs to be invested in improving the specification of the different functional forms of the model and the estimation procedures". On the other hand, for modelling high-frequency financial data, martingale cum GARCH type specifications have proven to be quite successful, e.g. Baillie and McMahon (1989). This process induces fat tails and by definition incorporates the clustering of volatility phenomenon. Obstfeld (1987) provides a theoretical argument as to why, within the class of monetary cum peso models, heteroskedasticity arises in a natural way. Obstfeld shows that this stems from the regime switches in the money supply process. Within the setup of the EMS, if an exchange rate approaches the boundary of the band this triggers official intervention and thereby affects the random nature of the money supply process, causing a change in the volatility.

The other strand of the literature on target zones starts from the observation that due to the forward looking nature of rational expectations models the presence of a band exerts an influence on the current movements of exchange rates. By adopting the continuous time framework, assuming normal innovations on the fundamentals and a band from which the exchange rate cannot escape, Krugman (1992) shows that exchange rates follow a regulated Brownian motion. This produces the elegant S-shape behaviour of exchange rates. The basic model can be extended to incorporate the effects of discrete interventions (Flood and Garber, 1992), or to allow for the possibility of a realignment (Krugman and Rotemberg, 1992). This analysis of realignments nicely combines the theory on speculative attacks with the theory on target zones.

While the target zone literature provides an intuitive account of the influence of the band, empirical support is still weak. Meese and Rose (1990) test (nonparametrically) for the presence of the nonlinear terms introduced by the regulated Brownian motion but fail to turn up evidence in favour of these terms. The S-shaped behaviour of the exchange rate within a band is the key element implied by the basic target zone model. Regarding this "bending with the band", little evidence has been found either, see e.g. Flood et al. (1991). More disturbing is that Smith and Spencer (1992) show that empirical models of target zones are not very successful in reproducing the most important stylized facts of exchange rate returns.

In the next section we derive a discrete time target zone model which possesses the features exhibited by the continuous time model, i.e. a forward looking solution under rational expectations, zero arbitrage opportunities, inducing an S-shape behaviour of the exchange rate when the band is fully credible. In addition, the model also allows for explicit incorporation of the stylized facts, such as ARCH, as well as the mean-reversion effect. One of the main advantages of such a discrete time specification over a continuous time target zone model is the ease with which these separate building blocks are included and analyzed. For an alternative discrete time target zone model, we refer to Pesaran and Samiei (1992).

In the third section we first investigate the empirical value of the model. The model is estimated for six bilateral EMS rates relative to the DM. Our specification allows us to test for the presence of the S-shape effect and the volatility effect separately. Simple prediction formulae are derived to compute one-week-ahead realignment probabilities for all six rates. To further evaluate the model we have constructed several different investment strategies which exploit the realignment predictions. These predictions are generated by constant and conditional variance models. The returns based on the latter models dominate the returns based on the former models.

2 Theory

First, it is shown that the standard continuous time target zone model can be well approximated by a linear discrete time model which preserves all the essential features. Next, the mean-reversion effect and the stylized facts are incorporated in a straightforward manner.

For a survey of the target zone literature we refer to Bertola (1993) or Svensson (1992). For an in-depth illustration of the target zone model, see Svensson (1991). Starting point in this paper is the continuous time model as presented in Krugman (1992). The reduced form monetary model of the logarithmic exchange rate $s(t)$ reads

$$s(t) = f(t) + \Psi E[ds(t)]dt, \qquad 0 < \Psi < 1, \tag{1}$$

where the fundamental $f(t)$ follows a standard Brownian motion, i.e.

$$df(t) = dz(t), \tag{2}$$

and where z is a Wiener process. Under a free float the solution to eq. (1) is

$$s(t) = f(t). \tag{3}$$

Through the integral representation of eqs. (2) and (3), the 'linearized discrete time' analogue of eq. (3) is easily seen to be

$$s(t+1) = s(t) + \varepsilon(t+1), \tag{4}$$

where $\varepsilon(t)$ are i.i.d. standard normal variates. Thus $s(t)$ follows a discrete time symmetric random walk with standard normal innovations. It is well-known that this simple model of high frequency exchange rate returns fails on two accounts: it does not adequately capture the fat tail property and discards the dependency in the conditional second moments. This can be remedied by giving $\varepsilon(t)$ a GARCH structure. Note that this extension does not affect the martingale nature of eq. (4), and is therefore consistent with the no arbitrage condition. But endowing $\varepsilon(t)$ in eq. (4) with a GARCH structure does not permit a straightforward return to the continuous time framework of eq. (3).

Suppose now that $f(t)$ is regulated at the symmetric upper and lower boundaries $\overline{f} = -\underline{f} > 0$ through infinitesimal interventions. Application of Ito's lemma to eq. (1) then yields a second order stochastic differential equation which can be solved as follows

$$\begin{aligned} s(f(t)) &= f(t) - \tau \sinh(\lambda f(t)), \\ &\quad \text{where} \quad \tau = 1/[\lambda \cosh(\lambda \overline{f})] \quad \text{and} \quad \lambda = \sqrt{(2/\Psi)}. \end{aligned} \tag{5}$$

As a result of the regulation, both $\{s(t)\}$ and $\{f(t)\}$ become stationary mean reverting processes. The unconditional distribution of $f(t)$, moreover, can be shown to be uniform on $[\underline{f}, \overline{f}]$. And the unconditional density of $s(t)$ can be found by a transformation of variable using the inverse of (5). Due to the typical S-shaped behaviour of $s(t)$ its density is U-shaped, i.e. bimodal with more mass towards the boundaries of the band. The smooth approach of $s(t)$ towards the boundaries stems from the forward looking nature of eq. (1) which implies that future interventions affect the current spot rate.

Conditional upon information up to time t eq. (5) may be approximated by a Taylor expansion around the central rate, i.e. where $s(t) = f(t) = 0$. The Taylor expansion yields

$$s(f(t)) = f(t) - \tau[\lambda\, f(t) + \frac{\lambda^3}{3!} f(t)^3 + \frac{\lambda^5}{5!} f(t)^5 + \ldots]\,. \tag{6}$$

From (6) the linearized solution is immediate:

$$s(f(t)) = (1 - \tau\lambda)\, f(t). \tag{7}$$

Note that $0 < \tau\lambda < 1$ for $\overline{f}$ and Ψ finite, and hence $0 < 1 - \tau\lambda < 1$. Comparing the free float solution (3) with the linearized target zone solution (7), we see that $s(t)$ as a function of $f(t)$ is rotated towards the x-axis. This is the S-effect in linearized format. Throughout the band, $s(t)$ moves less elastically with respect to the fundamentals than the free float solution due to the rationally anticipated future interventions. Pesaran and Shamiei (1992) explicitly solve a special discrete time model and show $s(t)$ as a convexoconcavo function of $f(t)$ around the central parity to which (7) is a first order approximation.

Next, Ito's lemma is used to obtain a discrete time approximation:

$$\begin{aligned} s(f(t+\Delta t)) &= s(t) + \left[1 - \tau\lambda - \tau\frac{\lambda^3}{2}\, f(t)^2 - \ldots\right] \Delta z \\ &\quad + \frac{1}{2}\left[-\tau\lambda^3\, f(t) - \ldots\right] \Delta t. \end{aligned}$$

Because we lack a good model of the fundamentals, the empirical analysis will gain robustness if one can sidestep specifying the fundamentals. Thus we seek the analogue of eq. (4) instead of eq. (3). Note that from (6) we have

$$f(t) = \frac{1}{1-\tau\lambda}\, s(t) + \frac{\tau}{1-\tau\lambda} \left[\frac{\lambda^3}{3!}\, f(t)^3 + \ldots\right].$$

Substitute this latter expression into the previous expression and obtain the following approximation

$$s(t+1) \simeq \left[1 - \frac{\tau\lambda^3}{2\,(1-\tau\lambda)}\right] s(t) + [1-\tau\lambda]\,\varepsilon(t+1), \tag{8}$$

where $\varepsilon(t+1) = \Delta z$ is a truncated standard normal innovation. The truncation occurs at the edges of the band, thereby implying a build up of probability mass at the edges (consistent with the continuous time model). Conditional upon information at time t, the size of the approximation error is of order $O(\overline{f}^2)$. Iterating eq. (8) forward instead of using eq. (5) may of course increase the size of the error. But for our purpose of calculating the one step ahead devaluation probabilities this need not overly concern us as these are conditional probabilities.

Let $\beta = 1 - \frac{\tau\lambda^3}{2\,(1-\tau\lambda)}$ and rescale $[1-\tau\lambda]\,\varepsilon(t+1)$, so that eq. (8) can be rewritten as

$$s(t+1) = \beta\, s(t) + \varepsilon(t+1). \tag{9}$$

Considering that under a free float $\tau = 0$ and hence $\beta = 1$, we assume $\frac{\tau\lambda^3}{2\,(1-\tau\lambda)}$ is small and positive. This notion is also supported by the estimated values of parameter δ in Table 2 in the next section, according to which β satisfies $0.90 < \beta < 1.00$. Hence, the exchange rate in eq. (9) follows a stationary AR(1) process.

Given that any model is an approximation to reality, we now show that model (9) displays the essential features of (5). Assume for simplicity that the $\varepsilon(t)$ of eq. (9) are i.i.d. uniform on $[\overline{f}, \underline{f}]$. It is then easy to show that the unconditional distribution of $s(t)$ has bounded support $[\underline{f}/(1-\beta), \overline{f}/(1-\beta)]$, as is required if the band on $s(t)$ is to be fully credible. Evidently $s(t)$ is a stationary and mean reverting process. Most importantly, eq. (9) generates an S-shaped behaviour, in the sense that $s(t+1)$ as a function of $s(t)$ is rotated towards the x-axis, c.f. the free float solution (4). Moreover, $s(t)$ approaches the boundaries in a smooth manner.

One of the main advantages of the discrete time model over the continuous time model is the ease with which the stylized facts of exchange rate returns can be incorporated. Fat tails and clustering of volatility in the exchange rate innovations can be modelled by endowing $\{\varepsilon(t)\}$ in eq. (9) with an ARCH structure:

$$\varepsilon(t) = X(t)\, H(t) \tag{10}$$

$$H^2(t) = \omega + \gamma\,\varepsilon(t-1)^2, \quad \omega > 0,\ 0 < \gamma < 1,$$

and $X(t)$ is uniformly distributed on [-1, 1].

The model (9) - (10) as it stands, still lacks one essential aspect of a target zone like the EMS. The band on $s(t)$ is fully credible. Given the number of realignments that have occured and given the current divergence between the real rates within the EMS, this assumption is not tenable. To remedy this problem we drop the assumption that the $X(t)$ in (10) are uniform and hence that the $\varepsilon(t)$ have bounded support. Instead we assume that the $X(t)$ in (10) are standard normal variates, rendering the well known ARCH(1) model originally formulated by Engle (1982). Hence with positive probability, $s(t)$ will cross the upper or lower boundary, but nevertheless the mean reverting property is retained if $\beta < 1$. This new tack also produces the desired fat tail property in the unconditional distribution of $\varepsilon(t)$, see e.g. Koedijk et al. (1990) for evidence on this for the EMS countries. The model in equations (9) and (10) retains the mean reversion property of the original Krugman model, unaffected by the discrete time approach. With regard to the conditional variance however, there is a distinct difference between the original model and the one in (9) - (10). In the original model, the changing conditional variance is an inherent property and depends on the previous level of the fundamental. In the model (9) - (10) on the other hand, the changing conditional variance is added as an extra property which models a stylized fact of exchange rate behaviour. An illustration of how to incorporate realignments in a target zone model is given by Bertola and Caballero (1992) or Koedijk, Stork and de Vries (1993).

We are now in a position to formulate the model which is to be estimated. We replace the central rate, which was placed at 0, with a more general central parity $c(t)$, which is used to standardize $s(t)$. Moreover, the boundaries of the target zone are usually stated in terms of $s(t)$ and not of $f(t)$. Let b and u denote the lower and upper boundaries of the standardized $s(t)$. Thus b and u determine the fluctuation margins of $s(t)$ around $c(t)$. Note that in case of a realignment $c(t)$ changes, but that b and u do not change if the band width remains the same. For estimation and testing purposes we write the autoregressive parameter as follows $\beta = 1 - \delta$, $0 < \delta < 1$. To allow for the possibility of a one way drift in the fundamentals we also introduce one extra parameter α. If $\alpha \neq 0$, while $\delta = 0$, then the model in (9) - (10) becomes a super- or submartingale. Because the GARCH(1,1) scheme with an autoregressive part in the variance function is often found to dominate the ARCH specification, we employ the GARCH(1,1) scheme with parameters ω, ϑ and ζ. If $\alpha = \delta = \gamma = \zeta = 0$ then $s(t)$ follows a random walk. The model to be estimated reads

$$s(t+1) = s(t) + \mu(t+1), \tag{11}$$

$$\mu(t+1) = \alpha - \delta(s(t) - c(t)) + \varepsilon(t+1), \tag{12}$$

$$\varepsilon(t+1) = x(t+1)\, h(t+1), \tag{13}$$

$$h(t+1)^2 = \omega + \gamma\, \varepsilon(t)^2 + \zeta\, h(t)^2, \tag{14}$$

and the $x(t)$ are i.i.d. standard normal innovations. Note that this specification allows one to test for the S-shape induced mean-reversion effect (that is whether or not δ is positive) separately from the volatility clustering effect. This is the main advantage of the discrete time approach. In the currently existing continuous time specifications, the detection of the S-effect is marred by the clustering effect. In the present set-up, fat-tail and the clustering effects are separately captured by γ and ζ, while α signifies a drift.

The estimated model is assessed by traditional specification tests. In addition, however, we subject the model to a prediction test. Assume that a realignment occurs whenever $s(t)$ moves outside its fluctuation margins. From eqs. (11)-(14) the one step ahead probability on this event is easily calculated. The probability of a realignment at $t+1$ given information up to and including time t is: $1 - P\{b < s(t+1) < u\}$. From eqs. (11)-(14) we find

$$\begin{aligned} P\{b < s(t+1) < u\} \quad = \quad & P\left\{\frac{b - \alpha - (1-\delta)\, s(t) - \delta c(t)}{h(t+1)}\right. \\ & < x(t+1) < \\ & \left.\frac{u - \alpha - (1-\delta)\, s(t) - \delta c(t)}{h(t+1)}\right\}, \end{aligned} \tag{15}$$

and where

$$h(t+1) = [\omega + \gamma\, (s(t) - (1-\delta)\, s(t-1) - \delta c(t-1) - \alpha)^2 + \zeta\, h(t)^2]^{\frac{1}{2}}. \tag{16}$$

In case of the ARCH(1) model, where $\zeta = 0$, equations (15) and (16) together with the probability law on $x(t+1)$ directly yield the one step ahead realignment probability. In case of the GARCH(1,1) model when $\zeta > 0$, eq. (16) is iterated recursively in time to produce $h(t+1)$. In the next section the model is confronted with empirical reality.

3 Empirical Results

3.1 Data Description

Weekly quotations of exchange rates and Euro interest rates are taken from Datastream, covering the period March 1979 - September 1990, i.e. 602 observations in total. All quotations are middle rates, the average of bid and ask rates. Germany is taken as the benchmark country and all exchange rates are expressed as the number of German marks per unit of foreign currency.

Countries included in the analysis are Belgium, Denmark, France, Germany, Ireland, Italy and The Netherlands. For Belgium 7-day Euro interest rates are available only from January 1981 onward and for Denmark only from June 1985 onward, amounting to 507 and 274 observations respectively. We prefer Euro currency interest rates to domestic ones as they are not subject to capital controls, more homogeneous and available for shorter maturities. The log differences of exchange rates display the usual features like fat tails, non-constant variance and some skewness which is due to the strength of the DM.

3.2 Estimation Results

In order to estimate the parameters of the variance equations (11)-(14), we used the common maximum likelihood procedure available in the software package GAUSS. The results are depicted in Table 1, with t-ratio's between brackets.

Table 1 Parameter estimates of the GARCH(1,1) model

	Belgium	Denmark	France	Holland	Ireland	Italy
α	-1.05E-6	-3.21E-7	-2.17E-7	0.00E-7	-3.53E-7	-5.34E-7
	(-4.15)	(-2.08)	(-2.71)	(0.15)	(-2.49)	(-2.44)
δ	7.68E-2	1.41E-2	6.76E-2	9.69E-2	1.77E-2	0.51E-2
	(4.29)	(2.12)	(8.32)	(4.84)	(1.01)	(0.55)
ω	1.51E-7	6.26E-6	4.90E-6	8.69E-8	5.60E-6	9.14E-6
	(1.72)	(5.98)	(6.85)	(2.06)	(5.06)	(5.84)
γ	0.19	0.51	3.61	0.24	0.95	0.30
	(5.78)	(5.67)	(8.35)	(4.75)	(7.06)	(3.68)
ζ	0.83	0.28	0.00	0.79	0.27	0.49
	(37.65)	(4.23)	(0.20)	(22.80)	(4.34)	(6.78)

The sum of the parameters γ and ζ is less than 1 for Denmark and Italy and exceeds 1 for the other four countries, implying an infinite variance. This phenomenon is quite common in empirical studies on financial data (Koedijk et al., 1990, and Hols and De Vries, 1991). In general one finds that intra-EMS rates are more heavily tailed than rates of EMS currencies versus the US dollar. The reason is that the latter rates are more or less on a free float, while the intra-EMS rates are restricted in their movements except at times of realignment when large changes occur, see Koedijk et al. (1990). For France the point estimate for γ seems implausibly high, which has to be investigated in future research.

Hard empirical support for the tendencies of intra-EMS exchange rates to revert to the central parity rate is relatively scarce, although Rose and

Svensson (1991) and Svensson (1991b) find some evidence on its existence. The model in eqs. (11) - (14) allows for an explicit representation of the mean-reversion phenomenon through $\delta > 0$.

Before interpreting the results for δ some caveats have to be taken into account. First, it can be shown that exchange rate $s(t)$ is non-stationary for most currencies over the sample, while on the other hand the EMS exchange rates in deviation from the central parity are stationary over time, e.g. Kofman, de Vaal and de Vries (1993) or Nieuwland (1993, pp. 149-152).

Second, to test the null hypothesis $\delta = 0$ against $\delta > 0$ one may not use the simple critical values in the case of i.i.d. errors. Hence, the t-ratio's have to be interpreted cautiously. The results for parameter δ show that for Belgium, France and Holland the mean-reversion parameter is significantly different from zero and positive as was predicted. The mean-reversion parameter for Denmark is positive but not very significant. For Ireland and Italy, however, no evidence of mean-reversion was found.

As was indicated in the theoretical section, we subjected the model to a prediction test by calculating the one-period-ahead realignment probabilities. These probabilities are compared with news around the realignment dates. To further evaluate the model we constructed five different investment strategies, two of which use conditional variance models to make ex-ante decisions on whether or not to take a long position in weak EMS currencies. Both issues are dealt with in the next subsections.

3.3 Realignment and Rumours

Between the inception of the EMS in March 1979 and September 1990 (the period under consideration), 13 realignments have occurred. All currencies, except for the Dutch guilder, were devalued against the German mark between 6 and 8 times. A second noteworthy fact is that between January 1987 and September 1990 there has been only one realignment. Estimates of an adjusted model and realignment probabilities, until September 1992, i.e. covering some of the recent turmoil in the EMS, can be found in Koedijk, Stork and de Vries (1993).

The estimates of the GARCH with mean-reversion model are employed to compute one-period-ahead realignment probabilities. These probabilities are recorded in a convenient way in Figures 1 through 6 below. For all figures the format is as follows: the horizontal axis measures time in weeks and the vertical axis the one-step-ahead realignment probability in percentage points. The dashed bars with dates printed alongside in a vertical format indicate the date the respective currency was devaluated against the German mark. The other bars denote the one-step-ahead realignment probabilities.

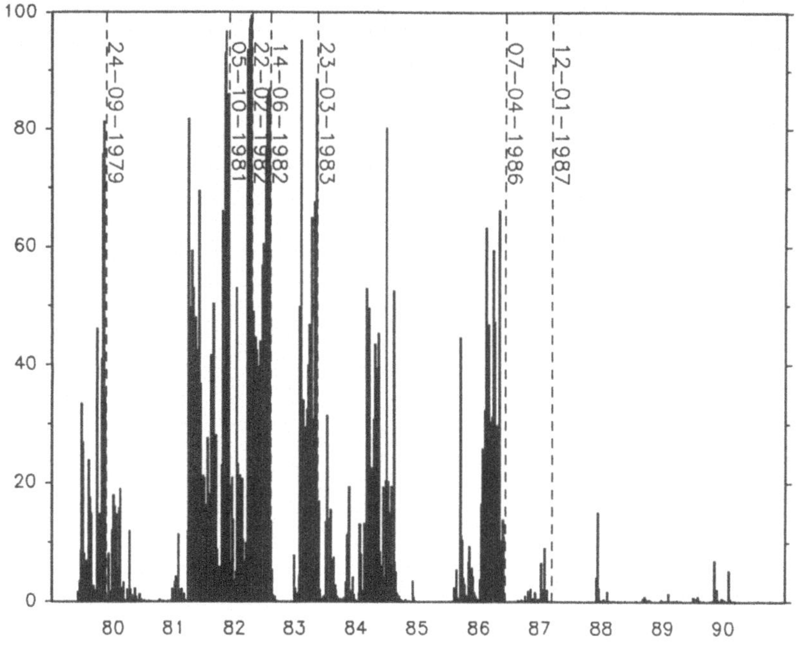

Figure 1 Belgium

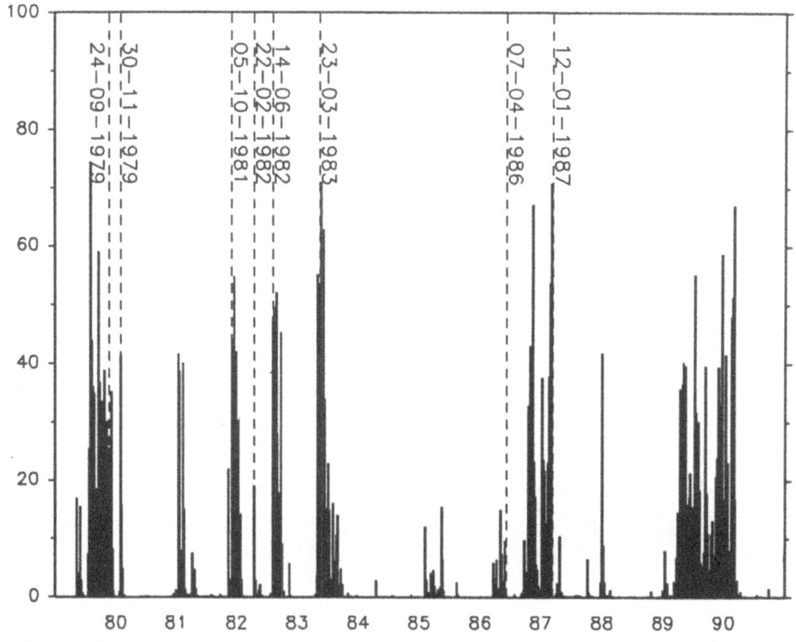

Figure 2 Denmark

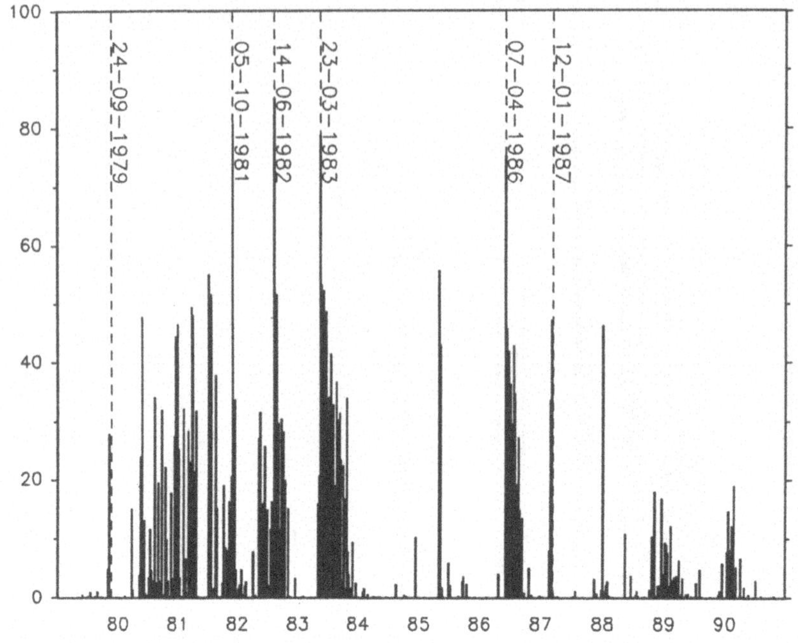

Figure 3 France

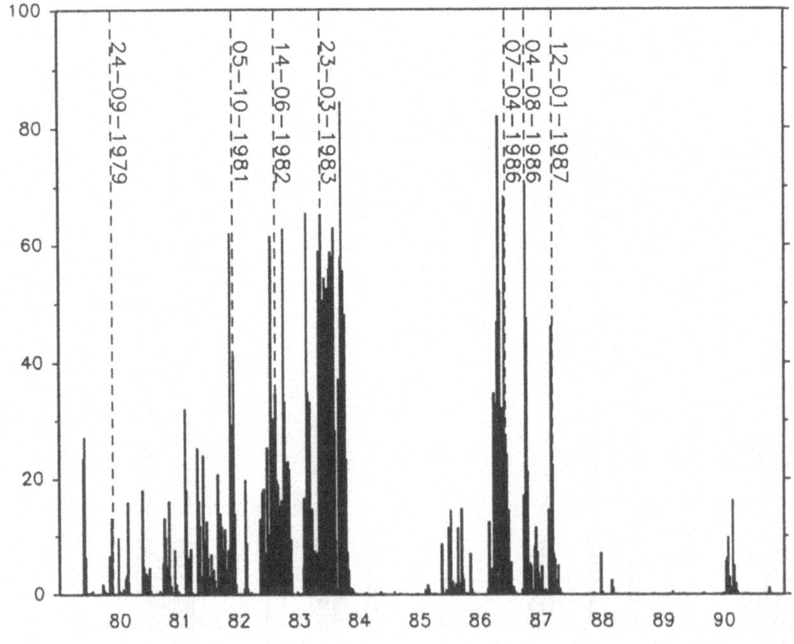

Figure 4 Ireland

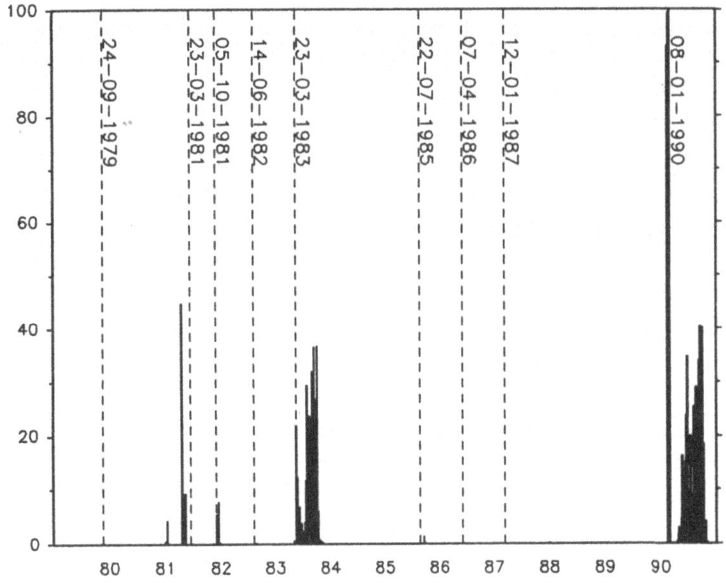

Figure 5 Italy

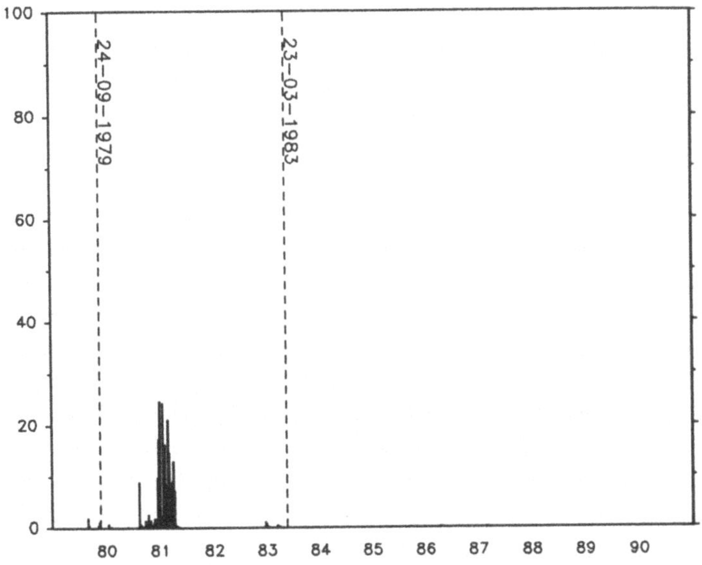

Figure 6 The Netherlands

The general impression that emerges from Figures 1 to 6 is that realignment probabilities are most prominent between 1979 and 1987. After the devaluation in 1987, realignment probabilities were reduced. During those years the notion that the EMS was gaining credibility was prevalent. The current upheaval in the EMS clearly contradicts this fictitious stability. The figures are now assessed in more detail by comparing the signals given by the figures with abstracts from the Financial Times around the realignment dates[4]. Nearly all the realignments which were anticipated by the Financial Times were also foreseen by the rising probabilities in the figures. Importantly, there is a number of realignments which come as a complete surprise to the news media, but for which the figures do provide an early warning sign.

Belgium is the first country we discuss in detail, see Figure 1. The first thing to note is that prior to seven out of the eight realignments the one step ahead probabilities are quite high. These periods of increased tension seem to come in surging waves during which the probabilities jump up and down. From the figure it is apparent that it provides early warning signs of possible realignments. Another aspect which manifests itself rather nicely is that immediately after a realignment the probabilites decrease substantially. This indicates that in general the realignment sufficed to take away the tensions between the Belgian franc and the German mark.

Three realignments deserve more discussion. The first one is the realignment of 22 February 1982. This realignment seems to come out of the blue: there is little indication from the one-step ahead probabilities that a realignment was imminent. The only comforting fact with respect to this realignment is that it was also reported in the newsmedia as a complete surprise. The Financial Times of 22-02-1982 reports: *"EMS members unite against Belgium's 12% realignment proposal and by the fact that it had appeared to encourage Denmark to lodge a request for a 7 percent devaluation of the krone. The Danish move was considered opportunistic ... and not justified by any undue strains on the currency within the EMS"*. Public discussion about a devaluation of the Franc started early 1981 to remedy the poor economic performance of Belgium. It was strongly opposed by the central bank on the grounds that it would trigger a new round of wage and price indexing. The revaluation of the German mark at the end of 1981 seemed to take away some of the tension and supported the belief in the public that the central bank view was dominant. With the government imposed devaluation of February 1982, the government sought to provide a shock signal to break the inflation spiral. The government's view proved to be right, no indexation requests followed. But the devaluation also signalled the end of the no devaluation policy rule. This triggered a period of prolonged uncertainty in the exchange market: which explains why the realignment probabilities remained

[4]Complete transcripts of the relevant Financial Times abstracts are available from the second author upon request.

high until the second realignment in 1982.

The third and final realignment we focus on is the realignment of 23-03-1983. The realignment probabilities clearly show that the realignment was long forecasted by our model. The fact that this realignment was anticipated in the market is corroborated by the Financial Times. This newspaper reports on 23-03-1983: *"This was the most widely anticipated of all seven EMS realignments"*.

The realignment probabilities for the Danish krone are reported in Figure 2. The Danish currency has been hit by eight realignments in the past twelve years. Of these eight realignments, five were preceded by higher than normal realignment probabilities. The other three realignments came to a large extent as a surprise. The realignment at 29-11-1979 is a special one because at this date the Danish krone was the only currency which was devalued. The realignment of February 1982 is also special in this sense, as only the Belgian franc and the Danish krone were devalued. From the figures the impression arises that multiple realignments are better predicted than single ones.

Comparing the figures with the abstracts from the Financial Times it turns out that the first realignment on 24-09-1979 was anticipated. The Times reports: *"Speculative selling of the Belgian franc and the Danish krone has forced both currencies very close to the lower end of the 2.25% fluctuation band"* and *"once again fears of currency unrest are overshadowing international bond markets"*. The second realignment of 29-11-1979 came largely unexpected, which is illustrated by the Financial Times: *"The EMS was subject of some discussion last week ... the renewed strength of the Danish krone makes it unlikely that the Scandinavian currency will be devalued again at the forthcoming review of the EMS"* and *"the surprise devaluation of the Danish krone"*. As for the Belgium franc the realignment on 23-03-1983 was widely anticipated by both the newsmedia and the probabilities. The probability results for the realignment on 12-01-1987 are especially successful. As early as two month prior to this realignment, probabilities start rising, providing warning signals of an impending realignment.

Figure 3 contains the realignment probabilities for France. The French franc has been devaluated six times against the German mark. Except for the devaluation in 1986, realignment probabilities rose drastically before every realignment. Especially noteworthy are the results for the two realignments when there was a major devaluation of the French franc, 14-06-1982 and 23-03-1983: both these realignments were correctly anticipated by rising probabilities several weeks prior to the actual realignment.

Figure 4 contains the results for Ireland. The case of Ireland seems quite convincing. In total there have been seven realignments where the Irish punt was included, six of which were preceded by relatively high probabilities. Only the first realignment of 24-09-1979 was not anticipated. The fact that probabilities sometimes built up fast suggests that using daily instead of weekly data might produce even better results.

Figure 5 contains the results for Italy. For Italy we used the actual fluctuation margin of 6% until the devaluation in January 1990, when it switched to a 2.25% margin. Consequently, this wide fluctuation band is responsible for the consistently low realignment probability estimate[5]. This is due to the fact that the lira hardly ever came close to its 6% boundary and in practice did not even exceed its fictive 2.25% margin very frequently (see also Ungerer et al., 1990). Also, realignments sizes often were in the same order of magnitude as the size of the margin.

An interesting period concerns the end of 1989 when for all currencies, except for the Italian lira and Dutch guilder, probabilities rose and built up until on January 5 1990 when the Italian lira was devalued. The Financial Times indicates that the realignment around that time was expected: *"The Italian lira fell to a record low against the D-mark yesterday amid heightened speculation about a possible realignment of currencies in the EMS"*, but that in the meantime it was regarded not unlikely that several other currencies would be realigned as well. This is confirmed by the sustained periods of tension in some of the other figures.

Figure 6 contains the results for the Netherlands. The results reported in this figure show that the Dutch guilder has been under stress only once, i.e. around December 1980. The Dutch guilder/German mark exchange rate was realigned only twice. The fact that the probabilities did not even jump once in the last ten years is in line with the fact that the monetary policy of the Netherlands has been linked very closely to that of Germany, and with the fact that a lot of effort has been put in keeping the guilder close to the central rate.

3.4 An Evaluation of Speculative Strategies

Another way of examining the results presented in Figures 1 to 6 is by means of a horse-race: comparing the excess returns that could have been earned by pursuing different investment strategies. Our evaluation consists of comparing five strategies. With strategy A we assume that an investor borrows a certain amount of German marks for one week and invests the borrowed amount over the same period in either one of the following currencies: the Belgian franc, the Danish kroner, the French franc, the Italian lira and the Dutch guilder, after which the positions are closed. The total return on each strategy is the sum of two components, the interest differential and the change in the bilateral exchange rate. The a priori known interest differential is positive and adds to the return on the investment. As the weak currencies are expected to depreciate and devaluate over time, the second component which represents

[5]Realignment probabilities for Italy using (0.75 * 6.00) 4.50% and 2.25% are available from the authors upon request. When these fictive margins are used, probabilities in general rise significantly prior to realignment dates.

the open position in the weak currency is likely to be negative, especially at the time of a devaluation.

The other strategies, marked B to E, introduce an ex-ante decision rule for investment. With these strategies the investor abstains from investing if the one-step-ahead probabilities are above a pre-determined subjective threshold. The main results are quite independent of the precise threshold level, and for this application a threshold level of 40% was chosen. We assume the investor refrains from investment until the probabilities on a realignment have come down and have remained below the threshold for two consecutive weeks.

The difference between strategies B, C, D and E are as follows: strategy B gives the excess returns if we use the one-step ahead realignment probabilities using a constant variance model, i.e. h_t is held fixed and equal to the unconditional variance. Strategy C denotes the excess returns if we use the GARCH(1,1) model to decide on the investment in the weaker EMS currencies. Hence, the difference between strategies B and C represents the advantage of using the realignment probabilities from the GARCH(1,1) model over those from the constant variance model. Strategy B and C differ from strategy D and E in the sense that for the first two we only take into account the realignment probabilities for each exchange rate separately, whereas with strategies D and E the realignment probabilities of the other currencies are taken into account as well. This is done to capture the multicurrency aspect of the EMS arrangement. So with strategies D and E the investor closes his long position in a specific weak-EMS currency not only if the realignment probability of that currency rises above the threshold level, but also if the realingment probability of any of the other weak EMS currencies rises above the threshold level. The intuitive idea behind this multiple currency procedure for strategy D and E is that if, say, a realignment is triggered by the position of the Belgian franc, this increases the probability that the French franc, the Danish kroner and the Italian lira will be devalued as well.

Before turning to a discussion of the results, it is important to stress that the returns made on investment B to E do not necessarily need to be superior to the return on investment A. If all agents are risk neutral and if markets are efficient, then one would expect all strategies to yield the same mean return. The reason is that if a devaluation is anticipated by the markets, then the interest differential will rise to compensate for the increased risk. Thus, indirectly we test for market efficiency and/or risk aversion. If one of the investment strategies C or E dominates strategy A, then predicting realignments on basis of the volatility clustering effect dominates the signal provided through a rising interest differential. Alternatively, if the returns B-E do not differ significantly from strategy A, a risk averse investor may still prefer B-E as these involve less volatility.

In addition to presenting full period results, we also present results for the same strategies for the sub-period April 1983 to September 1990. We

Table 2 Annual Excess Returns: March 1979 - September 1990

	A	B	C	D	E
Belgium	1.76	0.89	1.47	0.58	1.22
	1.24	0.65	1.09	0.40	0.90
	507	431	444	355	367
Denmark	3.07	2.34	2.20	2.83	2.75
	2.79	1.96	1.95	2.28	2.35
	274	242	253	217	227
France	1.73	1.79	1.77	2.87	3.20
	1.82	1.83	1.83	4.04	4.78
	602	558	560	433	444
Italy	3.76	3.93	3.80	4.53	4.85
	3.03	3.17	3.10	4.02	4.42
	602	598	592	433	444
Netherlands	0.29	0.41	0.29	0.66	0.48
	0.55	0.80	0.55	1.20	0.95
	602	600	602	433	444

separately calculated excess returns on the strategies for the second part of the EMS period, 1983-1990, as it is often argued that the functioning of the EMS has significantly changed after March 1983, so that the two sub-periods need to be distinguished. The first period, 1979-1983, is characterized by strong deflationary policies in all countries involved in the EMS, with different timing and different speeds, and by frequent realignments of the EMS parities. From March 1983 onwards, the system appears to have stabilized with realignments becoming scarcer and smaller in magnitude. The results of the different strategies are reported in Tables 2 and 3. The format of Tables 2 and 3 is as follows: under each heading A to E we report the mean annual excess return on exploiting the specific strategy, the t-ratios (also known as Sharpe-ratios) and the number of weeks the investor has a long position in the weaker EMS currencies. The excess returns on investing in the Irish punt are not reported since no Euro-interest rate data on Irish punt deposits are available.

Several noteworthy results are apparent from Table 2. First, note that the mean excess returns on investing in the Danish krone, the French franc and the Italian lira are significantly different form zero, see under the heading A. For the Belgium franc and the Dutch guilder no profitable opportunities appear to exist with this strategy. Second, we should keep in mind that fair comparison of the various strategies is hindered by not knowing the risk attitude or utility function of the investor. Here we will use the so-called "Sharpe-ratios", e.g. Sharpe and Alexander (1990, pp. 750-752). A strategy offering a higher Sharpe-ratio can in general be considered to be superior to one with a lower Sharpe-ratio. Hence, if we compare the results for strat-

Table 3 Annual Excess Returns: April 1983 - September 1990

	A	B	C	D	E
Belgium	2.89	2.07	2.12	2.41	2.34
	3.11	2.19	2.25	2.43	2.54
	389	359	371	303	317
Denmark	3.07	2.34	2.20	2.83	2.75
	2.79	1.96	1.95	2.28	2.35
	274	242	253	217	227
France	2.47	2.46	2.63	2.94	3.07
	3.04	2.92	3.27	3.72	4.31
	389	368	368	303	317
Italy	3.82	4.10	4.15	4.17	4.43
	3.26	3.52	3.56	3.15	3.48
	389	385	381	303	317
Netherlands	0.67	0.67	0.67	0.39	0.37
	1.39	1.39	1.39	0.83	0.78
	389	389	389	303	317

egy B (constant variance) with strategy C (GARCH), we notice that there is not much gain from using GARCH instead of the constant variance model to predict the single currency realignment probabilities. The gains from using GARCH come to the fore when we compare strategy D and E which report the excess returns using the multiple currency realignment probabilities. For four out of five currencies the GARCH model outperforms the constant variance model on the basis of the Sharpe-ratios. Especially noteworthy are the GARCH-results for France and Italy with respectively excess returns of 3.20% and 4.85% per year, and Sharpe-ratios of 4.78 and 4.42 respectively.

The results in Table 3 are similar to those in Table 2. Using Sharpe-ratio's, a strategy following the GARCH model outperforms the constant variance model for seven out of the ten cases. Two of the three dismal results are caused by the Dutch guilder, for which all mean excess returns are insignificant anyway. The GARCH model in a multicurrency setting, i.e. strategy E, outperforms strategies B-D for three currencies: Belgium, Denmark and France. Finally, we conclude this comparison by observing that according to a simple T-test on differences between mean returns of the various strategies, only in the first period there is a significant outperformance of one strategy over the other, namely the difference between strategies A and E for France. When, finally, we compare strategy A with E, we see that in the first period the latter one outperforms the first one for three out of the five currencies, whereas in the second period the no-frills strategy A is superior for three out of the five currencies.

4 Conclusion

The aim of this paper was to exploit the recent integration of the speculative attack and target zone literature for the case of the EMS. The target zone literature started with the work of Krugman (1992). By adopting the continuous time framework, assuming normal innovations and a band from which the exchange rate cannot escape, Krugman showed that exchange rates follow a regulated Brownian motion which implies the intuitive S-shape behaviour of exchange rates. The empirical validity of target zone models is however disputable and little evidence has been found for the theory being in accordance with empirical reality.

In this paper, we derived a discrete time approximation from the standard continuous time model. The discrete time model possesses all the features exhibited by the continuous time version. Moreover, the model allows for explicit incorporation of the stylized facts on intra-EMS exchange rates, i.e. heteroskedasticity and fat tails, as well as the mean reversion effect. The theoretical model also allowed us to derive simple prediction formulae for upcoming realignments for EMS currencies against the German mark between 1979 and 1990.

The rise and fall of realignment probabilities are indicative for the periods of tension within the EMS. The figures presented in this paper show that in many cases realignment probabilities rise drastically prior to actual realignments, thereby providing an early warning sign. To further evaluate the model we have constructed five investment stategies, two of which use conditional variance models to make ex-ante decisions on whether or not to take a long position in weak EMS currencies. The first investment strategy ignored the information provided by the model and always invested, independent from the realignment probabilities. From the exercise it appears that the GARCH model which incorporates the effect of the EMS band, outperforms the constant variance model in several cases. This comes to the fore when the GARCH and the variance model are compared in a multicurrency setting. Especially in the case of France and Italy the gains that can be made from the use of the GARCH model are substantial. As was remarked by a referee, ideally we would also compare the various investment strategies in an out-of-sample experiment. Because of a shortage of data and time however, we did not include such an experiment in the current version, but we do plan to incorporate it in future research.

References

Baillie R T and McMahon P C (1989) The Foreign Exchange Market. Cambridge. Cambridge University Press

Bertola G and Caballero (1992) Target Zones and Realignments. American Economic Review 82, 520-536

Bertola G (1993) Continuous-Time Models of Exchange Rate and Intervention. Van der Ploeg F (ed) Handbook of International Economics. London, Basil Blackwell, forthcoming

Blanco H and Garber P M (1986) Recurrent Devaluation and Speculative Attacks on the Mexican Peso. Journal of Political Economy, 148-166

Bollerslev T (1986) Generalized Autoregressive Conditional Heteroscedasticity. Journal of Econometrics 31, 307-327

Engle R F (1982) Autoregressive Conditional Heteroskedasticity with Estimates of the Variance of U.K. Inflation. Econometrica 50, 987-1008

Flood R P and Garber P M (1984) Collapsing Exchange-Rate Regimes: Some Linear Examples. Journal of International Economics 16, 1-14

Flood R P and Garber P M (1992) The Linkage between Speculative Attack and Target Zone Models of Exchange Rates: Some Extended Results. Krugman P and Miller M (eds). Exchange Rate Targets and Currency Bands, Cambridge. Cambridge University Press, 17-34

Flood R P Rose A K and Mathieson D J (1991) An Empirical Exploration of Exchange Rate Target-zones. Carnegie Rochester Conference Series on Public Policy. 35, 7-66

Hols M C A B and de Vries C G (1991) The Limiting Distribution of Extremal Exchange Rate Returns. Journal of Applied Econometrics 6, 287-302

Koedijk K G Schafgans M M A and de Vries C G (1990) The Tail Index of Exchange Rate Returns. Journal of International Economics 29, 93-108

Koedijk K G and Kool C J M (1992) Betting on the EMS. Open Economies Review, forthcoming

Koedijk K G Stork P A and de Vries C G (1993) Heteroskedasticity, Realignments and the EMS. Tinbergen Institute Discussion Paper, forthcoming

Kofman P de Vaal A and de Vries C G (1993) Fixing Soft Margins. Journal of International Economics 34, 359-374

Krugman P (1992) Exchange Rates in a Currency Band: a Sketch of the New Approach, in: Krugman P and Miller M (eds). Exchange Rate Targets and Currency Bands. Cambridge. Cambridge University Press

Krugman P and Rotemberg J (1992) Speculative Attacks on Target Zones, in: Krugman P and Miller M (eds). Exchange Rate Targets and Currency Bands. Cambridge. Cambridge University Press, 117-139

Meese R A and Rose A K (1990) Nonlinear, Nonparametric, Nonessential Exchange Rate Estimation. American Economic Review 80: Papers and Proceedings. 192-196

Nieuwland F G M C (1993) Speculative Market Dynamics. Unpublished PhD Dissertation

Obstfeld M (1987) Peso Problems, Bubbles, and Risk in the Empirical Assessment of Exchange-Rate Behavior. NBER working paper 2203

Pesaran M H and Samiei H (1992) An Analysis of the Determination of Deutsche Mark / French Franc Exchange Rate in a Discrete-Time Target Zone Model. The Economic Journal 102, 388-401

Rose A K and Svensson L E O (1991) Expected and Predicted Realignments: The FF / DM Exchange Rate during the EMS. International Finance Discussion Paper #395. Washington

Sharpe W F and Alexander G J (1990) Investments. Englewood Cliffs N J: Prentice Hall

Smith G W and Spencer M G (1992) Estimation and Testing in Models of Exchange Rate Target Zones and Process Switching. In: Krugman P and Miller (eds), Exchange Rate Targets and Currency Bands. Cambridge. Cambridge University Press, 211-238

Svensson L E O (1991a) Target Zones and Interest Rate Variability. Journal of International Economis 31, 27-54

Svensson L E O (1991b) Assessing Target Zone Credibility: Mean Reversion and Devaluation Expectations in the EMS. Institute for International Economic Studies, Seminar paper 493

Svensson L E O (1992) An Interpretation of Recent Research on Exchange Rate Target Zones. The Journal of Economics Perspectives, 119-144

Ungerer H T, Hauvonen J H, Lopez-Claros A and Mayer T (1990) The European Monetary System: Developments and Perspectives. Occasional Papers 73. IMF

Risk and Return in January: Some UK Evidence[1]

By Antonis Demos[2], Enrique Sentana[3] and Mushtaq Shah[4]

Abstract: A large body of empirical research has found that stock returns tend to be higher in January than in other months. One possible explanation is that there is seasonality in the risk-return structure. We examine the risk-return relationship for the UK equity market. We use monthly sectorial data to estimate a dynamic version of the APT that explicitly allows for a different conditional factor structure in January from the rest of the year. While we confirm the US finding that the risk-return relationship is different in January, our results depart from the existing literature in two ways. First, we find a consistently positive and statistically significant relationship between non-diversifiable risk and return in non-January months. Second, we find some evidence against the APT restrictions on our model in January, in that the price of January risk may not be common across assets.

1 Introduction

A large body of empirical research has found that stock returns tend to be higher in January than in other months. Moreover, this anomaly appears to be more pronounced in companies with relatively small market capitalisations (e.g. see Keim (1983)). While most of the initial studies only examined US data, subsequent work has found that the "January effect" is very much an international phenomenon, being actually stronger in many countries than in the US (see e.g. Gultekin and Gultekin (1983)).

Various explanations have been posited for such a finding and they can be broadly divided into two types. Some have argued that the January effect just reflects end-of-year tax-loss selling (e.g. see Chan (1986), Dyl (1977) and Reinganum (1983)); others that it is due to seasonality in the risk-return structure, induced either by extensive repositioning of professionally managed

[1]The authors have benefited from helpful discussions with John Campbell, Greg Connor and Sushil Wadhwani. They are also grateful to seminar participants at Chicago, Princeton, HEC, LSE and CEMFI as well as an anonymous referee for useful comments. Of course, the usual caveat applies. Financial support from the ESRC and the LSE Financial Markets Group is gratefully acknowledged.

[2]Antonis Demos, Department of Economics, University of Reading, Whiteknight, Reading RG6 2AA, UK

[3]Enrique Sentana, CEMFI, Casado del Alisal 5, 28014 Madrid, Spain and LSE Financial Markets Group

[4]Mushtaq Shah, Goldman Sachs International, 133 Fleet St., London EC4A 2BB, UK

portfolios at the turn of the year after evaluation, or by the unusually large availability of company reports of small firms in January. As the UK tax year ends on April 5, the tax explanation does not apply to the data used in this paper[5], and hence, we can concentrate on analysing the risk-return relationship.

Although there appears to be a consensus view that the cross-correlation structure of stock returns is different in January from the rest of year (see e.g. Cho and Taylor (1987), Connor and Korajczyk (1992)), there is disagreement on how it affects risk premia. The earliest finding of any differences in the risk-return relationship was documented by Rozeff and Kinney (1976). They examined the estimates of an unconditional CAPM and found that there was a relatively high risk premium in January compared to other months. However, Tinic and West (1984) found that not only is January different from other months, but it was the only month to show a consistently positive and statistically significant relationship between risk and return. Gultekin and Gultekin (1987) obtained a similar result when they estimated seasonal risk premia within an unconditional APT framework.

Nevertheless, Keim and Stambaugh (1986) point out that examining this issue in an unconditional setting may not be appropriate, since most recent asset pricing models call for conditional moments rather than unconditional ones. Their results are somewhat mixed, but in general they find that there is less risk-return seasonality conditionally than unconditionally, and in some sub-samples there is no significant difference between January and non-January months. More recently, Ng, Engle and Rothschild (1992) found that a conditional version of the CAPM does a reasonably good job in explaining US stock returns, but a model in which two factors are included in addition to the market portfolio provides a more adequate description. Importantly for our purposes, their second factor is closely related to a January dummy, but they do not test for the extra cross equation restrictions implied by the additional factors.

In this paper we use monthly UK sectorial returns data (see the data appendix in Demos et al. (1993) for details) to estimate a dynamic version of the APT that explicitly allows for a different conditional factor structure in January from the rest of the year. Specifically, we consider a conditional two factor model in which the second factor only influences returns in January (cf. Connor and Korajczyk (1992)). Importantly, we do not divide our sample observations into January and the rest of the year, but rather estimate our model using all months simultaneously. In so doing, not only should we obtain more efficient estimates, but also we ensure that the first factor, which could be identified as close to the market portfolio, is the same all year round. Notice that having two factors in January allows a more flexible relation

[5]However, if the tax code is an adequate explanation of the January effect in the US, there could be an indirect tax effect on the UK via "contagion".

between risk and return in that month. Nevertheless, we also investigate a conditional one factor model with seasonal factor variance as an important special case of our model.

While we confirm the US finding that the risk-return relationship is different in January compared to other months, our results depart from the existing literature in two ways. First, we find a consistently positive and statistically significant relationship between non-diversifiable risk and return in *non-January* months. Second, we find some evidence against the APT restrictions on our model in January, in that the price of January risk may not be common across assets. This seems to be in contrast to Ferson and Harvey (1991) who suggest that risk premia in January are higher in absolute terms but their cross-sectional structure is largely unaffected.

The rest of the paper is organised as follows. Section 2 discusses our basic model and its estimation procedure. Section 3 reports our results, while the final section contains our conclusions.

2 Theory and Estimation

2.1 A Seasonal Factor Model of Asset Returns with Time-Varying Volatility

We begin by assuming that excess returns for each asset have a conditional factor representation:

$$r_{it} = \mu_{it} + \beta_{i1t} f_{1t} + \ldots + \beta_{ikt} f_{kt} + v_{it} \quad (i = 1, 2, \ldots) \tag{1}$$

where μ_{it} is the asset risk premium, f_{jt} $(j = 1, \ldots, k, finite)$ are common factors which capture systematic risk affecting all assets, β_{ijt} $(i = 1, 2, \ldots; j = 1, \ldots, k)$ are the associated factor loadings that measure the sensitivity of the asset to the common factors, while v_{it} are idiosyncratic terms which reflect unsystematic risk. To guarantee that the unanticipated component, $r_{it} - \mu_{it}$, has zero expectation conditional on the information set available at time $t-1$, we assume that $E_{t-1}(v_{it}) = 0$ and $E_{t-1}(f_{jt}) = 0$. We also assume that the factors are conditionally orthogonal, i.e. $E_{t-1}(f_{jt} f_{lt}) = 0$ for $j \neq l$, and that they have time-varying factor variances, $\lambda_{jt} > 0$ $(j = 1, \ldots, k)$. As for the asset-specific risks, v_{it}, we assume that they are conditionally uncorrelated to each other, which corresponds to an exact conditional k factor structure (cf. Chamberlain and Rothschild (1983)). For tractability reasons, we finally assume that the idiosyncratic terms have constant variances, $\gamma_i > 0$, so that all time variation in variances and covariances is systematic.

Given the conditional factor structure for risk, the Arbitrage Pricing Theory of Ross (1976) implies that if investors can diversify away idiosyncratic risk and if some regularity conditions are satisfied, the risk premium for each of the assets can be written as a linear combination of the volatility of the factors, with weights given by the corresponding factor loadings (see King, Sentana and Wadhwani (1992)), i.e.:

$$\mu_{it} = \beta_{i1t}\lambda_{1t}\tau_{1t} + \ldots + \beta_{ikt}\lambda_{kt}\tau_{kt} \tag{2}$$

where τ_{jt} is the price of risk associated with the j-th factor, which can be interpreted as the amount of expected return that agents are willing to give away to reduce the variability of the factor by one unit. Given that $cov_{t-1}(r_{it}, f_{jt}) = \beta_{ijt}\lambda_{jt}$, we can also re-write (2) as:

$$\mu_{it} = \tau_{1t}cov_{t-1}(r_{it}, f_{1t}) + \ldots + \tau_{kt}cov_{t-1}(r_{it}, f_{kt}) \tag{3}$$

Equation (3) then says that the risk premium of an asset is a linear combination of the conditional covariances of its returns with each factor, weighted by the corresponding prices of risk. In the case of only one factor whose representing portfolio is actually the "market", then $\mu_{it} = \beta_{i1}\lambda_{1t} = \tau_{1t}cov_{t-1}(r_{it}, f_{1t})$, and our model can be related to a standard conditional CAPM restriction. In general, (3) could be interpreted as saying that risk premia are determined by the covariance of the asset returns with the (orthogonal) systematic risk components, which are undiversifiable.

Notice that since λ_{jt} and τ_{jt} are not asset dependent, (2) is a cross-equation restriction on the relative pricing of any subset of assets based on an arbitrage argument. To transform this period by period restriction into an estimable model of the time-variation in risk premia, we need to specify the number of factors k and the evolution of β_{ijt}, λ_{jt} and τ_{jt}.

In this paper we consider a two factor model for the excess returns of 27 industrial sector portfolios of the London Stock Exchange. The first factor has a time varying conditional variance that follows a GARCH(1,1)-type process. Given that the factors are in principle unobservable, much care has to be exercised when dealing with their conditional variance (see Harvey, Ruiz and Sentana (1992)). For that reason we assume that $\lambda_{1t} = \alpha_0 + \alpha_2 E_{t-1}(f_{1t-1}^2) + \alpha_3\lambda_{1t-1}$, so that λ_{1t} is a measurable function of the information set. Since $E_{t-1}(f_{1t-1}^2) = E_{t-1}^2(f_{1t-1}) + V_{t-1}(f_{1t-1})$, the conditional variance of the first factor contains a correction term, $V_{t-1}(f_{1t-1})$, which reflects the uncertainty about the factors. The GARCH formulation, however, is not capable of capturing the common view that a decline in share prices increases volatility by more than a price increase of the same size: the so-called "leverage effect". To allow for this possibility we actually estimate a GQARCH(1,1)-type model for λ_{1t}, which augments the above equation with the term $\alpha_1 E_{t-1}(f_{1t-1})$ (see Sentana (1991)). The GQARCH(1,1) formulation nests a GARCH(1,1)-type process if $\alpha_1 = 0$, ARCH(1) if $\alpha_3 = 0$, and homoskedasticity if α_2 is also 0. Its main distinctive feature is that it allows for a dynamic asymmetric (linear) effect, so that if $\alpha_1 < 0$, negative shocks have a bigger effect on the future conditional variance than positive ones.

The second factor is a seasonal one with constant variance in January and zero variance otherwise. Hence, we are effectively assuming a seasonal factor structure in which the number of factors in January (two) is different from the rest of the year (one). Our model is therefore in line with the empirical findings of Connor and Korajczyk (1992) and Cho and Taylor (1987). However, we do not divide our sample observations into January and rest of the year, but rather estimate our model using all months simultaneously. In so doing, we ensure that the first factor is the same all year round.

An arbitrary element of the model is the scaling of the factors. We solved this by assuming that the first factor has unit unconditional variance, and that the variance of the second factor in January is one. Notice that in such a case α_0 is not a free parameter as it is given by one minus the sum of α_2 and α_3 (see Sentana (1991)). We then assume that for this scaling of the factors, the factor loadings and prices of risk are time invariant, i.e. $\beta_{ijt} = \beta_{ij}$ and $\tau_{jt} = \tau_j$. As a consequence, the only sources of time-variation in the conditional means and variance-covariance matrix of excess returns are the factor variances. Notice, though, that if we alternatively scale the factors so that they always have unit conditional variance, the above assumption is equivalent to $\beta_{ijt} = \beta_{ij}\lambda_{jt}^{1/2}$ and $\tau_{jt} = \tau_j\lambda_{jt}^{1/2}$. Hence our model can also be interpreted as a time-varying factor betas model with constant-variance factors in which the betas of different assets on the first factor change proportionally, and the betas on the second factor are zero for all months but January.

Hence we consider the following model:

$$r_{it} = \beta_{i1}\lambda_{1t}\tau_1 + \beta_{i2}d_t\tau_2 + \beta_{i1}f_{1t} + \beta_{i2}d_tf_{2t} + v_{it} \quad (i = 1, 2, \ldots, 27) \tag{4}$$

where $d_t = 1$ for January and 0 otherwise. In vector notation for the 27 assets at hand, the above model can be written as:

$$\mathbf{r}_t = \mathbf{b}_1\lambda_{1t}\tau_1 + \mathbf{b}_2d_t\tau_2 + \mathbf{b}_1f_{1t} + \mathbf{b}_2d_tf_{2t} + \mathbf{v}_t \tag{5}$$

where f_{2t} is 0 in non-January months and bold letters denote vectors of dimension 27.

If the N testable restrictions $\mathbf{b}_2 = \theta\mathbf{b}_1$ and $\tau_2 = \theta\tau_1$ are imposed in (5), where θ is a scalar, our model reduces to a one factor model all year round with the factor variance being seasonal. Specifically, equation (5) becomes:

$$\mathbf{r}_t = \mathbf{b}_1\lambda_t^*\tau_1 + \mathbf{b}_1f_t^* + \mathbf{v}_t \tag{6}$$

with $f_t^* = f_{1t} + \theta d_tf_{2t}$ and $\lambda_t^* = \lambda_{1t} + \theta^2d_t$. This special case has an interesting property from the asset pricing point of view. It implies that if $\tau_1\mathbf{b}_1 > 0$, risk premia will be higher in January than in the rest of the year, but the relative pricing of the assets will be the same (cf. Ferson and Harvey (1991)).

Our assumptions also imply that a portfolio of assets with weights given by the vector w can be represented as:

$$r_t^p = b_1^p \lambda_{1t} \tau_1 + b_2^p d_t \tau_2 + b_1^p f_{1t} + b_2^p d_t f_{2t} + v_t^p \tag{7}$$

where $r_t^p = w' r_t$, $b_1^p = w' b_1$, $b_2^p = w' b_2$ and $v_t^p = w' v_t$. Note that the factors and prices of risk in the above equation are the same as in equation (5), whereas the factor loadings are the linear combinations of the corresponding factor loadings.

If the portfolio is well diversified then $v_t^p = 0$, and in addition the restrictions $b_2 = \theta b_1$ and $\tau_2 = \theta \tau_1$ are imposed on (7), we obtain:

$$r_t^p = b_1^p \lambda_{1t}^* \tau_1 + b_1^p f_{1t}^* \tag{8}$$

i.e. a GARCH-M model with seasonal variance. However, if one were to estimate (8) as a univariate GARCH model with a seasonal dummy in the variance, one should include a correction term in the variance constant term so that the seasonal effect would not be carried through to other months (see Baillie and Bollerslev (1989)). The advantage of estimating (8) in terms of a restricted two factor model, one of which is seasonal, is that such a correction is implicitly made.

It is illustrative to relate our model to the standard CAPM. Assuming that the market portfolio r_t^M is well diversified, the market beta for an asset, i.e. $\beta_{jMt} = cov_{t-1}(r_{jt}, r_t^M)/V_{t-1}(r_t^M)$, will be given by:

$$\frac{\beta_{j1}}{b_1^M} + \frac{b_2^M(\beta_{j2} - \beta_{j1} b_2^M / b_1^M)}{b_1^{M2} \lambda_{1t} + b_2^{M2}} d_t$$

while the market price of risk, $\tau_t^M = E_{t-1}(r_t^M)/V_{t-1}(r_t^M)$, will be:

$$\frac{\tau_1}{b_1^M} + \frac{b_2^M(\tau_2 - \tau_1 b_2^M / b_1^M)}{b_1^{M2} \lambda_{1t} + b_2^{M2}} d_t$$

Hence our model allows for both a seasonal market beta and a seasonal market price of risk. Our asset pricing restriction, though, is derived using the APT and not the CAPM. Under the extra assumption that $\tau_t^M = \tau_1 / b_1^M = \tau_2 / b_2^M$ so that factor risk is priced through the market, both models coincide.

2.2 EM-Algorithm

For estimation purposes we assume that the common factors and idiosyncratic noises have a joint conditional normal distribution. We then have to estimate the following parameters: a 27×2 matrix of factor loadings, $B = (b_1, b_2)$, the 27 constant idiosyncratic variances in the diagonal of the matrix, Γ, the 3 free parameters in the conditional variance of the first factor and the two prices of risk, i.e. a total of 86 parameters. To speed up the procedure we employ the EM-based algorithm suggested in Demos and Sentana (1992) to obtain good initial values for a standard quadratically convergent method.

The rationale for using the EM (Expectation-Maximization) algorithm stems from the fact that if the factors were observed, maximising the joint likelihood function of the complete data set i.e. the 27 excess returns and the 2 unobservable factors would be obtained by running 27 univariate regressions and estimating one univariate GQARCH model for the first factor. Given that the factors are actually unobserved, the EM algorithm maximises instead the expected value of this joint log-likelihood function conditional on the observed data set and the current parameter values. Unfortunately, a straightforward application of the EM algorithm to our model is not possible. However, the standard EM algorithm for conditionally homoskedastic factor models could still be applied provided that the extra parameters were known. On this basis, Demos and Sentana (1992) develop a feasible two-level procedure which, on the one hand, uses the speed of the EM algorithm to estimate the vast majority of the parameters, i.e. the 54 B's and 27 idiosyncratic variances, keeping the conditional variance parameters and the prices of risk constant, and on the other, employs a Quasi-Newton technique to maximise with respect to the remaining 5 parameters. Consequently the speed and robustness of the EM algorithm are combined with the feasibility of the Quasi-Newton procedure.

For the standard EM part of the algorithm, expectations conditional on the observed data set are derived using the Kalman filter. Taking the common factors as the state, it is straightforward to derive the updating equations (see Harvey, Ruiz and Sentana (1992)):

$$E_t(f_t) = f_{t|t} = \Lambda_t(b_1, b_2 d_t)'\Sigma_t^{-1}[r_t - b_1\lambda_{1t}\tau_1 - b_2 d_t \tau_2] \tag{9a}$$

$$V_t(f_t) = \Lambda_{t|t} = \Lambda_t - \Lambda_t(b_1, b_2 d_t)'\Sigma_t^{-1}(b_1, b_2 d_t)\Lambda_t \tag{9b}$$

where $\Lambda_t = \begin{pmatrix} \lambda_t & 0 \\ 0 & d_t \end{pmatrix}$ and $\Sigma_t = (b_1, b_2 d_t)\Lambda_t(b_1, b_2 d_t)' + \Gamma$.

Then, the p-th EM iteration estimates are computed as follows:

$$B^{(p)} = \sum_{t=1}^{T} r_t \phi_{t|t}^{\prime(p-1)} \left[\sum_{t=1}^{T} \phi_{t|t}^{(p-1)} \phi_{t|t}^{\prime(p-1)} + \Lambda_{t|t}^{(p-1)}\right]^{-1} \tag{10a}$$

$$\Gamma^{(p)} = \sum_{t=1}^{T} \left[r_t r_t' - B^{(p)} \phi_{t|t}^{p-1} r_t' \right] \tag{10b}$$

where $\phi_{t|t}^{(p-1)} = \Lambda_{t|t}^{(p-1)} \tau^{(p-1)} + f_{t|t}^{(p-1)}$, and $f_{t|t}^{(p-1)}$ and $\Lambda_{t|t}^{(p-1)}$ are $E_t(f_t)$ and $V_t(f_t)$ evaluated at the previous iteration estimates.

3 Empirical Evidence

3.1 Univariate Results

To investigate the nature of the UK January effect we initially consider univariate models for the FTA Allshare returns in Figure 1 along the lines described in Section 2.1. In this respect, and given that it is a broadly based index, we assume in what follows that it does not contain any idiosyncratic risk. First of all, we estimate a constant mean and variance model with and without a dummy variable in the mean that takes the value of one in January and zero elsewhere. The results for the period 71m2-92m5 are presented in Table 1. In line with international evidence for a January effect (see e.g. Gultekin and Gultekin (1983)), we can comfortably reject the null of a constant expected return throughout the year (t-value for January dummy = 3.05). Indeed in this model the expected return in January is over twenty times that in other months. The size of the UK January effect, though, may be unduly affected by the fact that in January 75 there was a 51.6% surge in stock market prices. Still, for the period 75m2-92m5 the expected return in January is almost six times that in other months (t-value for January dummy = 2.12).

Table 1 Tests on Univariate Model

Test For January Effect In Constant Variance Model	LR = 9.21 ($\chi^2_{1,0.05} = 3.84$)
Test For Time-Varying Variance	LR = 61.1 ($\chi^2_{3,0.05} = 7.87$)
Test For January Effect In Time-Varying Variance Model	LR = 4.07 ($\chi^2_{1,0.05} = 3.84$)
Test For Seasonality In Factor	LR = 5.33 ($\chi^2_{2,0.05} = 5.99$)

However, it is possible that this anomaly could be due to the inappropriate modelling of risk. More specifically, recent evidence suggests that the conditional variance of stock returns is time-varying (see Bollerslev, Chou and Kroner (1992) for a comprehensive survey). For this reason, we then go on to model the conditional variance as a GQARCH(1,1) process and make the risk premium proportional to it. The results of this estimation can be found in Table 2. A likelihood ratio test rejects the null of a constant variance comfortably at the 5% level (see Table 1). The estimated conditional variance is plotted in Figure 2. In accordance with the results in Sentana (1991) for the FT500, there seems to be a fair amount of variation over time and a fair degree of persistence. There is also some evidence for a dynamic asymmetric effect, in that negative shocks have a bigger effect on the future conditional variance than positive ones (LR=17.33). This finding is consistent with the results of Braun, Nelson and Sunier (1990) in the US. When we added the January dummy to the mean, though, it was still statistically significant, so that the anomaly does not appear to be caused only by assuming a constant variance.

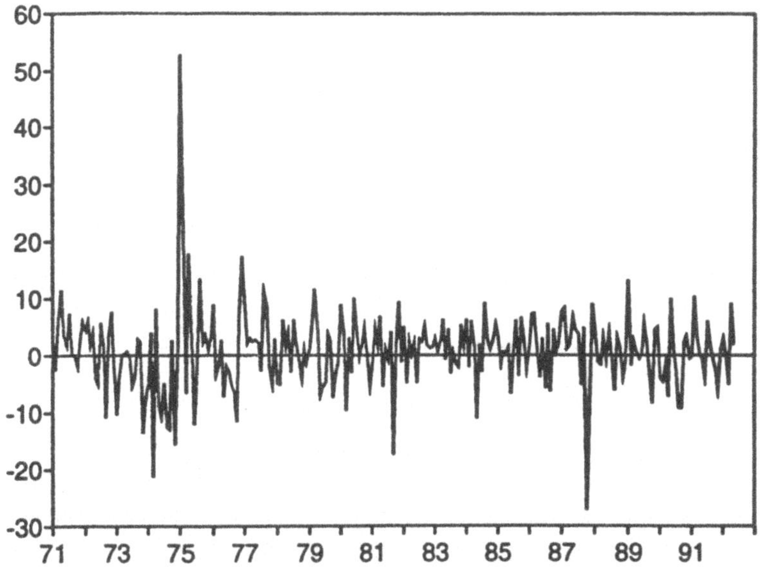

Figure 1 Excess returns on FT Allshare

Table 2 GQARCH(1,1) Parameter estimates for univariate Model

$$\sigma_t^2 = \delta_0^2 + \delta_1^2(\varepsilon_{t-1} - \delta_2)^2 + \delta_3^2\sigma_{t-1}^2 = \gamma_0 + \gamma_1\varepsilon_{t-1} + \gamma_2\varepsilon_{t-1}^2 + \gamma_3\sigma_{t-1}^2$$

Parameters	Estimate (Std. Error)	Parameters	Estimate
δ_0	0.0147 (0.0192)	γ_0	0.00076
δ_1	0.3276 (0.1205)	γ_1	-0.01795
δ_2	0.0835 (0.0399)	γ_2	0.10734
δ_3	0.8100 (0.0603)	γ_3	0.65621

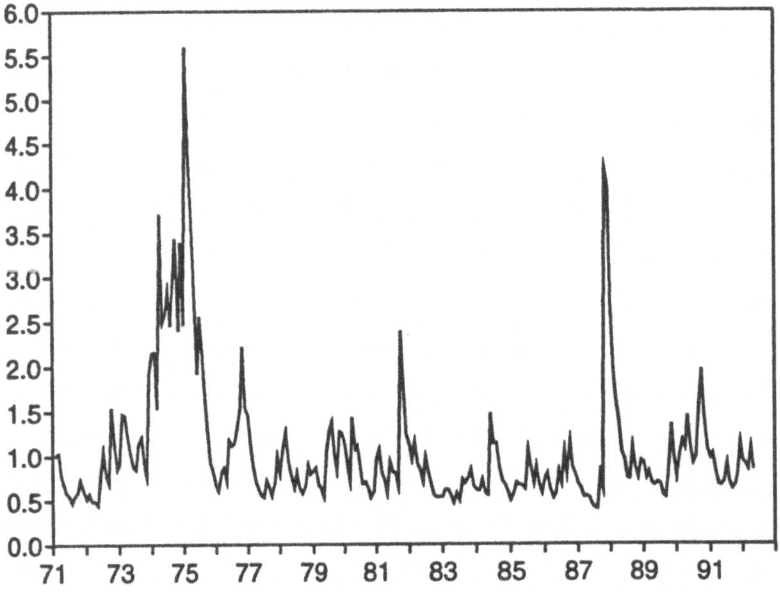

Figure 2 Conditional Variance of Market

Nevertheless, we could still be inappropriately modelling risk if there were seasonality in the variance of the market that the GQARCH(1,1) formulation cannot capture. In order to investigate this possibility we estimate the seasonal two factor model in equation (7) under the assumption that the market is well diversified. We find, though, little evidence for seasonality in the market since the likelihood ratio test gives a value of 5.33, which is insignificant at the 5% level. However, due to the small sample size it seems likely that this test lacks power. Moreover, there are problems of interpretation with (7). Since we are only dealing with one asset, in this case the market portfolio, we cannot tell whether the extra term in the mean in January is a genuine risk premium for that month or something else. In particular, the following model is observationally equivalent if $b_2^p \neq 0$:

$$r_t^p = b_1^p \lambda_{1t} \tau_1 + \varphi d_t + b_1^p f_{1t} + b_2^p d_t f_{2t} \tag{7'}$$

whether or not φ / b_2^p is equal to τ_2.

3.2 Multivariate Results

To deal with these problems, we move on to the multivariate estimation and proceed along similar lines to the univariate tests. Thus, we first estimated (1) with a single unobservable factor with constant variance. The factor loadings and average weights of the factor are presented in Table 3. Interestingly, the extracted factor is highly correlated with excess returns on the FTA all share index (0.98), although the weights are very different from the market value weights (cf. Sentana and Shah (1992)). When we added a January dummy we found that we could easily reject the null of the same constant risk premia throughout the year (see Table 4).

We then re-estimated the same one factor model, but with a time-varying variance and risk premia, and again we allowed for a dynamic asymmetric effect in the conditional variance. The parameter estimates are presented in Table 3. Once more, the null of constant variance is clearly rejected. The conditional variance of this unobservable factor is plotted in Figure 3. Notice that it does bear some resemblance to the conditional variance of the FTA index in Figure 2.

To see whether the assumed asset pricing model provides an adequate representation of UK sectorial risk premia, we first tested whether the cross-equation restriction of a common τ_1 in (2) was valid by doing a likelihood ratio test against an unrestricted model which allowed each asset to have a different price of risk. Second, we allowed a constant in the mean of each equation to capture the possibility that idiosyncratic risk is priced because investors in UK shares are not well diversified. We could not reject the null hypothesis in either case at the 5% level (see Table 4). Hence, this basic model apparently does a pretty good job in pricing sectorial assets in the UK.

Table 3 Estimates of b and $b\tau$ in single Factor Model with Time-varying Variance

Sector	b	$b\tau$	Portfolio Weight	Mkt. Cap Weight
Banks	6.55 (0.33)	0.88 (0.38)	1.66	10.44
Brewers & Distillers	6.14 (0.30)	0.82 (0.36)	2.85	10.98
Building Materials	7.89 (0.30)	1.06 (0.45)	5.78	2.80
Chemicals	5.97 (0.28)	0.80 (0.34)	3.32	4.90
Contracting, Construction	8.38 (0.33)	1.12 (0.48)	3.94	0.78
Electricals	6.75 (0.29)	0.90 (0.39)	2.93	0.55
General Engineering	6.73 (0.26)	0.90 (0.39)	8.38	2.53
Food Manufacturing	6.14 (0.22)	0.82 (0.35)	4.98	6.32
Food Retailing	6.47 (0.28)	0.87 (0.37)	2.15	6.29
Insurance Brokers	6.61 (0.34)	0.88 (0.38)	1.21	0.56
Insurance Composite	6.50 (0.31)	0.87 (0.38)	2.30	2.53
Insurance Life	7.03 (0.32)	0.94 (0.41)	2.09	2.29
Investment Trusts	6.43 (0.26)	0.86 (0.37)	3.31	3.73
Health & Leisure	7.15 (0.27)	0.96 (0.41)	5.37	3.18
Merchant Banking	7.85 (0.36)	1.05 (0.45)	1.98	0.80
Metals	6.73 (0.31)	0.90 (0.39)	4.10	0.73
Miscellaneous	6.72 (0.26)	0.90 (0.39)	7.75	5.22
Other Financial	6.24 (0.29)	0.83 (0.36)	3.49	0.71
Motors	6.52 (0.35)	0.87 (0.38)	5.06	1.16
Oil	5.15 (0.41)	0.69 (0.30)	0.45	12.68
Paper	6.76 (0.27)	0.90 (0.39)	6.30	2.00
Property	6.90 (0.36)	0.92 (0.40)	1.86	1.76
Shipping & Transport	5.38 (0.31)	0.72 (0.31)	2.61	3.59
Stores	7.06 (0.30)	0.94 (0.41)	3.14	8.36
Textiles	6.60 (0.30)	0.88 (0.38)	3.60	0.75
Engineering & Aerospace	6.60 (0.26)	0.88 (0.38)	7.11	1.00
Electronics	6.52 (0.30)	0.87 (0.38)	2.26	3.36
τ	0.133 (0.05)			

Table 4 Tests on single Factor Models

Test For January Effect In Constant Variance Model	LR = 44.32 ($\chi^2_{27,0.05} = 40.1$)
Test For Time-Varying Variance	LR = 102.9 ($\chi^2_{3,0.05} = 7.87$)
Test For Equality of Price of Risk	LR = 21.76 ($\chi^2_{26,0.05} = 38.9$)
Test For Pricing of Idiosyncratic Risk	LR = 20.52 ($\chi^2_{27,0.05} = 40.1$)
Test For January Effect In Time-Varying Variance Model	LR = 46.66 ($\chi^2_{27,0.05} = 40.1$)
Test For January Effect In Proportionality Model	LR = 44.14 ($\chi^2_{27,0.05} = 40.1$)

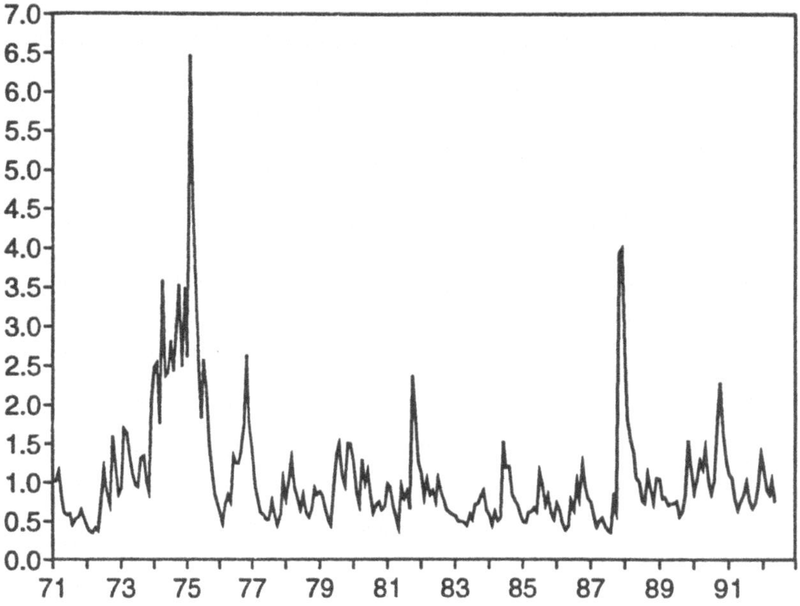

Figure 3 Conditional Variance of Factor

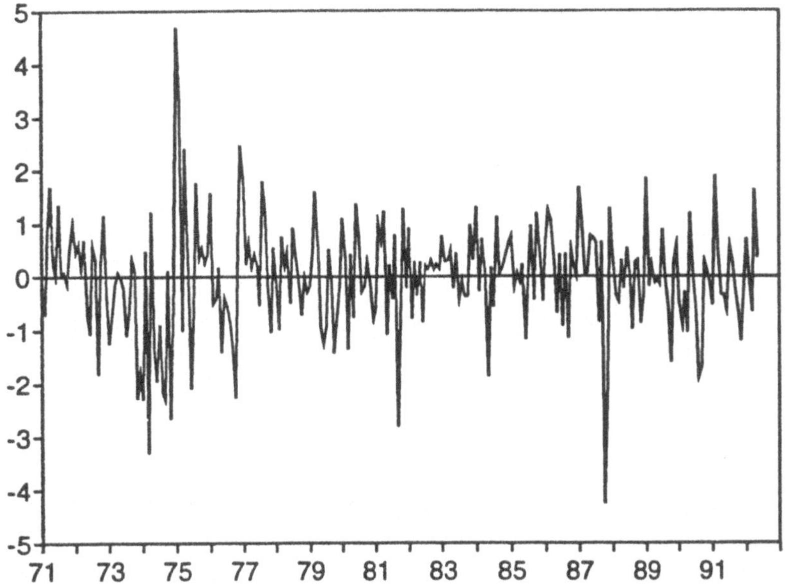

Figure 4 First Factor

But when we added a January dummy variable in the mean, it was again significant (see Table 4, row 5). Again, this could be due to seasonality in the variance of the single unobservable factor, the existence of January specific risk and a different risk-return relationship in this month or something else. The advantage of working with multivariate data is that we can now differentiate between these explanations.

To capture the first possibility, we estimated model (6) which has the same price of risk across months, but allows the absolute level of the January risk premium to be proportionally higher in January (cf. Ferson and Harvey (1991)). In this respect, we find that a seasonal one factor model does a better job than an unseasonal one at explaining UK returns. Table 4 though, shows than an unrestricted January dummy variable in the mean is still significant. Given that the extracted factor is very close to the market, this model is empirically very similar to a CAPM model with constant betas in which the risk premium for the market is proportional to its seasonal conditional variance with a constant price of risk. Not surprisingly, if we estimate an unrestricted market model by regressing each sectoral return on the market and test for a January effect, we reject the null hypothesis (Wald $= 48.63, \chi^2_{27,0.05} = 40.1$).

We then moved on to our most general model which allows for a different covariance structure and risk-return relationship in January and so nests the previous model. Specifically, we estimate model (5), so that in January we allow ourselves an extra factor and a different price of risk. The results are reported in Tablc 5 and the estimated factors are plotted in Figures 4 and 5.

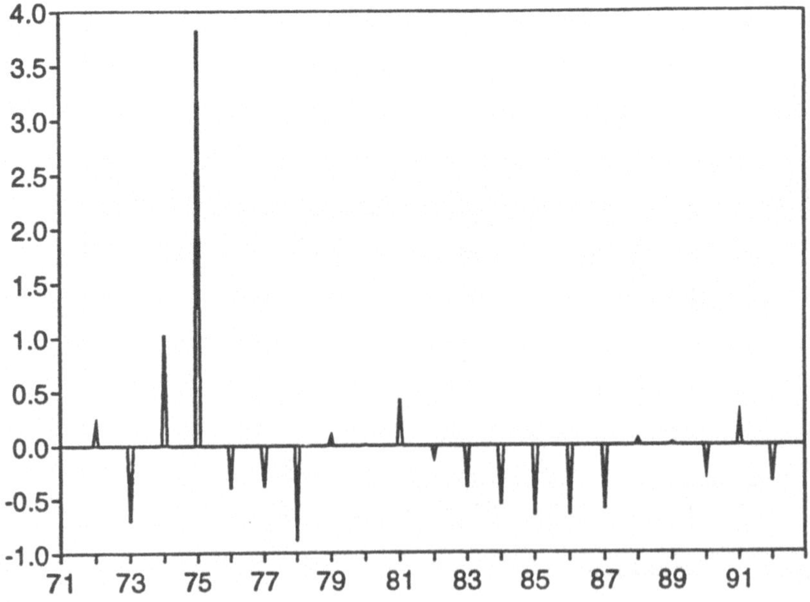

Figure 5 January Factor

Table 5 Estimates of b and $b\tau$ in two Factor Model with Time-varying Variance

Sector	b_1	$b_1\tau_1$	b_2	$b_2\tau_2$
Banks	6.32 (0.57)	0.70 (0.37)	5.83 (2.31)	0.33 (1.39)
Brewers & Distillers	5.92 (0.51)	0.66 (0.34)	5.52 (2.10)	0.32 (1.32)
Building Materials	7.63 (0.62)	0.85 (0.44)	7.03 (2.61)	0.41 (1.68)
Chemicals	5.88 (0.51)	0.65 (0.34)	4.34 (2.11)	0.25 (1.05)
Contracting, Construction	8.10 (0.67)	0.90 (0.47)	7.53 (2.74)	0.43 (1.79)
Electricals	6.57 (0.56)	0.73 (0.38)	5.57 (2.25)	0.32 (1.33)
General Engineering	6.82 (0.54)	0.75 (0.39)	3.15 (2.26)	0.18 (0.77)
Food Manufacturing	5.80 (0.48)	0.64 (0.34)	6.78 (2.13)	0.39 (1.62)
Food Retailing	6.09 (0.53)	0.68 (0.36)	7.35 (2.23)	0.42 (1.75)
Insurance Brokers	6.25 (0.58)	0.70 (0.37)	7.33 (2.48)	0.42 (1.75)
Insurance Composite	6.36 (0.56)	0.71 (0.37)	4.98 (2.22)	0.29 (1.19)
Insurance Life	6.68 (0.58)	0.74 (0.39)	7.33 (2.47)	0.42 (1.75)
Investment Trusts	6.08 (0.51)	0.67 (0.36)	7.18 (2.40)	0.41 (1.71)
Health & Leisure	6.93 (0.56)	0.77 (0.40)	6.27 (2.41)	0.36 (1.50)
Merchant Banking	7.53 (0.65)	0.84 (0.44)	7.65 (2.72)	0.44 (1.83)
Metals	6.93 (0.59)	0.77 (0.40)	2.02 (2.33)	0.12 (0.51)
Miscellaneous	6.71 (0.54)	0.74 (0.39)	3.86 (2.22)	0.22 (0.93)
Other Financial	6.52 (0.57)	0.71 (0.38)	0.72 (2.14)	0.04 (0.22)
Motors	7.08 (0.60)	0.79 (0.41)	-1.76 (2.24)	-0.10 (0.41)
Oil	4.65 (0.52)	0.52 (0.27)	7.86 (2.18)	0.45 (1.87)
Paper	6.81 (0.56)	0.76 (0.39)	3.36 (2.28)	0.19 (0.82)
Property	6.76 (0.61)	0.75 (0.39)	5.26 (2.33)	0.30 (1.26)
Shipping & Transport	5.41 (0.49)	0.60 (0.32)	2.75 (2.09)	0.16 (0.67)
Stores	6.81 (0.57)	0.75 (0.39)	6.33 (2.33)	0.36 (1.51)
Textiles	6.64 (0.57)	0.74 (0.38)	3.36 (2.31)	0.19 (0.82)
Engineering & Aerospace	6.64 (0.54)	0.74 (0.38)	3.42 (2.18)	0.20 (0.83)
Electronics	6.25 (0.55)	0.70 (0.36)	6.31 (2.18)	0.36 (1.50)
τ	0.111 (0.06)		0.058(0.23)	

This model does a much better job in capturing the cross-sectional correlation structure in returns than a one factor model with seasonal variance. In addition, we find that the null of a common price of non-January risk cannot be rejected, and moreover, that adding constants to the mean equations yields jointly insignificant results, so the idiosyncratic risk does not appear to be priced (see Table 6). However, our model fares less well when we allow the risk premia on the January factor to be different across assets. Such a restriction is rejected by the data (p value $\simeq$ 0.002). Thus, we are unable to fully explain the January effect in the UK within the context of our dynamic seasonal version of the APT, despite the fact that such a model provides a reasonable overall representation of returns.

Our results, though, may be affected by the behaviour of the UK stock market in January 75, when there was a 51.6 increase in the index, but a fair degree of heterogeneity across sectors. For this reason, we have re-estimated

Table 6 Tests on two Factor Model

Test for Proportionality between Risk Premia in January & other Months	LR = 145.4 ($\chi^2_{27,0.05} = 40.1$)
Test For Equality of the Price of Non-January Risk	LR = 19.54 ($\chi^2_{26,0.05} = 38.9$)
Test For Equality of the Price of January Risk	LR = 51.66 ($\chi^2_{26,0.05} = 38.9$)
Test For Pricing of Idiosyncratic Risk	LR = 21.33 ($\chi^2_{27,0.05} = 40.1$)

our model starting in 75m2. While the performance of our model for non-January months is largely unaffected, the evidence against it in January is much weaker. The test for the APT cross-equation restriction in the January component of the risk premia is only 34.42 (p-value $\simeq$ 0.12). Whether this result is due to a loss of power is an unresolved issue.

4 Conclusions

In this paper we use monthly UK sectorial returns to estimate a dynamic seasonal version of the APT that allows for a different conditional factor structure in January from the rest of the year. Our results are different from the existing literature in two significant ways. First, we find a positive and statistically significant relationship between non-diversifiable risk and return in *non-January* months. This is in contrast to earlier findings that there is only a consistent relationship between systematic risk and expected returns *in January*. Second, although we do allow for a different risk structure in January, the price of risk may not be common across assets, thus rejecting the cross equation restriction implied by the APT. This result, though, is not robust to excluding January 75. In any case, we find little support for the conjecture that risk premia in January are proportionately higher, but still the price of risk is common across assets.

We can think of at least three reasons why our results are different from previous studies. First, we model the time-variation in the risk premia, rather than assume that it is constant. Second, we allow for a different covariance structure in January by explicitly considering an extra factor in that month. Last, we use UK data whilst most other studies use US data. All these differences deserve further investigation so that we can reconcile our results in a more satisfactory manner.

On one level our results are encouraging for proponents of existing asset pricing models, in that they shift the emphasis from January being the only month in which returns move in line with theory, to the only month in which they may not. Hence, the APT would provide a satisfactory explanation for what is happening in 11/12 of a year rather than 1/12 as previously.

However, our results are also somewhat negative in that they do not fully resolve the January puzzle. Of course, it is possible that a more general model for seasonal risk may well explain the January effect. Searching for such a model provides an interesting avenue for further research.

References

Baillie R T and Bollerslev T (1989) The Message in Daily Exchange Rates: A Conditional-Variance Tale, Journal of Business and Economic Statistics 7, 297-305

Bollerslev T (1986) Generalised Autoregressive Conditional Heteroskedasticity, Journal of Econometrics 31, 307-328

Bollerslev T, Chou R Y and Kroner K F (1992) ARCH Modelling in Finance: A Review of the Theory and Empirical Evidence, Journal of Econometrics 52, 5-59

Braun P A, Nelson D B and Sunier A M (1990) Good News, Bad News, Volatility and Betas, University of Chicago Graduate School of Business Working Paper 90-93

Chamberlain G and Rothschild M (1983) Funds, Factors and Diversification in Arbitrage Pricing Models, Econometrica 51, 1305-1324

Chan K C (1986) Can Tax-Loss Selling Explain the January Seasonal in Stock Returns? Journal of Finance, 1115-1128

Cho D C and Taylor W M (1987) The Seasonal Stability of the Factor Structure of Stock Returns, Journal of Finance 42, 1195-1211

Connor G and Korajczyk R (1992) A Test for the Number of Factors, LSE Financial Markets Group Discussion Paper 137

Demos A and Sentana E (1992) An EM-based Algorithm for Conditionally Heteroskedastic Factor Models, LSE Financial Markets Group Discussion Paper 140

Demos A, Sentana E and Shah M (1993) Risk and Return in January: Some UK Evidence, LSE Financial Markets Group Discussion Paper

Dyl E A (1977) Capital Gains Taxation and Year-End Stock Market Behaviour, Journal of Finance, 165-175

Ferson W E and Harvey C R (1991) The Variation of Economic Risk Premiums, Journal of Political Economy 99, 385-415

Gultekin M N and Gultekin N B (1983) Stock Market Seasonality: International Evidence, Journal of Financial Economics 12, 469-481

Gultekin M N and Gultekin N B (1987) Stock Return Anomalies and the Tests of the APT, Journal of Finance 42, 1213-1224

Harvey A, Ruiz E and Sentana E (1992) Unobserved Component Time Series Models with ARCH Effects, Journal of Econometrics 52, 129-157

Keim D B (1983) Size Related Anomalies and Stock Return Seasonality: Further Empirical Evidence, Journal of Financial Economics 12, 13-32

Keim D B and Stambaugh R F (1986) Predicting Returns in the Stock and Bond Markets, Journal of Financial Economics 17, 357-390

King M, Sentana E and Wadhwani S (1993) Volatility and Links between National Stock Markets, mimeo, LSE

Ng V, Engle R F and Rothschild M (1992) A Multi-Dynamic-Factor Model for Stock Returns, Journal of Econometrics 52, 245-266

Reinganum M R (1983) The Anomalous Stock Market Behaviour of Small Firms in January: Empirical Tests for Tax-Loss Selling Effects, Journal of Financial Economics 12, 89-104

Ross S A (1976) The Arbitrage Theory of Capital Asset Pricing, Journal of Economic Theory 13, 641-60

Rozeff M S and Kinney W R (1976) Capital Market Seasonality: The Case of Common Stock Returns, Journal of Financial Economics 3, 379-402

Sentana E (1991) Quadratic ARCH Models: A Potential Re-interpretation of ARCH Models, mimeo, LSE
Sentana E and Shah M (1992) An Index of Co-movements in Financial Time Series, mimeo, LSE
Tinic S M and West R R (1984) Risk and Return: January vs. the Rest of the Year, Journal of Financial Economics 13, 561-74

Markov-Switching Models for Exchange-Rate Dynamics and the Pricing of Foreign-Currency Options[1]

By Juergen Kaehler and Volker Marnet[2]

Abstract: Mixtures of normal distributions and Markov-switching models are applied to model the leptokurtosis and heteroskedasticity of exchange-rate dynamics. The mixtures of normal distributions capture well the leptokurtosis of the data whereas the Markov-switching models capture both the leptokurtosis and the heteroskedasticity. There is strong evidence against Gaussian white noise in high-frequency data. Foreign-currency option prices derived under the assumption of Gaussian white noise differ systematically and significantly from prices derived under the assumptions of a mixture model or a Markov-switching model. The typical "smile effects" are caused by the implied peakedness and fat tails of the models.

1 Introduction

The problem of decomposing an empirical frequency distribution into several components is a very old statistical problem. We are approaching the centenary of Karl Pearson's classical paper (Pearson, 1894) in which he introduced the method of moments to estimate the parameters of a two-component mixture of normal distributions and in which he applied the model to the distributions of some measures of the forehead of crabs and of the dental distance in prawns.

Over the years, the statistical analysis of finite mixture distributions has found a great variety of applications in such diverse fields as fisheries research, geology, crime and comet frequencies and medicine[3]. In finance, mixtures of normal distributions have been applied to model the price dynamics of stocks (see Barnea and Downes (1973), Ball and Torous (1983), Fielitz and Rozelle (1983), Kon (1984), Akgiray and Booth (1987), and Akgiray, Booth and Loistl

[1]The paper was presented at ESEM 1993, the annual meeting of the Verein für Socialpolitik 1993, and in seminars at the Universities of Tübingen and Zürich. An earlier, more technical version was presented at the ZEW conference on "Financial Markets Econometrics". We are grateful to conference and seminar participants for helpful comments.

[2]Juergen Kaehler and Volker Marnet, ZEW, Kaiserring 14-16, D-68161 Mannheim.

[3]See Everitt and Hand (1981) and Titterington, Smith and Makov (1985) for comprehensive surveys.

(1989)) and exchange rates (see Boothe and Glassman (1987), Akgiray and Booth (1988), and Tucker and Pond (1988))[4].

From a theoretical perspective, mixtures of distributions can be motivated as models of information arrival on financial markets (see Kon (1984)). It is typically assumed that the model consists of two (or more) distributions with different variances. Drawings from the high-variance distribution represent information events while drawings from the low-variance distribution represent non-information periods which can be associated with background noise of normal trading. Alternatively, Kon (1984) suggested a three-components mixture model for stock returns based on the idea that the returns are drawn from a non-information distribution, a firm-specific information distribution, and a market-wide information distribution. Mixture models may also be related to "anomalities" of the stock market such as excess returns and volatilities on Mondays and other calendar effects. In applications to exchange rates, it has been suggested that the components of the mixture represent periods with central bank intervention and periods without intervention or, alternatively, that the two components of a mixture can be associated with news from the two countries whose exchange rate is considered (Friedman and Vandersteel (1982)).

From a statistical perspective, mixture models may be motivated as models which imply leptokurtosis. Extensive empirical analysis has revealed that leptokurtosis is a strong and robust empirical regularity of short-run price dynamics in financial markets. Under time-aggregation, however, leptokurtosis vanishes, i.e. the null hypothesis of a normal distribution can, in general, be rejected for daily and weekly data but not for monthly and quarterly data (see Fama (1976)). It can be shown (see Section 2) that arbitrary scale-mixtures of normal distributions imply leptokurtosis. Hence, this class of models is compatible with the strong stylized facts of leptokurtosis and convergence to normality. The latter follows, of course, from the central limit theorem.

There are a number of competing probability models, however, which also imply leptokurtosis. The work along these lines was initiated by Mandelbrot (1963) who introduced the family of stable Paretian distributions into economics and finance. However, stable Paretian distributions are not compatible with convergence to normality and, besides, have some unattractive analytical features. The other main competitors are the Student's distribution, introduced into the modelling of financial data by Praetz (1972), and the compound Poisson process, introduced by Press (1967). It is interesting to note that all four probability models can be viewed within the framework of scale-compounded normal distributions where the variance is random with an independent distribution. The mixture model attaches a multinomial distribution to the variance, the Student's distribution attaches an inverted

[4]It is quite remarkable that the finance literature on mixture models seems to have been unaware of the statistics literature on the same subject. For instance, Ball and Torous (1983) and Kon (1984) deal with estimation problems which had long been solved.

gamma-distribution, the compound Poisson process attaches a Poisson distribution and the stable Paretian distributions attach positive stable distributions to the variance. In this way, the choice among the models can be regarded as a choice between variance functions for a normal distribution.

There is mounting empirical evidence for the rejection of the stable Paretian distribution as a valid model for price dynamics in financial markets (see Lau et al. (1990), Jansen and de Vries (1991), and Kaehler (1991)). In comparative studies with daily and weekly data on stock returns and exchange-rate dynamics, it turned out that the compound Poisson process and mixtures of normal distributions are superior to stable distributions and Student's distributions in their fit to the data (see Kon (1984), Akgiray and Booth (1987, 1988), Boothe and Glassman (1987), Tucker and Pond (1988), and Akgiray, Booth and Loistl (1989)).

In this paper we consider the mixture of normal distributions and a generalization of it for the modelling of financial data and we apply the model to daily, weekly, monthly, and quarterly exchange-rate dynamics. In Section 2 we show that heteroskedasticity is another strong empirical regularity of the data and in Section 3 we demonstrate that the mixture model does not capture this regularity. Section 4 introduces an extension of the mixture model which incorporates heteroskedasticity by letting drawings from the component distributions follow a first-order Markov chain. This Markov-switching model for mixture distributions is due to Lindgren (1978) based on the work of Baum et al. (1970). In a series of papers, Hamilton extended the model and adapted it to the modelling of interest rates, exchange rates and the business cycle (see Hamilton (1988, 1989, 1990, 1991a,b), and Engel and Hamilton (1990)).

The stochastic specification of financial models is of fundamental importance in almost every branch of finance. We study the implications of mixture models and Markov-switching models for the pricing of foreign-currency call options in Section 4. In Section 5 we draw some conclusions from our study and suggest directions for future research.

2 Stylized Facts of Exchange-Rate Dynamics

The data to be analysed are the exchange rates of the U.S. dollar against the German mark, the British pound, the Swiss franc and the Japanese yen. The data are on a daily basis but also weekly, monthly and quarterly data are used. For these series, end-of-period data were derived from daily exchange rates. The data are from July 1st, 1974 to June 28th, 1991. Due to differences in bank holidays between countries, there are different numbers of observations in the daily data: 4260 for the mark, 4299 for the pound, 4266 for the franc, and 4226 for the yen. For all currencies, the number of observations in the weekly series is 886, in the monthly series it is 203 and in the quarterly series it is 67. Data sources are the IMF's International Financial Statistics and the monthly reports of the Swiss National Bank. The exchange-rate dynamics are analysed in the form of $x_t = 100(e_t - e_{t-1})$ where e_t is the logarithm of the exchange rate at time t.

Table 1 reports some descripitive statistics and tests for the daily, weekly, monthly, and quarterly exchange-rate dynamics. Overall, the results are in line with earlier studies of price dynamics in financial markets (see e.g. Taylor (1986)). First, the means of the series are, in general, not significantly different from zero. It is only in the daily and weekly yen series that we find some weak evidence against a mean of zero. But note that the underlying t-test assumes normality and that this assumption is very questionable for these data as will be shown below.

Second, there is some evidence of negative skewness (β_1, defined as the 3rd standardized moment) in the daily and weekly data of the mark, the franc, and the yen. However, there is no strong evidence against the null hypothesis of a symmetric distribution ($H_0 : \beta_1 = 0$) in monthly and quarterly data.

Third, we find very strong leptokurtosis in all daily and weekly series. It has repeatedly been found that returns and price movements in financial markets have excess kurtosis, i.e. kurtosis which is significantly greater than 3 (the value for a normal distribution). Kurtosis β_2, defined as the ratio of the 4th central moment to the square of the variance, increases both with excessive mass in the tails or at the centre of the distribution (peakedness). A test of $H_0 : \beta_2 = 3$ is a test of mesokurtosis with the two-sided alternatives of platykurtic ($\beta_2 < 3$) and leptokurtic ($\beta_2 > 3$) distributions[5]. Whereas leptokurtosis is highly significant in daily and weekly data, it is only significant (at the 5 percent level) for the monthly series of the mark, the pound and the franc and all distributions of quarterly data are platykurtic (but not significantly). We may conclude, therefore, that leptokurtosis is a phenomenon of short-run exchange-rate dynamics and that there is convergence to normality under time-aggregation.

In order to further investigate deviations from normality, we applied the Anderson-Darling (AD) test for normality which, like the well-known Kolmogorov-Smirnov test, is based upon the vertical difference between the empirical distribution function and the theoretical distribution function. But the AD test has more power than the Kolmogorov-Smirnov test (see Stephens (1986)). As Table 1 shows, the results from the AD test are quite similar to those of the kurtosis test. Normality is overwhelmingly rejected for daily and weekly data. It is quite peculiar, however, that the only monthly series

[5]Since the skewness and kurtosis statistics have unknown distributions and show strong non-normality even in large samples, we applied to both statistics some transformations (as described by D'Agostino (1986)) to improve the approximation to a standard normal distribution. We used the S_u approximation for β_1 and the Anscombe-Glynn approximation for β_2.

Table 1 Statistical Properties of Exchange-Rate Dynamics

		mark	pound	franc	yen
day	mean	-0.008	0.009	-0.015	-0.017 *
	variance	0.473	0.454	0.660	0.406
	skewness	-0.225 ***	-0.048	-0.086 **	-0.450 ***
	kurtosis	7.423 ***	7.341 ***	8.095 ***	7.363 ***
	AD	26.675 ***	44.891 ***	32.603 ***	42.780 ***
	$Q_x(40)$	41.412	43.233	40.732	58.488 **
	$Q_{xx}(40)$	567.435 ***	968.832 ***	926.047 ***	760.990 ***
week	mean	-0.039	0.044	-0.073	-0.083 *
	variance	2.153	2.137	2.891	1.786
	skewness	-0.209 **	-0.015	-0.229 ***	-0.728 ***
	kurtosis	5.380 ***	6.242 ***	4.749 ***	6.186 ***
	AD	5.992 ***	4.386 ***	4.976 ***	9.683 ***
	$Q_x(40)$	39.122	28.852	31.353	75.048 ***
	$Q_{xx}(40)$	168.753 ***	194.851 ***	172.655 ***	127.254 ***
month	mean	-0.175	0.188	-0.318	-0.379
	variance	11.770	11.329	14.707	11.381
	skewness	0.176	-0.315 *	0.215	-0.224
	kurtosis	4.084 **	3.850 **	4.003 **	3.470
	AD	0.784	0.488	0.482	2.038 **
	$Q_x(40)$	36.835	28.213	39.486	47.721
	$Q_{xx}(40)$	26.653	26.113	28.729	39.83
quarter	mean	-0.569	0.543	-0.949	-1.153
	variance	40.155	32.942	53.325	37.544
	skewness	0.174	0.053	-0.361	-0.450
	kurtosis	2.596	2.437	2.767	2.667
	AD	0.210	0.556	0.297	0.583
	$Q_x(15)$	19.955	21.728	10.205	15.456
	$Q_{xx}(15)$	15.146	11.169	10.256	9.728

Significance levels: * 10 percent, ** 5 percent, *** 1 percent.

for which normality is rejected is the yen series whereas in the kurtosis test, this series was the only monthly series for which mesokurtosis could not be rejected. This demonstrates that these tests are sensitive to different distributional aspects. The H_0 of normality cannot be rejected with the AD test for any of the quarterly series.

Table 1 also reports results from a test of serial independence. We applied the Ljung-Box statistic $Q_x(M)$ which is based on the autocorrelation function (ACF) of x_t where M is the highest lag in the ACF. Under the H_0 of white noise, $Q_x(M)$ has asymptotically a χ^2 distribution with M degrees of freedom. We report a heteroskedasticity adjusted version of the Ljung-Box statistic (see Diebold (1988)). Only the daily and weekly yen series have significant autocorrelations. We, therefore, conclude that mean effects are absent in three of the four exchange rates.

In order to quantify the heteroskedasticity of the series, we computed the ACF of the squared data x_t^2. McLeod and Li (1983) have established that under the H_0 of white noise, the standard errors of squared-data autocorrelations are the same as for the usual ACF. Hence also the Ljung-Box statistic $Q_{xx}(M)$ for squared data is applicable without modifications. As with the test for normality, we find that there are marked differences between short-run, i.e. daily and weekly, and medium-run, i.e. monthly and quarterly exchange-rate dynamics. Whereas there is extremely strong serial dependence of volatility in daily and weekly data, this dependence disappears completely in monthly and quarterly data. Furthermore, all individual autocorrelation coeffecients for the daily data are positive and they are significant up to $M = 40$. For the weekly data, some autocorrelation coefficients are negative but all significant coefficients are positive. Hence, there is a strong clustering of small and of large exchange-rate fluctuations in the short-run data.

To summarize the statistical properties, we find very strong leptokurtosis and heteroskedasticity in daily and weekly but a convergence to Gaussian white noise under time-aggregation. In the following two sections, we shall aim to build a model compatible with these three empirical regularities.

3 Mixtures of Normal Distributions

As noted in the introduction, the mixture of normal distributions has often been applied to capture the stylized facts of price dynamics in financial markets. A finite mixture of normal distributions is defined by:

$$f(x_t \mid \Theta) = \sum_{i=1}^{I} p_i f_i(x_t \mid \mu_i, \sigma_i) \tag{1}$$

with

$$\sum_{i=1}^{I} p_i = 1 \quad \text{and} \quad 0 < p_i < 1 \quad \text{for all } i \tag{2}$$

and

$$f_i(x_t \mid \mu_i, \sigma_i) = \frac{1}{\sqrt{2\pi}\sigma_i} \exp\left\{-\frac{(x_t - \mu_i)^2}{2\sigma_i^2}\right\}. \tag{3}$$

In equation (1), Θ is the parameter vector $\Theta = (p_1, \ldots, p_{I-1}, \mu_1, \ldots, \mu_I, \sigma_1, \ldots, \sigma_I)$ where p_I is redundant because of the restriction that the probabilities p_i sum to 1. Scale mixtures of normal distributions are defined as special cases of (1) with $\mu_1 = \ldots = \mu_I$.

It is straightforward to show that scale mixtures for arbitrary I are leptokurtic[6]. It is more convenient to define leptokurtosis here in terms of the fourth cumulant κ_4 which is related to central moments by

$$\kappa_4 = \nu_4 - 3\nu_2^2, \tag{4}$$

where ν_k is the k-th central moment. Leptokurtosis can also be defined by the condition $\kappa_4 > 0$. It is easy to show that for scale mixtures

$$\nu_2^2(X) = \left(\sum_{i=1}^{I} p_i \sigma_i^2\right)^2 \tag{5}$$

and

$$\nu_4(X) = 3\sum_{i=1}^{I} p_i \sigma_i^4. \tag{6}$$

Inserting both terms into (4) yields

$$\kappa_4(X) = 3\left[\sum_{i=1}^{I} p_i \sigma_i^4 - \left(\sum_{i_1}^{I} p_i \sigma_i^2\right)^2\right] = 3 \text{ var } (\sigma^2) > 0 \tag{7}$$

since the variance σ^2 is non-constant by assumption. Furthermore, the convergence to normality under addition follows simply from the central limit theorem.

The mixture of normal distributions of equation (1) can only be estimated if I is specified. In order to identify I we applied the Schwarz information criterion (SIC) and found that the optimal I was either 2 or 3 for the series of exchange rates. There were also some numerical problems when I was greater than 3. Distinguishing between mean mixtures, which impose the restriction $\sigma_1 = \ldots = \sigma_I$, scale mixtures, which impose the restriction $\mu_1 = \ldots = \mu_I$, and mean-scale mixtures, which impose no such restrictions, we found by applying the SIC that mean mixtures are never optimal and that mean-scale mixtures are only optimal for the two yen series. Otherwise, scale mixtures with either two or three components were optimal for the other series. However, in most three-components models there was one component with a very small probability p_i of 0.05 or less. For instance, for the weekly franc series we estimated $p_2 = 0.02$ along with $\mu_2 = 2.63$ and σ_2^2 =0.05. Compared with the overall mean of μ = -0.07 and the overall variance of σ^2 =2.89,

---

[6]Gridgeman (1970) proved only the peakedness of general scale mixtures of normal distributions. Mean mixtures of normal distributions are not generally leptokurtic. For instance, the kurtosis of a two-component normal mixture with $\sigma_1 = \sigma_2 = 1$ and $\mu_1 = -\mu_2 = 1$ is 1.25, i.e. this distribution is platykurtic.

it is clear that this component picks up a bunch of strong depreciations of the Swiss franc. The small values of the p_2 and σ_2^2 are disturbing because they indicate that there might be a problem with singularities, or near singularities, in the likelihood function (see Titterington, Smith and Makov (1985)). Furthermore, one of the diagnostic tests for independence which we applied to the model (see below) could not be performed for some of the three-components models because of some low component probabilities p_i. Therefore, we report only the results from the two-component models in this paper. The estimates are given in Table 2 and asymptotic standard errors are in brackets.

Several important observations may be drawn from Table 2. First, there are no significant mean effects in the daily and weekly series of the mark, pound and franc but both yen series have components which are significantly different in their means with opposite signs. On the other hand, the components of all short-run exchange-rate series can clearly be distinguished with respect to their variances. The first component is always associated with the lower variance and σ_2^2 is larger than σ_1^2 by a factor of at least 5 in daily data and by a factor of at least 4 in a weekly data. In general the low-variance component has a higher probability than the second component, the only exception being the weekly mark series.

The results are somewhat different for medium-term exchange-rate dynamics, i.e. for monthly and quarterly data. The low-variance component has the smaller probability for these data (with the exception of the monthly pound series). It may also be surprising that the first component is associated with the high-variance state in quarterly data but note that the "ranking" of states is arbitrary and unimportant in this model. We also find some strong mean effects in the lower frequency data. All quarterly series have components which are significantly different in their means with opposite signs. Some of the mean effects, however, are disturbing. For instance, the second component for the quarterly mark series has a large mean, a small variance and a probability of 4.5 percent. With a total of 68 quarterly observations, this probability implies an expected number of approximately 3 observations from the second component in this series. This means that the second component represents a small number of large depreciations of the mark against the dollar. In more extreme cases, the mixture model may converge to a singularity where the mean of one component is equal to the value of one observation (often an extreme one) and where the variance of this components goes to zero. The likelihood function will then go to infinity and this is a major problem for maximum-likelihood estimation of the model. In order to avoid this singularity problem, one may try to keep all σ_i^2 away from zero through simple restrictions on the parameter space or through the introduction of a penalty function (which also has the interpretation of a Bayesian prior) as in Hamilton (1991a). Empirical applications often apply the restrictions of mean mixtures but we decided not to impose the restrictions of equal variances because we have good reason to believe that scale effects are

Table 2 Estimates of the Mixture of Normal Distributions

		mark	pound	franc	yen
day	p	0.749 (0.053)	0.519 (0.045)	0.807 (0.030)	0.689 (0.035)
	μ_1	0.002 (0.012)	-0.010 (0.010)	0.010 (0.012)	0.032 (0.010)
	μ_2	-0.036 (0.041)	0.029 (0.022)	-0.121 (0.060)	-0.125 (0.034)
	σ_1^2	0.232 (0.024)	0.101 (0.016)	0.332 (0.021)	0.151 (0.012)
	σ_2^2	1.192 (0.145)	0.834 (0.057)	2.013 (0.207)	0.955 (0.073)
	$\tilde{\beta}_1$	-0.086	0.071	-0.192	-0.315
	$\tilde{\beta}_2$	5.330	4.954	6.077	5.578
	LR	400.05 ***	585.56 ***	524.80 ***	573.45 ***
	runs	6.704 ***	9.971 ***	7.950 ***	9.311 ***
	Markov	44.175 ***	99.056 ***	63.084 ***	86.564 ***
week	p	0.335 (0.084)	0.830 (0.141)	0.612 (0.094)	0.636 (0.073)
	μ_1	-0.015 (0.057)	0.025 (0.058)	0.071 (0.071)	0.139 (0.051)
	μ_2	-0.050 (0.076)	0.136 (0.262)	-0.300 (0.180)	-0.469 (0.147)
	σ_1^2	0.293 (0.143)	1.313 (0.319)	1.154 (0.224)	0.592 (0.108)
	σ_2^2	3.084 (0.332)	6.143 (2.625)	5.533 (0.836)	3.630 (0.504)
	$\tilde{\beta}_1$	-0.021	0.073	-0.236	-0.544
	$\tilde{\beta}_2$	4.125	5.172	4.662	5.145
	LR	75.627 ***	63.215 ***	65.848 ***	120.20 ***
	runs	3.399 ***	4.711 ***	2.247 **	5.662 ***
	Markov	11.310 ***	21.934 ***	4.994 **	31.336 ***
month	p	0.297 (0.200)	0.926 (0.173)	0.200 (0.138)	0.265 (0.184)
	μ_1	-0.225 (0.426)	0.188 (0.273)	0.047 (0.597)	0.364 (0.500)
	μ_2	-0.155 (0.365)	0.188 (3.003)	-0.409 (0.367)	-0.647 (0.520)
	σ_1^2	2.262 (2.218)	9.376 (1.982)	2.458 (2.140)	0.787 (1.366)
	σ_2^2	15.701 (3.498)	34.911 (44.730)	17.642 (2.910)	14.856 (2.992)
	$\tilde{\beta}_1$	0.015	0.000	-0.059	-0.216
	$\tilde{\beta}_2$	3.824	4.059	3.509	3.840
	LR	8.459 **	3.701	4.317	20.649 ***
	runs	-0.223	-0.234	-	-0.145
	Markov	0.058	0.046	-	0.058
quarter	p	0.955 (0.030)	0.736 (0.083)	0.935 (0.033)	0.750 (0.166)
	μ_1	-1.201 (0.752)	-2.013 (0.907)	0.149 (0.812)	1.471 (1.312)
	μ_2	12.723 (0.591)	7.683 (0.776)	-16.708 (0.763)	-9.005 (3.307)
	σ_1^2	32.604 (6.365)	17.339 (5.923)	37.541 (7.530)	16.537 (6.473)
	σ_2^2	0.734 (6.436)	5.429 (2.769)	2.044 (1.532)	15.904 (13.942)
	$\tilde{\beta}_1$	0.196	0.089	-0.379	-0.462
	$\tilde{\beta}_2$	2.921	2.225	3.053	2.763
	LR	3.870	5.129 *	6.698 **	5.258*
	runs	0.554	-2.671 ***	0.236	2.166 **
	Markov	0.155	6.298 **	0.362	4.376 **

more important than mean effects in our data. The only series where we got serious problems with singularities was the monthly pound series. The fully parameterized model converged for none of the starting values which we tried. We, therefore, imposed the restriction of equal means for this series.

In order to judge whether the estimated models are compatible with the stylized facts of the data, we computed the implied skewness $\tilde{\beta}_1$ and the implied kurtosis $\tilde{\beta}_2$ of the models from

$$\tilde{\beta}_1 = \frac{\sum_{i=1}^{I} p_i(3\sigma_i^2\delta_i + \delta_i^3)}{\left[\sum_{i=1}^{I} p_i(\sigma_i^2 + \delta_i^2)\right]^{\frac{3}{2}}} \tag{8}$$

and

$$\tilde{\beta}_2 = \frac{\sum_{i=1}^{I} p_i(3\sigma_i^4 + 6\sigma_i^2\delta_i^2 + \delta_i^4)}{\left[\sum_{i=1}^{I} p_i(\sigma_i^2 + \delta_i^2)\right]^2} \tag{9}$$

with $\delta_i = \mu_i - \mu$, where μ is the overall mean. The results, reported in Table 2, show a rather close agreement between the pattern of skewness and kurtosis in the data and the implied skewness and kurtosis. If we impose a 5 percent significance level, we find significant negative skewness in several daily and weekly series (see Table 1) and we find also for all those series a negative implied skewness. As regards implied kurtosis, we get leptokurtosis for all daily, weekly, and monthly series but the degree of leptokurtosis decreases under time-aggregation, as it does in the data (see Table 1). The implied kurtosis is somewhat smaller than the kurtosis of the data for daily and weekly series but there is a quite close agreement between implied leptokurtosis and actual leptokurtosis for the monthly data.

We also report in Table 2 the results from a likelihood-ratio (LR) test against the H_0 of Gaussian white noise. There is, however, a problem with the application of the LR test to mixture models since the degrees of freedom are unclear for mean-scale mixtures. We may either impose the restriction $p \equiv p_1 = 0$ (or alternatively: $p = 1$) which reduces the mixture model to Gaussian white noise or we may impose the restrictions $\mu_1 = \mu_2$ and $\sigma_1 = \sigma_2$. In the first case we would have one degree of freedom (from one restriction) in the LR test and in the second case we would have two degrees of freedom. Another related problem with the LR test is that p is on the boundary of the parameter space under H_0 and that, therefore, the regularity conditions for the application of the χ^2 distribution are not satisfied.

We took here the pragmatic position of being on the safe side with a conservative rule that the degrees of freedom are two. The choice of degrees of freedom is immaterial for daily and weekly data where the H_0 of Gaussian white noise is overwhelmingly rejected. For monthly and quarterly data, we find much weaker evidence against normality but this is no surprise in view of the stylized facts reported in the previous section.

Finally, we applied two tests of serial dependence to examine the dynamic properties of the model. In order to test for independence we introduce the unobservable state variable s_t which determines at time t from which component a realization is drawn, i.e. if $s_t = i$ then there will be a drawing from component i at t . From Bayes's theorem we get

$$p(s_t \mid x_t) = \frac{f_i(x_t \mid \mu_i, \sigma_i)\, p_i(s_t)}{\sum_{i=1}^{I} f_i(x_t \mid \mu_i, \sigma_i)\, p_i(s_t)} \tag{10}$$

and we can estimate the integer s_t by maximizing $f_i(x_t \mid \mu_i, \sigma_i)p_i(s_t)$ This gives an estimated series of states which can be tested for independence.

The first test is the multiple runs test of Barton and David (1957). A run is defined as a sequence of s_t's with the same value. A positive value of the test statistic indicates that there are less runs than expected under the H_0 of randomness. Table 2 shows that for all high-frequency series randomness is indeed rejected and that there are always less runs than expected, i.e. there is positive dependence in the states. Given that the components of the mixture are mainly different with respect to their variances, this result corresponds to the results from the ACF for squared data in Table 1. Again, there is a marked difference to low-frequency (i.e. monthly and quarterly) data where the runs test leads to a rejection of independence for the quarterly pound and yen series only[7].

The second test for independence is a conventional χ^2 test within the framework of a Markov chain for s_t. The results are very similar to the ones from the runs test. There is strong rejection of independence for all daily and weekly data but no rejection in the monthly data. For quarterly data, independence can be rejected for the pound and the yen at the 5 percent level. In all cases of rejections, the dependence is caused by the fact that the states s_t have a greater degree of persistence than expected, i.e. there is positive serial dependence of states.

We may conclude from the above analysis that the model of two mixtures of normal distributions captures well the stylized facts of non-normality and leptokurtosis in short-run exchange-rate data. With the exception of the yen series, the dominant effect is the scale effect and not the mean effect. For monthly and quarterly data, however, we find much weaker evidence for a mixture model. This, of course, is in accordance with the stylized fact of convergence to normality under time aggregation. But a general deficiency of the model is that it cannot capture the heteroskedasticity of the high-frequency data. The rejection in the test of independence for the state variable s_t indicates this deficiency. In the next section we will discuss an extension of this model which removes this deficiency by introducing a Markov chain process for the state variable.

---

[7]The run test could not be computed for the monthly franc series because, according to (10), all observations are classified as belonging to the second component.

4 Markov-Switching Models

A natural way to add dynamics to the mixture model is to assume that the state variable s_t follows a time-homogeneous or stationary first-order Markov process, i.e.

$$p(s_t = j \mid s_{t-1} = i, s_{t-2}, \ldots, s_1, x_t, x_{t-1}, \ldots, x_1) = p(s_t = j \mid s_{t-1} = i) = p_{ij}. \quad (11)$$

For a Markov-switching model with two states (or regimes) we get a 2×2 transition matrix of states with two independent probabilities p_{11} and p_{22}. Of course, it follows that $p_{21} = 1 - p_{11}$ and that $p_{12} = 1 - p_{22}$. This Markov chain together with the mixture model (1) and the specification of the normal distribution (3) gives a seven parameter model with parameter vector $\Theta = (p_{11}, p_{22}, \mu_1, \mu_2, \sigma_1, \sigma_2, \psi)$ where $\psi = p(s_1 = 1)$. We need ψ, the probability of being in state 1 in time period $t = 1$, to start off the Markov chain and a natural choice is to set ψ equal to the stationary probability of being in state 1, i.e.

$$\psi = \frac{1 - p_{22}}{2 - p_{11} - p_{22}}. \quad (12)$$

Estimation of the Markov-switching model is quite involved since the state variable s_t is not observable. The basic idea of the model is due to Baum et al. (1970) who suggested to estimate the model with the expectation-maximization (EM) algorithm. Furthermore, they derived the essential properties of the EM algorithm within a general model with Markov-chain dependence. They showed that, under certain regularity conditions, the EM algorithm increases the likelihood function monotonically and that it converges to the maximum-likelihood (ML) estimates. Lindgren (1978) detailed the steps needed to implement the EM algorithm for the Markov-switching model, extended the model to the case of switching regressions and examined the properties of the ML estimator. The switching-regressions model may be written as

$$x_t = z_t \theta^i + u_t^i \quad \text{with} \quad u_t^i \sim N(0, \sigma_i^2) \quad (13)$$

$$s_{t-d} = i \quad \text{for} \quad i = 1 \ldots I \quad (14)$$

where z_t is a vector of exogenous or lagged endogenous variables, θ^i is a vector of regression parameters for the i-th state, u_t is a Gaussian white-noise disturbance term with state-dependent variance σ_i^2 and d is a delay parameter for the state variable s_t.

It may be noted that the switching-regressions model of (13) - (14) describes a broad class of models including the switching model of Goldfeld and Quandt (1973) and the threshold models of Tong (1983, 1990) and Priestley (1988). The specifications differ only in their assumptions about the state variable s_t. The Markov-switching model obtains from (13) - (14) when $z_t = 1$ and when we assume a Markov chain for s_t as in (11). We also assume that the delay parameter d is zero. Our motivation for ignoring mean effects of exogenous and lagged endogenous variables derives from Section 2 where we found no strong mean effects in the statistical properties of the exchange-rate data.

The estimates of the Markov-switching model are presented in Table 3 where asymptotic standard errors are given in brackets. First, we note that the large values of p_{11} and p_{22} indicate great persistence of states. We can calculate the expected duration of state i, λ_i, from $\lambda_i = (1 - p_{ii})^{-1}$ and find that, for instance, the expected duration of state 2 is 50 days for the daily mark series. For daily data, the expected duration of states varies between 29.4 days and 50.0 days, for weekly data λ_i varies between 9.7 weeks and 31.3 weeks, for monthly data λ_i varies between 2.3 months and 12.0 months, and for quarterly data λ_i varies between 1 quarter and 14.3 quarters. The extreme values for the quarterly data were caused by the franc series where the problem of convergence to singularities occurred. For some series and states, the λ_i's are roughly consistent across time horizons. For instance, the λ_1's for the mark-dollar exchange rate are 47.6 for daily data, 9.7 for weekly data and 2.9 for monthly data. On the other hand, λ_2 is equal to 16.4 for the weekly yen series and equal to 16.7 for the monthly yen series, and this appears to be inconsistent. In general, the λ_i's of quarterly data are surprisingly high.

We also computed the stationary state probabilies $\bar{p_1}$ and $\bar{p_2}$ from $\bar{p_1} = \psi$ (see (12)) and $\bar{p_2} = 1 - \bar{p_1}$. It is surprising that the low-variance states, in general this is state 1, have in most cases a smaller stationary probability than the high-variance states. Only for two series is $\bar{p_1}$ greater than 0.5 (it is 0.526 for the daily pound series and 0.558 for the daily franc series, see also the last column in Table 4). This result is in conflict with the estimates from the mixture model where p_1 was greater than 0.5 for nearly all of the daily and weekly series.

Table 3 Estimates of the Markov-Switching Model

		mark	pound	franc	yen
day	p_{11}	0.979 (0.004)	0.975 (0.005)	0.977 (0.004)	0.966 (0.006)
	p_{22}	0.980 (0.005)	0.973 (0.005)	0.971 (0.006)	0.979 (0.004)
	μ_1	0.002 (0.010)	0.010 (0.009)	0.013 (0.011)	0.018 (0.008)
	μ_2	-0.018 (0.020)	0.008 (0.020)	-0.051 (0.026)	-0.039 (0.016)
	σ_1^2	0.153 (0.008)	0.147 (0.014)	0.225 (0.010)	0.072 (0.056)
	σ_2^2	0.781 (0.033)	0.793 (0.045)	1.204 (0.050)	0.610 (0.021)
	LR	513.490***	389.732***	465.268***	651.809***
week	p_{11}	0.897 (0.029)	0.897 (0.020)	0.924 (0.041)	0.922 (0.025)
	p_{22}	0.940 (0.021)	0.968 (0.004)	0.967 (0.036)	0.939 (0.028)
	μ_1	-0.062 (0.051)	-0.086 (0.062)	-0.116 (0.080)	0.087 (0.063)
	μ_2	-0.025 (0.078)	0.082 (0.059)	-0.055 (0.082)	-0.217 (0.113)
	σ_1^2	0.416 (0.066)	0.284 (0.070)	0.597 (0.185)	0.388 (0.092)
	σ_2^2	3.154 (0.240)	2.679 (0.140)	3.867 (0.560)	2.851 (0.313)
	LR	66.692***	64.356***	55.204***	78.094***
month	p_{11}	0.657 (0.369)	0.568 (0.105)	0.767 (0.075)	0.857 (0.023)
	p_{22}	0.840 (0.307)	0.908 (0.043)	0.917 (0.013)	0.940 (0.012)
	μ_1	-0.179 (0.449)	0.654 (0.457)	0.156 (0.477)	0.026 (0.210)
	μ_2	-0.174 (0.412)	0.089 (0.398)	-0.488 (0.305)	-0.541 (0.334)
	σ_1^2	2.967 (4.456)	2.108 (1.426)	3.347 (1.007)	1.568 (0.483)
	σ_2^2	15.820 (6.103)	13.171 (1.561)	18.582 (1.839)	15.116 (1.914)
	LR	0.123	0.246	5.585**	7.548***
quarter	p_{11}	0.814 (0.120)	0.807 (0.070)	0.930 (0.036)	0.647 (0.068)
	p_{22}	0.881 (0.099)	0.606 (0.216)	0.000 (0.541)	0.752 (0.148)
	μ_1	-4.115 (1.074)	-2.554 (1.044)	0.169 (0.808)	2.269 (0.706)
	μ_2	1.762 (1.651)	6.955 (1.684)	-16.696 (0.756)	-3.535 (1.437)
	σ_1^2	17.122 (6.724)	14.755 (4.570)	37.260 (7.445)	12.696 (4.288)
	σ_2^2	40.604 (10.664)	8.122 (6.641)	2.058 (1.548)	40.066 (7.082)
	LR	0.483	5.370**	0.526	3.310

From the parameter estimates of the model we can also compute the conditional probability $\pi_i(t \mid \tau) = p(s_t = i \mid x_1, ..., x_\tau; \theta)$ in a recursive way (see Lindgren (1978) and Hamilton (1989)). If we set $\tau = t$, we get "filter" probabilities about the probable state at time t whereas for $\tau = T$ we get "smoothed" probabilities based on the full sample. In practice, both alternatives give very similar results. In Figure 1 we plot the smoothed probabilities of state 1 for the weekly mark series together with the series x_t. It is apparent from this figure that state 1 is associated with tranquil (i.e. low variance) periods. The probability smoother identifies the period from November 1975 until November 1977 as being associated with state 1 if the criterion is that $\pi_1(t \mid T) > 0.5$. The corresponding plot of x_t shows that this was also a period of relatively small weekly exchange-rate fluctuations. The only other periods of prolonged tranquillity are the ones from July until December 1974 and from February until September 1979. This seems to indicate that the early period of the post-Bretton-Woods era was more tranquil than the more recent one. It is also interesting to note that the smoother attaches a probability of zero to $\pi_1(t \mid T)$ to both the strongest appreciation of the mark in the sample (the 7.8 percent appreciation in the wake of the Plaza agreement in September 1985) and the strongest depreciation (the 7.0 percent depreciation after the introduction of support measures for the dollar in November 1978).

As regards the estimates of means μ_i, we get results that are very similar to the ones of the mixture model. We find no strong mean effects in daily, weekly and monthly data with the exception of the daily yen series. It is only with quarterly data that we find strong mean effects with μ_1 and μ_2 having opposite signs. This result confirms the finding of Engel and Hamilton (1990) that there are significant mean effects in the three quarterly dollar exchange rate they analysed (mark, pound and French franc). It is, however, somewhat puzzling that we should find mean effects in quarterly data but not in higher-frequency data. A possible explanation for this might be significant high-order autocorrelations in the high-frequency data, a phenomenon that was also discussed in the context of business-cycle analysis (see Cochrane (1988)). Applications of the variance-ratio test to exchange-rate data seem to confirm this conjecture (see Liu and He (1991)).

As regards the estimates of variances σ_i, we find the variance-effect to be dominant in daily, weekly and monthly data but also to be prevalent in quarterly data. We noted in the previous section that the presence of singularities in the likelihood is a major problem for the estimation of mean-scale mixtures. The same problem arises in the estimation of Markov-switching models with mean-and-variance effects. But, fortunately, this problem did not bother us much in our application to exchange rates. The only series where this problem occured was the quarterly franc series.

Finally, it is interesting to compare the Markov-switching models and the mixture models with LR tests. Table 3 shows that for daily and weekly data we can reject the mixture models in favour of the corresponding Markov-switching models at very high significance levels (note that we apply a χ^2 distribution with one degree of freedom to the LR statistic). However, the evidence in favour of the Markov-switching model is much weaker in the low-frequency data. Only three of the eight LR's for monthly and quarterly data are significant at the 5 percent level. It is only the monthly yen series where the LR statistic rejects the mixture model against the Markov-switching model *and* it rejects the H_0 of Gaussian white-noise against the mixture model. If we apply the LR test to a direct comparison between the Markov-switching model and Gaussian white noise, we are again confronted with the methodological problems mentioned in the last section. However, if we apply a χ^2 distribution with 2 degrees of freedom to this direct comparison we find that Gaussian white noise is rejected in six of the eight low-frequency series.

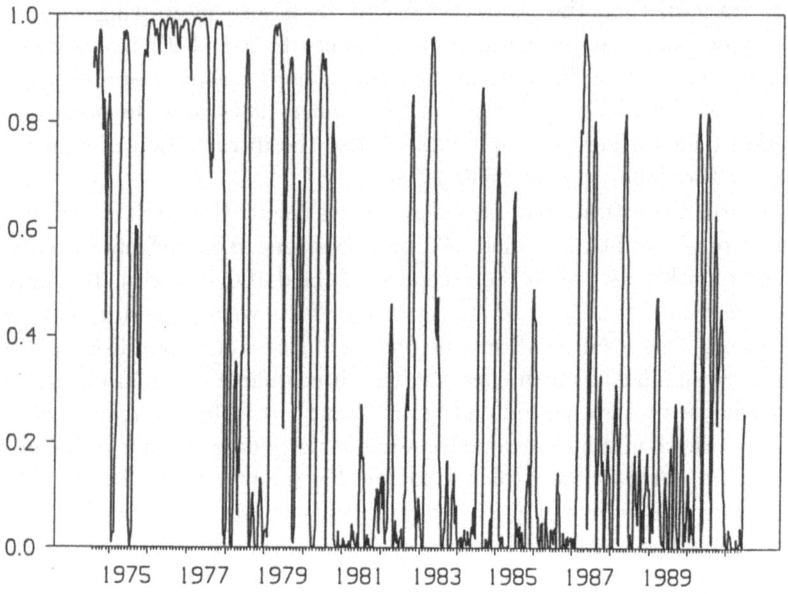

Figure 1a Smoothed probabilities of state 1: weekly mark series

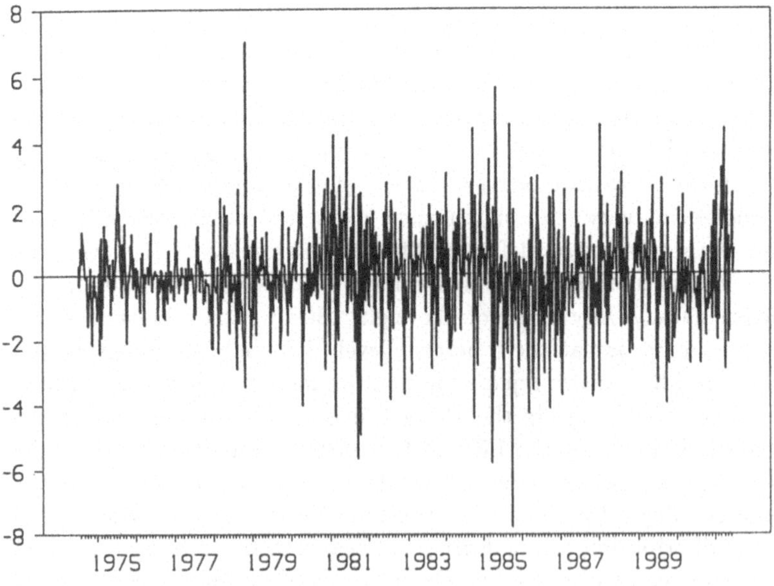

Figure 1b Exchange-rate dynamics: weekly mark series

We motivated the application of mixture models to the modelling of exchange-rate dynamics in Section 3 with reference to the stylized facts of the data, i.e. with the statistical properties of leptokurtosis and convergence to normality under time-aggregation. The extension to the Markov-switching model was motivated by the fact that the mixture model cannot capture the stylized fact of heteroskedasticity whereas this property is incorporated in Markov-switching models with scale components. We have now to ask ourselves whether leptokurtosis and convergence to normality still obtain in a Markov-switching model. The question of leptokurtosis is very easy to answer. In order to compute the moments of the distribution of X, we simply have to compute the stationary probabilities as in (12) and then proceed as in the case of a mixture model. This means that we have the same condition for leptokurtosis as in the mixture model with p_i replaced by $\bar{p}_i$ and that we may use equations (8) and (9) with $\bar{p}_i$ substituted for p_i. It follows that Markov-switching models with variance effects but without mean effects always imply leptokurtosis.

The question of convergence to normality under time-aggregation is more difficult to address since the property of independence is lost and, therefore, we cannot invoke a simple central limit theorem. There is, however, some reason to conjecture that convergence to normality obtains for non-degenerate and non-pathological Markov-switching models. Lindgren (1978) established the asymptotic independence of the X_i variables and this ought to be half the way to the proof of convergence to normality[8]. We leave it to future research to provide the remaining steps of a complete proof of convergence since we want to concentrate here on the aspects of application of the model. However, in Table 4 we offer some illustrations of asymptotic independence for the estimated models. We report there the estimates of the n-step transition probabilities $p_{ii}^n = p(s_t = i \mid s_{t-n} = i)$ for daily and weekly data. The n-step transition probabilities are obtained from the n-th power of the transition matrix. The last column reports the stationary transition probabilities for $n \to \infty$. Independence obtaines if $p_{11}^n + p_{22}^n = 1$, and we find this condition quite closely satisfied at a yearly time interval, i.e. for $n = 250$ with daily data and for $n = 52$ with weekly data.

We may conclude from the analysis in this section that the Markov-switching model captures well the major stylized facts of the exchange-rate data. It does so especially for the short-run, i.e. daily and weekly, data.

[8]Lindgren (1978) proved asymptotic independence by showing that the "mixing" conditions are satisfied. The use of the term "mixing" might cause some confusion in this context since the "mixing" conditions are not related in any way to the mixing of densities as in (1).

Table 4 Estimates of the n-Step Transition Probabilities

day		n=5	n=20	n=60	n=250	$n \to \infty$
mark	p_{11}^n	0.903	0.708	0.530	0.490	0.490
	p_{22}^n	0.906	0.719	0.548	0.510	0.510
pound	p_{11}^n	0.888	0.688	0.545	0.526	0.526
	p_{22}^n	0.876	0.654	0.495	0.474	0.474
franc	p_{11}^n	0.896	0.709	0.576	0.558	0.558
	p_{22}^n	0.869	0.632	0.464	0.442	0.442
yen	p_{11}^n	0.847	0.579	0.401	0.381	0.381
	p_{22}^n	0.907	0.741	0.632	0.619	0.619
week		n=1	n=4	n=12	n=52	$n \to \infty$
mark	p_{11}^n	0.897	0.678	0.444	0.369	0.369
	p_{22}^n	0.940	0.812	0.674	0.631	0.631
pound	p_{11}^n	0.897	0.663	0.369	0.235	0.234
	p_{22}^n	0.968	0.897	0.807	0.766	0.766
franc	p_{11}^n	0.924	0.696	0.479	0.305	0.303
	p_{22}^n	0.967	0.868	0.773	0.698	0.697
yen	p_{11}^n	0.922	0.704	0.532	0.439	0.439
	p_{22}^n	0.939	0.769	0.634	0.562	0.562

5 Implications for the Pricing of Foreign-Currency Options

The concept of choice under uncertainty is the cornerstone of financial theory. Therefore, the stochastic specification of financial models is of fundamental importance in almost any branch of modern finance. A convenient and natural choice for the underlying probability model is the normal distribution in the static context and the corresponding Wiener process in the continuous-time context.

The assumption of a Wiener process for the price (or return) process is also central for the seminal option-pricing model of Black and Scholes (1973). The fact that this assumption is at odds with the empirical regularities of stock prices has early been recognized (see the Introduction). But early attempts to adapt the Black-Scholes model to the stylized facts of financial data have only considered the effect of non-normality, i.e. leptokurtosis. A popular alternative to the Wiener process has been Merton's (1976) model of a jump-diffusion process which incorporates a compound Poisson process. Empirical applications have shown that this model provides a better fit to the data than the assumption of Gaussian white noise but when option prices are computed from the estimated parameters of compound Poisson processes, they differ only little from Black-Scholes prices (see Ball and Torous (1985)).

The issue of heteroskedasticity has only recently been addressed in the finance literature under the label of "stochastic volatility" (Jarrow and Wiggins

(1989) and Taylor (1992) provide surveys of this literature). The approaches which have been applied can be grouped under two headings: the continuous-time-finance approach and the econometric approach. In the continuous-time-finance approach, the price process

$$dE/E = \alpha dt + \sigma dW \tag{15}$$

(where E is the price of the underlying asset, say the exchange rate, W is a standard Brownian motion, α is a constant and σ is the instantaneous standard deviation) is augmented by a specification of the volatility process as a geometric Wiener process

$$d\sigma/\sigma = \lambda dt + \gamma dV \tag{16}$$

(where λ and γ are constants and V is a standard Brownian motion) or as a Ornstein-Uhlenbeck process

$$d\sigma/\sigma = \lambda(\xi - \sigma)dt + \gamma dV \tag{17}$$

(where ξ is a constant) or some variants of (16) or (17). The two-equation system of either (15)-(16) or (15) and (17) has an additional parameter ρ, the correlation between dW and dV.

There are several problems with this approach. First, the specification of (16) or (17) is ad hoc and only motivated by the fact that it is convenient to work with popular stochastic processes. Second, the fundamental problem with any specification of an independent stochastic volatility process is that it becomes impossible to construct a perfect-hedge portfolio because volatility is non-observable and non-traded. Therefore, the great advantage of risk-neutral evaluation is lost. One can try to circumvent this problem by either assuming that the volatility risk can be diversified (see e.g. Hull and White (1987)), but this appears to be arbitrary, or by putting restrictions on the utility function of investors, such as logarithmic utility functions (see e.g. Wiggins (1987)).

Whereas the continuous-time-finance approach starts from a theoretical perspective, the econometric approach starts from an empirical one. This approach has only recently been applied and it has used the generalized autoregressive conditional variance (GARCH) model of Engle (1982) and Bollerslev (1986). The aim of this approach is to find a specification of the volatility process which adequately represents the stylized facts (see e.g. Duan (1991)). A problem with this approach is that it is often unclear under which conditions the specified volatility process is compatible with the risk-neutral valuation principle. Duan (1991), however, has established such conditions for the GARCH model.

In this section, we follow the econometric approach to study the impact of leptokurtosis and heteroskedasticity on option pricing. More specifically, we compute call option prices which would obtain under a mixture model and under a Markov-switching model and compare them with Black-Scholes prices which are derived under the assumption of Gaussian white noise. Of course, we cannot hope to derive closed-form solutions for option prices of mixture models and Markov-switching model. We, therefore, have to rely on simulations which are based on the expected value of the boundary condition, i.e. we compute the call option price as

$$C = \frac{1}{R}\sum_{r=1}^{R} \max\{E_r - B; 0\} \tag{18}$$

where B is the exercise price and R = 20,000 is the numer of repetitions in every experiment. We based our simulations on the parameter estimates of the daily mark series, as reported in Tables 1-3.

Table 5 reports the results from the simulation experiments when the current spot rate E_t is varied between 1.60 and 2.00. The time to maturity is set to 20 days and the exercise price B is set to 1.80. Note that, across each row of Table 5, the computed option prices are based on the same realizations of the random variable, whereas the drawings are distinct between rows. We could, of course, compute the Black-Scholes prices from a closed-form equation but in order to reduce the impact of sample variation, the Black-Scholes prices, reported under the heading of "Gauss", are based on simulations, too. Note, too, that we neglect the present-value factor in the boundary condition (18) since it would have no influence on the comparison of prices between models.

Although the simulations are based on 20,000 repetitions per row, the sample variations are still sizeable for out-of-the-money options. It is, of course, inconsistent to have call option prices for the Black-Scholes model and for the mixture model which are lower at a spot rate of $E_t = 1.64$ than at $E_t = 1.63$ but here we are interested in comparisons across rows and not between rows. Under the headings of "bias" we report the differences between Black-Scholes prices on the one hand and prices from the mixture model and the Markov-switching model on the other hand. The corresponding standard errors are given in brackets. Table 5 shows that the biases according to the mixture model are small and unsystematic. According to the standard errors, nearly all biases are statistically insignificant[9]. We find, however, a systematic pattern in biases if Black-Scholes prices are compared with prices computed from the Markov-switching model. For out-of-the-money options the bias is positive and increasing if we go from $E_t = 1.60$ to $E_t = 1.71$. It then decreases and becomes negative for at-the-money options. The bias is again positive

[9]Due to a computational error, an earlier version of this paper (Kaehler and Marnet (1993)) reportet wrong standard errors for option biases.

Table 5 Spot-rate effect for call options: daily mark series

E_t	Gauss	Mixture	Markov	$bias_{Mixture}$	$bias_{Markov}$
1.60	0.000000	0.000003	0.000013	0.000002 (0.000002)	0.000012 (0.000005)
1.61	0.000002	0.000002	0.000014	0.000000 (0.000001)	0.000013 (0.000005)
1.62	0.000006	0.000011	0.000030	0.000005 (0.000003)	0.000024 (0.000007)
1.63	0.000012	0.000022	0.000050	0.000010 (0.000005)	0.000038 (0.000010)
1.64	0.000010	0.000010	0.000071	-0.000000 (0.000004)	0.000061 (0.000011)
1.65	0.000031	0.000048	0.000121	0.000016 (0.000008)	0.000089 (0.000014)
1.66	0.000069	0.000092	0.000210	0.000024 (0.000010)	0.000142 (0.000018)
1.67	0.000134	0.000145	0.000308	0.000011 (0.000012)	0.000174 (0.000021)
1.68	0.000192	0.000218	0.000424	0.000026 (0.000015)	0.000233 (0.000024)
1.69	0.000368	0.000371	0.000569	0.000004 (0.000021)	0.000201 (0.000031)
1.70	0.000621	0.000639	0.000924	0.000018 (0.000026)	0.000303 (0.000037)
1.71	0.000992	0.000984	0.001366	-0.000008 (0.000032)	0.000374 (0.000043)
1.72	0.001398	0.001429	0.001717	0.000031 (0.000037)	0.000320 (0.000048)
1.73	0.002262	0.002330	0.002401	0.000068 (0.000046)	0.000138 (0.000056)
1.74	0.003329	0.003320	0.003422	-0.000009 (0.000052)	0.000093 (0.000063)
1.75	0.005169	0.005193	0.005097	0.000024 (0.000062)	-0.000072 (0.000073)
1.76	0.007003	0.007015	0.006707	0.000012 (0.000070)	-0.000296 (0.000079)
1.77	0.009605	0.009475	0.008915	-0.000130 (0.000079)	-0.000690 (0.000083)
1.78	0.012810	0.012674	0.011814	-0.000136 (0.000086)	-0.000995 (0.000088)
1.79	0.016543	0.016581	0.015555	0.000038 (0.000096)	-0.000988 (0.000090)
1.80	0.020855	0.020841	0.019793	-0.000014 (0.000102)	-0.001062 (0.000091)
1.81	0.026378	0.026222	0.025422	-0.000157 (0.000113)	-0.000956 (0.000097)
1.82	0.032268	0.032425	0.031619	0.000157 (0.000121)	-0.000649 (0.000099)
1.83	0.039193	0.038843	0.038593	-0.000350 (0.000127)	-0.000600 (0.000103)
1.84	0.045956	0.045926	0.045930	-0.000030 (0.000132)	-0.000027 (0.000108)
1.85	0.053905	0.053924	0.053992	0.000019 (0.000139)	0.000087 (0.000115)
1.86	0.062576	0.062522	0.062732	-0.000055 (0.000145)	0.000156 (0.000119)
1.87	0.070819	0.070960	0.071402	0.000140 (0.000147)	0.000583 (0.000127)
1.88	0.079893	0.080074	0.080399	0.000181 (0.000151)	0.000506 (0.000131)
1.89	0.089578	0.089608	0.090176	0.000029 (0.000154)	0.000598 (0.000136)
1.90	0.098772	0.099140	0.099507	0.000368 (0.000156)	0.000735 (0.000140)
1.91	0.108399	0.108739	0.108748	0.000340 (0.000160)	0.000350 (0.000143)
1.92	0.117965	0.117986	0.118355	0.000021 (0.000161)	0.000390 (0.000146)
1.93	0.128322	0.128344	0.128543	0.000022 (0.000165)	0.000221 (0.000150)
1.94	0.138264	0.138107	0.138489	-0.000157 (0.000164)	0.000225 (0.000150)
1.95	0.148130	0.148112	0.148246	-0.000017 (0.000164)	0.000116 (0.000153)
1.96	0.157830	0.157835	0.158127	0.000005 (0.000166)	0.000297 (0.000153)
1.97	0.167222	0.167193	0.167415	-0.000028 (0.000167)	0.000194 (0.000156)
1.98	0.178347	0.178564	0.178557	0.000217 (0.000168)	0.000210 (0.000156)
1.99	0.187682	0.187663	0.187869	-0.000019 (0.000170)	0.000186 (0.000157)
2.00	0.198572	0.198372	0.198444	-0.000200 (0.000170)	-0.000128 (0.000158)

Table 6 Maturity effect for call options: daily mark series

Maturity	Gauss	Mixture	Markov	$bias_{Mixture}$	$bias_{Markov}$
1	0.00490	0.00448	0.00458	-0.00042 (0.00002)	-0.00032 (0.00002)
2	0.00693	0.00657	0.00648	-0.00036 (0.00003)	-0.00045 (0.00003)
3	0.00831	0.00812	0.00777	-0.00019 (0.00004)	-0.00054 (0.00004)
4	0.00957	0.00934	0.00901	-0.00024 (0.00005)	-0.00056 (0.00004)
5	0.01079	0.01061	0.01007	-0.00018 (0.00005)	-0.00072 (0.00005)
6	0.01166	0.01150	0.01086	-0.00016 (0.00006)	-0.00080 (0.00005)
7	0.01302	0.01279	0.01231	-0.00023 (0.00006)	-0.00071 (0.00006)
8	0.01377	0.01365	0.01291	-0.00012 (0.00007)	-0.00086 (0.00006)
9	0.01432	0.01410	0.01360	-0.00022 (0.00007)	-0.00072 (0.00006)
10	0.01499	0.01479	0.01398	-0.00020 (0.00007)	-0.00101 (0.00007)
11	0.01584	0.01560	0.01487	-0.00024 (0.00008)	-0.00097 (0.00007)
12	0.01642	0.01616	0.01546	-0.00026 (0.00008)	-0.00096 (0.00007)
13	0.01719	0.01711	0.01613	-0.00008 (0.00008)	-0.00106 (0.00008)
14	0.01795	0.01786	0.01695	-0.00008 (0.00009)	-0.00100 (0.00008)
15	0.01834	0.01823	0.01737	-0.00010 (0.00009)	-0.00097 (0.00008)
16	0.01913	0.01898	0.01809	-0.00015 (0.00009)	-0.00104 (0.00008)
17	0.01963	0.01936	0.01861	-0.00027 (0.00009)	-0.00102 (0.00008)
18	0.01981	0.01980	0.01870	-0.00000 (0.00010)	-0.00111 (0.00009)
19	0.02030	0.02003	0.01924	-0.00027 (0.00010)	-0.00106 (0.00009)
20	0.02100	0.02112	0.02010	0.00012 (0.00011)	-0.00090 (0.00009)
21	0.02138	0.02127	0.02045	-0.00010 (0.00011)	-0.00093 (0.00009)
22	0.02222	0.02217	0.02103	-0.00005 (0.00011)	-0.00119 (0.00010)
23	0.02275	0.02271	0.02161	-0.00004 (0.00011)	-0.00114 (0.00010)
24	0.02302	0.02296	0.02183	-0.00006 (0.00011)	-0.00119 (0.00010)
25	0.02356	0.02347	0.02252	-0.00008 (0.00012)	-0.00104 (0.00010)
26	0.02421	0.02402	0.02308	-0.00019 (0.00012)	-0.00113 (0.00011)
27	0.02451	0.02444	0.02341	-0.00007 (0.00012)	-0.00110 (0.00011)
28	0.02473	0.02467	0.02359	-0.00006 (0.00012)	-0.00114 (0.00011)
29	0.02546	0.02549	0.02409	0.00003 (0.00013)	-0.00137 (0.00011)
30	0.02559	0.02565	0.02431	0.00006 (0.00013)	-0.00128 (0.00011)
31	0.02578	0.02569	0.02463	-0.00010 (0.00013)	-0.00115 (0.00011)
32	0.02612	0.02592	0.02489	-0.00020 (0.00013)	-0.00123 (0.00012)
33	0.02700	0.02692	0.02575	-0.00009 (0.00013)	-0.00125 (0.00012)
34	0.02682	0.02669	0.02571	-0.00013 (0.00013)	-0.00111 (0.00012)
35	0.02761	0.02763	0.02614	0.00002 (0.00014)	-0.00147 (0.00012)
36	0.02808	0.02791	0.02686	-0.00017 (0.00014)	-0.00122 (0.00012)
37	0.02783	0.02783	0.02662	-0.00000 (0.00014)	-0.00121 (0.00012)
38	0.02847	0.02849	0.02709	0.00003 (0.00014)	-0.00138 (0.00013)
39	0.02852	0.02843	0.02751	-0.00009 (0.00014)	-0.00101 (0.00013)
40	0.02893	0.02905	0.02769	0.00012 (0.00015)	-0.00124 (0.00013)

for in-the-money options with spot rates larger than 1.84. The largest bias obtains for a spot rate of 1.90 (at the money) and somewhat surprisingly, the bias is again negative for a spot rate of 2.00. The price biases can be explained by the fat-tail effects and the peakedness effects of the leptokurtic distributions. The fat right tail increases the probability of out-of-the-money options to come into the money; therefore, the option price increases. The effect of the fat left tail can be explained with the help of the call-put parity. A out-of-the-money put option increases in price if the probability in the left tail is increased and, therefore, the price of an in-the-money call option increases, too. Finally, the negative price biases of at-the money options can be explained by the peakedness effect. An excessive number of small price fluctuations (compared to the normal distribution) implies that the options do not go as deep into the money as expected under the normal distribution.

It is interesting to note that this pattern of biases mimics the patterns derived by Hull and White (1987) within the continuous-time-finance approach based on equations (15)–(16) and also mimics the results of Duan (1991) who found the same pattern of biases in an application of the GARCH model. Furthermore, the standard errors are small and indicate that the biases are statistically significant. Figure 2 plots the biases implied by the mixture model (bold line) and by the Markov switching model (solid line) together with the 95 percent confidence limits (dashed lines). The biases implied by the Markov-switching model show a pattern which is known as the smile effect whereas the pattern from the mixture model is unsystematic.

Results from experiments of varying the time to maturity are reported in Table 6. We computed call option prices for at-the-money options with a spot rate and an exercise price of 1.80. The simulations were based on the same parameter estimates as in the previous experiment and the time to maturity was varied between 1 and 40 days.

A comparison of option prices derived under the assumptions of Gaussian white noise and of a mixture distribution shows that for nearly all maturities, the Black-Scholes prices are larger than the mixture-distribution prices. This corresponds to the negative value of the bias obtained in Table 5 for a spot rate of 1.80. Surprisingly, however, for a maturity of 20 days we get a positive bias in Table 6. This indicates that there is sizeable sample variation for at-the-money options although we used 20,000 repetitions. The negative price bias is statistically significant only for options with short maturities.

If we compare Black-Scholes prices with Markov-switching prices, we find in Table 6 that the Black-Scholes model overprices the options at all maturities and this corresponds to the result in Table 5 for a spot rate of 1.80. The absolute value of the bias increases with the time to maturity. Figure 3 shows the maturity effects of biases implied by the mixture model (bold line) and by the Markov-switching model (solid line) together with the 95 percent confidence limits (dashed lines).

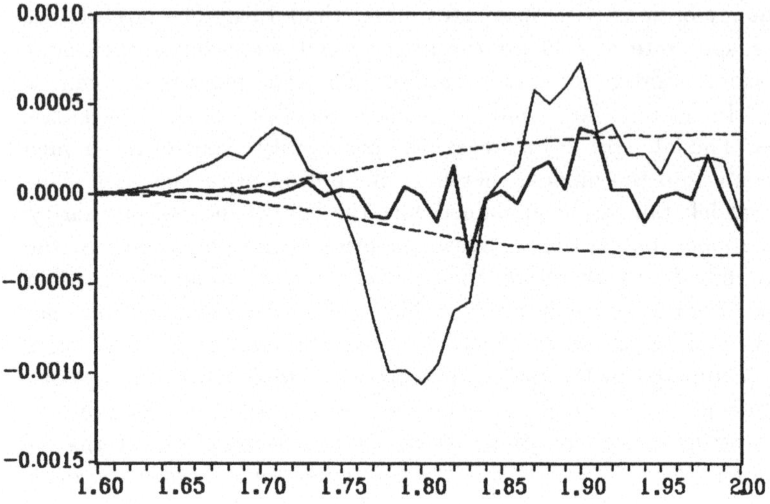

Figure 2 Spot-rate effect of option biases: daily mark series

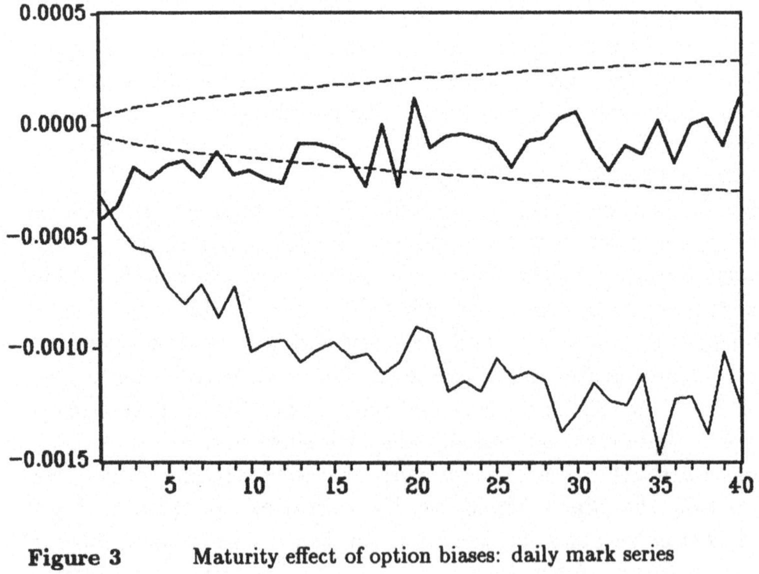

Figure 3 Maturity effect of option biases: daily mark series

Whereas only the short-maturity effects of the mixture model produce statistically significant biases, the negative biases from the Markov-switching model are clearly outside the confidence limits for all maturities. The biases increase (in absolute value) for maturities between 1 and 30 days but there is no clear tendency in the biases for longer maturities. We would, however, expect that the bias effects level off for long maturities because the convergence to normality under time aggregation leads to the equalization of Black-Scholes prices and Markov-switching prices. Figure 3 also shows that the plot of biases is quite erratic, i.e. there is still substantial sample variation in the simulations.

6 Conclusions

In this paper we have examined issues in the application of mixture models and Markov-switching models to the modelling of price dynamics in financial markets. We applied the models to exchange-rate data but the approach is readily extended to other financial prices, such as stock prices, since speculative prices share the stylized facts of leptokurtosis and heteroskedasticity.

Engel and Hamilton (1990) motivated their application of the Markov-switching model to quarterly exchange rates with a search for "long swings" in exchange rates, i.e. with a search for mean effects. Our motivation differs from it by emphazising that the most significant statistical properties of exchange-rate data are the leptokurtosis and heteroskedasticity of short-run, i.e. daily and weekly, data and by relating it to mixture models which have a long tradition in finance.

The estimation showed that Markov-switching models provide a significantly better fit than models of Gaussian white noise and mixture models and that this holds especially for short-run data. To a certain extent we can confirm the findings of mean effects in quarterly data, as in Engel and Hamilton (1990), but the dominant effect is the variance effect in daily and weekly data where we find no significant mean effects in seven of eight series.

The application of mixture models and Markov-switching models to the pricing of options showed that we can only find systematic and statistically significant differences to Black-Scholes prices if we adopt a Markov-switching model but not if we adopt a mixture model. Interestingly, the pattern of spot-rate effects implied by the Markov-switching model is of the "smile" type which was also found in earlier studies of stochastic-volatility models.

There are several points where our analysis is incomplete or where an extension would be interesting. We noted in Section 4 that currently we can only conjecture that the Markov-switching model is compatible with convergence to normality under time aggregation. We hope to provide a proof of this property in a subsequent paper. The greatest gap that our paper leaves is the fact that we only assume that option pricing in the framework of the risk-neutral-valuation principle is possible if we adopt a mixture model or a Markov-switching model. We leave it to future work to show under which conditions these models allow risk-neutral valuation and we suppose that we have to impose some restrictions on the utility function or the changes in aggregate consumption in order to derive the desired result. Finally, it would be interesting to compare the performance of the Markov-switching model in modelling speculative prices with the performance of GARCH-type models.

References

Akgiray V, Booth G G (1987) Compound Distribution Models of Stock Returns: An Empirical Comparison, Journal of Financial Research 10: 269-280

Akgiray V, Booth G G (1988) Mixed Diffusion-Jump Process Modeling of Exchange Rate Movements, Review of Economics and Statistics 70: 631-637

Akgiray V, Booth G G , Loistl O (1989) Statistical Models of German Stock Returns, Journal of Economics 50: 17-33

Ball C A, Torous W N (1983) A Simplified Jump Process for Common Stock Returns, Journal of Financial and Quantitative Analysis 18: 53-61

Ball C A, Torous W N (1985) On Jumps in Common Stock Prices and Their Impact on Call Option Pricing, Journal of Finance 40: 155-173

Barnea A, Downes D H (1973) A Reexamination of the Empirical Distribution of Stock Price Changes, Journal of the American Statistical Association 68: 348-350

Barton D E, David F N (1957) Multiple Runs, Biometrika 44: 168-178

Baum L E, Petrie T, Soules G, Weiss N (1970) A Maximization Technique Occuring in the Statistical Analysis of Probabilistic Functions of Markov Chains, Annals of Mathematical Statistics 41: 164-171

Black F, Scholes M (1973) The Pricing of Options and Corporate Liabilities, Journal of Political Economy 81: 637-654

Bollerslev T (1986) Generalized Autoregressiv Conditional Heteroskedasticity, Journal of Econometrics 31: 307-327

Boothe P, Glassman D (1987) The Statistical Distribution of Exchange Rates, Journal of International Economics 22: 297-319

Cochrane J H (1988) How Big is the Random Walk in GNP? Journal of Political Economy 96: 893-920

D'Agostino R B (1986) Tests for the Normal Distribution In: R B D'Agostino and M A Stephens (eds.), Goodness-of-Fit Techniques, New York (M. Dekker): 367-419

Diebold F X (1988) Empirical Modeling of Exchange Rate Dynamics, Berlin (Springer)

Duan J-C (1991) The GARCH Option Pricing Model, Faculty of Management, McGill University, Canada, mimeo

Engel C M, Hamilton J D (1990) Long Swings in the Dollar: Are They in the Data and Do Markets Know It? American Economic Review 80: 689-713

Engle R F (1982) Autoregressive Conditional Heteroscedasticity with Estimates of the Variance of UK Inflation, Econometrica 50: 987-1008

Everitt B S, Hand D J (1981) Finite Mixture Distributions, London (Chapman and Hall)

Fama E F (1976) Foundations of Finance New York (Basic Books)

Fielitz B D, Rozelle J P (1983) Stable Distributions and the Mixtures of Distributions Hypothesis for Common Stock Returns, Journal of the American Statistical Association 78: 28-36

Friedman D, Vandersteel S (1982) Short-Run Fluctuations in Foreign Exchange Rates, Journal of International Economics 13: 171-186

Goldfeld S M, Quandt R E (1973) A Markov Model for Switching Regressions, Journal of Econometrics 1: 3-15

Gridgeman N T (1970) A Comparison of Two Methods of Analysis of Mixtures of Normal Distributions, Technometrics 12: 823-833

Hamilton J D (1988) Rational-Expectations Econometric Analysis of Changes in Regime: An Investigation of the Term Structure of Interest Rates, Journal of Economic Dynamics and Control 12: 385-423

Hamilton J D (1989) A New Approach to the Economic Analysis of Nonstationary Time Series and the Business Cycle, Econometrica 57: 357-384

Hamilton J D (1990) Analysis of Time Series Subject to Changes in Regime, Journal of Econometrics 45: 39-70

Hamilton J D (1991a) A Quasi-Bayesian Approach to Estimating Parameters for Mixtures of Normal Distributions, Journal of Business and Economic Statistics 9: 27-39

Hamilton J D (1991b) Estimation, Inference, and Forecasting of Time Series Subject to Changes in Regime, To appear in C R Rao and G S Maddala (eds.), Handbook of Statistics, Vol 10

Hull J, White A (1987) The Pricing of Options on Assets with Stochastic Volatilities, Journal of Finance 42: 281-300

Jansen D W, de Vries C G (1991) On the Frequency of Large Stock Returns: Putting Boosts and Busts into Perspective, Review of Economics and Statistics 73: 18-24

Jarrow R A, Wiggins J B (1989) Option Pricing and Implicit Volatilities, Journal of Economic Surveys 3: 59-81

Kaehler J (1991) On the Modelling of Exchange-Rate Dynamics by Stable Paretian Distributions, Institut für Volkswirtschaftslehre und Statistik, Universität Mannheim, Discussion Paper No 448-91

Kaehler J, Marnet V (1993) Markov-Switching Models for Exchange-Rate Dynamics and the Pricing of Foreign-Currency Options. ZEW Discussion Paper No. 93-03

Kon S J (1984) Models of Stock Returns - A Comparison, Journal of Finance 39: 147-165

Lau A H-L, Lau H-S, Wingender J R (1990) The Distribution of Stock Returns: New Evidence Against the Stable Model, Journal of Business and Economic Statistics 8: 217-223

Liu C Y, He J (1991) A Variance-Ratio Test of Random Walks in Foreign Exchange Rates, Journal of Finance 46: 773-785

Lindgren G (1978) Markov Regime Models for Mixed Distributions and Switching Regressions, Scandinavian Journal of Statistics 5: 81-91

Mandelbrot B (1963) The Variation of Certain Speculative Prices, Journal of Business 36: 394-419

McLeod A I, Li W K (1983) Diagnostic Checking ARIMA Time Series Models Using Squared-Residual Autocorrelations, Journal of Time Series Analysis 4: 269-273

Merton R C (1976) Option Pricing When Underlying Stock Returns are Discontinuous, Journal of Financial Economics 3: 124-144

Pearson K (1894) Contributions to the Mathematical Theory of Evolution, Philosophical Transactions of the Royal Society 185: 71-110

Praetz P D (1972) The Distribution of Share Price Changes, Journal of Business 45: 49-55

Press S J (1967) A Compound Events Model for Security Prices, Journal of Business 40: 317-335

Priestley M B (1988) Non-linear and Non-stationary Time Series Analysis, London (Academic Press)

Stephens M A (1986) Tests Based on EDF Statistics In: R B D'Agostino and M A Stephens (eds.), Goodness-of-Fit Techniques, New York (M. Dekker): 97-193

Taylor S J (1986) Modelling Financial Time Series, Chichester (Wiley)

Taylor S J (1992) Modelling Stochastic Volatility. Department of Accounting and Finance, Lancaster University, UK, mimeo

Titterington D M, Smith A F M, Makov U E (1985) Statistical Analysis of Finite Mixture Distributions, Chichester (Wiley)

Tong H (1983) Threshold Models in Non-linear Time Series Analysis, New York (Springer)

Tong H (1990) Non-linear Time Series: A Dynamical Systems Approach, Oxford (Oxford University Press)

Tucker A L, Pond L (1988) The Probability Distribution of Foreign Exchange Prices Changes: Tests of Candidate Processes, Review of Economics and Statistics 70: 638-647

Wiggins J (1987) Option Values Under Stochastic Volatility: Theory and Empirical Estimates, Journal of Financial Economics 19: 351-372

The manufacturer's authorised representative in the EU is Springer Nature Customer Service Centre GmbH, Europaplatz 3, 69115 Heidelberg, Germany. If you have any concerns regarding our products, please contact ProductSafety@springernature.com

Printed and bound by CPI Group (UK) Ltd, Croydon, CR0 4YY
01/10/2026
02225951-0010